Autonomies
in Hungary and Europe

A COMPARATIVE STUDY

By Józsa Hévizi

The Regional and Ecclesiastic Autonomy
of the Minorities and Nationality Groups

CORVINUS SOCIETY
2005

Second Enlarged Edition

Title of the First Edition:

Regional and Ecclesiastical Autonomy in Historic Hungary

Reviewed by:

Dr. Ildikó Lipcsey

Dr. Lajos Arday

Translated By

Thomas J. DeKornfeld

Thanks to my mother for help,

and to Szabolcs Magyarody, whose initiative was written this work.

English Text Reviewed and Edited By

Helen D. Hiltabidle

Wrapper: Perhács Lászlóné

Back, maps: dr. Ottófi Rudolf

Art by Márta Buda

PRINTED IN THE UNITED STATES

ISBN 1-882785-17-7 cb
ISBN 1-882785-20-7 nb

Library of Congress Control Number 2005932694

Table of Contents

Foreword

It gave me great pleasure that the work entitled "The Regional and Ecclesiastic Autonomy in Historic Hungary" was published and was granted the status of a textbook. This is a reference manual not only in the field of textbook literature but it is just as much a reference manual for us who labor in the regions wrested from the historic Hungary, trying to reestablish our mutilated ecclesiastic and national autonomy in a contemporary guise.

I render thanks to God and to the author for the unexpected ideological, historical and theoretical help, coming from an unexpected source and at an unexpected time. It will contribute greatly to the better and "more fundamental" buttressing of our endeavors and of our ideas of autonomy.

February 29, 1996

LÁSZLÓ TŐKÉS
Episcopal Office of the
Királyhágómellék Reformed Synod

5

The Justification of Autonomy

According to Aristotle, in a democracy "supreme power belongs to the people" which in theory means that the power is exerted by the entire people and not just by one of its subgroups or segments. In spite of this, the democracies of the classic era did not grant citizenship to foreigners (the metoikos in Greece) and the status of the ethnic minorities did not change appreciably through the centuries.

According to the eminent 20th century Protestant thinker and teacher, Sándor Karácsony, "World history is the history of a single endeavor, the attempts of individuals to become independent from other individuals. The only thing that happened politically throughout history was that every period endeavored to curtail the overly developed autonomy of one man while furthering the diminished or yet undeveloped autonomy of another man." He was of the opinion that in the process of maturing of individuals the same principle was manifested as in the social and political development of nations, namely a striving for autonomy.

Although the national states evolved only in the 19th century, nations and ethnic groups have struggled from the beginning of history for their administrative, economic and cultural (religious and linguistic) autonomy essential for the preservation of their identity.

Ever since the union with Wales, Scotland and Ireland was established, England endeavored to abolish the administrative independence of these regions and to achieve linguistic assimilation. Religious matters were also part of this endeavor and only the Scottish Presbyterians maintained some independence. The Act of Union between England and Wales, promulgated in 1536, banned the use of the Welsh language in legal matters. In 1616, James I issued an edict banning the use of Gaelic in Scotland.

The Education Act of 1870 banned the use of Welsh in the schools. After the annexation of Wales, Scotland and Ireland to England only scattered remnants of autonomy remained. Following the Anglo-Welsh Union of 1536, Wales became entirely integrated into England but its autonomous cultural heritage was maintained to this day. The Union of Scotland and England (1707) did not lead to complete assimilation since Scotland's religious autonomy was left intact. Thus the continuation of the Scottish Kirk was assured and the Scottish legal and legislative practices were also preserved.

At the time of the religious wars in France in the 16th century, the victory of the Catholics over the Huguenots was accompanied by the central government doing away with the regional parliaments and with the regional separatism represented by them. Francis I (1515-1547) made French the official state language in 1539 and this process was completed when the French Revolution banned the use of Breton, Basque, German, Italian and Flemish.

The great philosophers and politicians of the French Revolution believed that enacting human and civic rights and promulgating individual rights would lead to democracy. Today we can see that such a law can come to life only by a compromise that attempts to balance complicated group interests and the mechanisms to integrate such divergent interests. Unfortunately, political life demonstrates that those in power tend to represent the interests of some group, e.g.- the economic lobbies.

If we raise the question whether interest groups on all sides, employer, worker (union) and government are listened to, we must admit that traditionally only the interests of the groups organized on an economic or social basis are considered worthy of consideration, while the ethnic issues or an approach on ethnic bases cannot be integrated into the system.

It may be a solution if ethnic considerations were the basis on which regional or territorial autonomy would be established. This has recently been shown to be correct in a number of Western-European countries.

When, as a result of the 1789 French Revolution, everybody became a citizen and the inequalities in the judicial system, in taxation and in other areas all disappeared, the elimination of privileges of the nobility and clergy was accompanied by the disappearance of the manifestations of regional interests. In lieu of a society consisting of groups with widely varying privileges, a society was established where all individuals had the same privileges and the same obligations. By terminating a naturally evolved regional organization, possibly indicating ethnic divisions, a consistently modern administrative system was established. It was in this way that the modern bourgeois state eliminated the inequalities between individuals, while at the same time it also eliminated the possibility of a collective protection of the interests of regional ethnic minority groups.

In Hungary, the Habsburg government allowed the establishment of an ecclesiastic autonomy that, in turn, could establish a certain framework for cultural and economic self-rule.

Thus, the modern state has replaced caste privileges with individual rights but failed to recognize that individual rights could be exercised only inadequately when the ethnic minorities could not protect themselves and their particular interests vis-à-vis the national majority. The citizen had become a taxpayer but in exchange for his taxes he does not enjoy those rights that are enjoyed by those belonging to the majority ethnic group holding the power. The majority enjoyed collective rights not available to those belonging to the minority. The interests of the members of the minority group coincided with those of the majority only to a limited extent and, so far as use of the mother tongue, education and preservation of their national identity were concerned, minorities functioned as a separate community of interest.

The concept of nation and nationality has not been clearly defined in the technical literature even today. These concepts are fundamentally a function of the perspective and treatment with which minorities and their problems have been handled in various countries or are being handled today. The minorities' historic origin may differ and they may be the descendants of the original inhabitants, settlers or later immigrants. We consider those communities as descendants of the original inhabitants who are linked to their region by their historic past, but who differ from the majority of the population by their ethnic or religious traditions and by their way of life. Two subsets may be identified: one consists of individuals who are ethnically and linguistically identical with the majority population of a neighboring country (separated from this majority by some arbitrary decision following a war). The other consists of minority groups who have no homeland.

The term ethnicity means the totality of the characteristics or attributes of a certain people or group of peoples. In practice a number of groups are called ethnic, and the term may refer to a linguistic-cultural nation, a national community or a racial minority. By a minority, we mean an ethnic element that represents a smaller group vis-à-vis the majority constituting the country. The minority wishes to live in harmony with its mother country beyond the frontier (Nationality minority). Some authors consider a nationality to be a group separated from its mother country and representing a minority in their present country, or an ethnic group without a motherland, but one that could develop into an independent nation. By nation, these authors mean a historically established, persistent human community whose members are united by a common culture, language and characteristic emotional structure even though boundaries and differing economic systems may stand between them.

In the Kingdom of Hungary, where foreign invasions constituted a constant and continuing threat (Cuman, Tartar, Turkish, etc.), the medieval monarchs settled the various newly arrived communities, granting them a variety of privileges. The privileges granted depended to some extent upon the role the new arrivals were going to play in the economic life of the nation or in the defense of the frontiers. The Székelys, Pechenegs, Cumans, Jazygians, Saxons and Croats were given territorial autonomy (corresponding in English political life to "home rule"). The regional autonomy given in exchange for military service had various forms, such as the Székely and Saxon areas where lower level administrators were elected locally, the Saxon "universitas" and the Cumanian and Jazygian regions. Such forms allowed these nationalities to establish their own administrative systems and, within these frameworks, defend their own interests.

In the feudal system, the Saxons had such a complete autonomy that they could not be viewed as a national minority by today's standards, in the Hungary of that day, or in the Transylvanian Principality. Their privileges were first curtailed by Joseph II but it was the bourgeois state, standing on the principle of individual equality, that did away with their separate status in 1868. The national group, enjoying feudal independence and equality before the law, became a nationality threatened in its ethnic identity.

The Croats enjoyed the most complete autonomy, since the Hungarian kings viewed Croatia for many centuries as a sister state. In the 16-17th century, the Romanians and Serbs lived outside the borders of Hungary in vassal states under Turkish dominion. When they migrated to Hungary in great numbers or were resettled within the borders of Hungary, they were given only ecclesiastic autonomy. Even Leopold I considered these settlements to be temporary expedients because he hoped that the Turkish domination of the Balkans would be terminated shortly.

The Ruthenian population in the northeastern part of the country was always exceedingly poor and, living with the Hungarian serfs, struggled against the local landowners. Their national consciousness developed only in the 19th century, similarly to the Slovaks in whom this process began with a fight for an independent Slovak language, distinctly different from Czech.

In the 18th century, the 30-40 thousand gypsies and the 80,000 Jews enjoyed a very special situation. Endeavors to settle the gypsies with some privileges proved unsuccessful. The great wave of Jewish settlement took place at the turn of the century and by this time their number had increased to 542,000. This was due largely to the Act of Emancipation of 1867 and to the Act of Legal Equality of 1895.[1]

The forms of autonomy, evolved in Hungary and Switzerland by the end of the 19th century, were the result of a long historic evolution and differed from the standard European practices.

It seems worthwhile, therefore, to examine the path taken by European minorities and the differing way in which this issue was handled in Hungary. Among the European examples, the path of the Scottish, Welsh and Irish minorities toward autonomy will be highlighted.

The struggle for autonomy reached completion only recently and the process illustrates that while general European political practice recognized only individual, and not collective, rights, this framework made it possible for autonomy to be achieved, albeit only by a fight for civil rights lasting for decades.

---

[1] István Soós: In Magyarok a Kárpát medencében, henceforth MOK (Hungarians in the Carpathia basin). Collected and edited by Ferenc Glatz, Pallas Publishing House, Bp. 1988, p. 197.

Regional Autonomy in the Kingdom of Hungary

Regional Autonomy
(self-government by communities and by nationality groups)

King Saint Stephen (997-1038) in his "Admonitions" to his son, Prince Imre, expressed the necessity of welcoming settlers and foreigners because, "a monoglot country lacking a diversity of customs is weak and likely to fall". The examples of self-government, taken from the feudal period, demonstrate how the local or regional ethnic groups managed local administration through their own representatives, preserving separatism, the legal system and the traditions of the community for a long period of time while slowly adapting themselves to the body politic of the entire country.

The various groups and nationalities (Pechenegs, Ismaelites, Székelys and Cumans) were granted different types and levels of autonomy in return for military service and defense of the frontiers against the Tartars and Turks. While the areas inhabited by Hungarians were divided into counties, the Saxons, Székelys and Cumans lived under a different administrative system. Voivode (Vajda), who were also the governors of Transylvania, administered the Hungarian counties. The Székelys were governed by bailiffs and the Saxons by the royal judge of Zips. They all lived in separate regions, under different laws, held their own regional meetings and voted for taxes or military service separately. The newly acquired southern-Slav regions were incorporated into Hungary as "Bánáts". Based on the precedent of the "Székely autonomy", **István Bocskai ennobled the Heyduks who participated in the war of independence of 1604-1606**. As a consequence of the large-scale settlements and immigration, the nationalities of Hungary represented 20-25% of the population by the end of the Middle Ages. Jenő Szűcs cites a contemporary Belgian chronicle relating how Walloons from Hungary, visiting Liege in 1447, told the story of their ancestors being given land by the King of Hungary, with the admonition not to forget their mother tongue.[2]

In the 11th century, King Saint László and King Kálmán, the Learned, tried to convert the Mohammedans to Christianity, admittedly under ecclesiastic urging, but these people, living in closed communities under their bailiffs and elders (villae Ismaelitanum), resisted. In the 12th century, under King Géza II, one Abu Hamid al Andalusi was given royal permission to explain the Koran to them.[3]

---

[2] Jenő Szűcs: A középkori Magyarország népei. (The Nationalities of Medieval Hungary) MOK. pp. 32-37.
[3] Jenő Szűcs, Ibid.

In the 13th century, the settlement villages in the Hungarian regions began the slow process of assimilation. The situation was similar for the Walloons and Pechenegs. The large bulk of the Székelys were settled by the beginning of the 13th century at their present location, the so-called Székelyföld, as a frontier defense group, according to the mandate of King András II. At the time the autonomous territory of the Saxons was established in Transylvania, the people living in that region (Szászváros-Háromszék) were moved further east. They were granted their privileges for having served in the armies of the king (Voivode and Reigning Prince).[4]

The Székelys (and Csángós)

They considered themselves descendants of Attila, based not only on legend but also on some documentary evidence. In the "Memorial" of the Székely National Assembly, held in 1700, they referred to their heroism in the service of the Hungarian kings and demanded the re-institution of their privileges from Leopold I, King of Hungary and Emperor of Austria. We learn that "their nation is very, very ancient and is a descendant of the Hun-Scythian nation who came from Asia to Europe where they became very populous. With their arms, they expelled the Goths and other nations from Dacia and settled permanently in that part of the region, which is known as Erdély (Transylvania). They remained there even when the other Scythian-Hun armies left to conquer Pannonia. Later, separating from the Scythians and Huns who had departed, they still retained their name Scythulus in Latin and Székely in Hungarian. Their descent is a subject for debate to this day. (Archeological research unearthed Avar findings). At the time of the conquest, they were already speaking Hungarian. Our present historiography leans toward a Volga area Bulgarian-Turk origin.

The names of their settlements reflect the names of the original tribes and nationalities. They originally consisted of six tribes (Örlőc, Medgyes, Adorján, Ábrán, Jenő and Halom), divided into 24 branches. Because of subsequent internal struggles, one part of them was resettled along the eastern border as guardians of the marches.[5]

Regional autonomy (the structure of self-government)
Their independent administrative units, known as "szék-s", stood in contrast to the county system that encompassed all those living in a villein-landowner relationship. The Szék (Literally: Seat) held economic, administrative, jurisdictional and military power over the community it served. They were ruled by the nationality judges, who formerly rendered judgments at the National Assemblies. At the side of the Judge stood the Lieutenant (Captain), the military commander of the Seat and judge of the military tribunal. These two shared the control over the Seat. The Judge and the Lieutenant kept track of

---

[4] László Makkai: Erdély betelepülése, (The settlement of Transyilvania) Historia, Bp. 1986 #2.
[5] Zoltán Szász: Székelyek. MOK p. 47. The charters are cited by Jakab-Szadecky in: Udvarhely vármegye története a legrégibb időtől 1849-ig (History of county Udvarhely from the earliest times to 1849) pp. 136-137.

the ownership rights, enforced obedience to royal commands and played a role at the investitures as well. (Ius Regium did not apply to the Székelyföld or Székelyland). They were assisted as advisors and fellow-justices by the noble Székelys, under the name of consul or senior. Starting in the 15th century, the governing body of the Seat was enlarged by the election of representatives (jurymen). First 12 and later 24 were elected to serve along the seniors. Half of them and occasionally 2/3 were Székely commoners.

The officials were elected, except the Bailiff (Székelyispán) who, as the commander of the Székely military, was a member of the Voivode's and later the Ruling Prince's council and thus one of the leading nobles of the land. He had judicial responsibilities and was responsible for the organization and command of the army. From time to time he had to check on the Lieutenant or Captain, to see how he organized and trained the army. He was also in charge of the royal revenues ("ox-roasts", castles, mines, forests and revenues of the boundary lands). At his installation he had to take an oath to defend the Székely freedoms and the safety of the Székelyföld. It was only after having taken the oath that he was given the emblems of authority, the flag, the staff and the sword. According to the 1429 military regulations of King Zsigmond of Luxenburg, the Bailiff was obliged to furnish two companies of soldiers of 500 men each. In 1433 he had to furnish 2,000 cavalrymen. Prior to his campaign against Naples, King Lajos the Great visited Transylvania since the Székelys were an important component of his armies. In 1463, in Buda, King Mátyás authorized the three Transylvanian nationalities, Hungarian, Székely and Saxon, to decide at their National Assemblies on the methodology of their going to war. The rules pertaining to Székelys contained the following, "During a general mobilization, the Székelys, according to their ancient traditions, will send two thirds of their nation to serve under the flag, while one third of the nation will remain at home in all events. Mobilization will be announced by the exhibition of a bloody saber, or by a letter from the Bailiff or from the Voivode of Transylvania, provided that he is also, at the same time, the Bailiff of the Székelys..."

The sequence of sentencing and the methodology of the appeal process denoted the hierarchy of the Seats:

The King (only territorial disputes of more than 3 forint value)
The Bailiff
The First Seat
The Maternal Seat
The Filial Seat

The type of settlement determined the form of military service. The smallest units of settlement were the "tizes" or denary units. They led independent lives under the control of the denary judge. The denary units functioned like economic cells and shared the agricultural work and the management of the livestock. The area jointly worked was re-divided from time to time and was increased, when indicated, by clearing some wooded area. Relatives lived side by side and also fought side by side. (Since the days of Prince Gábor Bethlen (1613-1629) the members of each denary unit rode in a single cart when called to arms.) By the 16th century the Székelys were firmly divided into social levels in spite of the their previous system of shared labor.

They were eligible for office on the basis of their wealth and social standing:
The Noble (primor)
The "Lófő" (primipilus): owned inherited land, was eligible for officer positions
The Commoners (pixidarius): members of the community, eligible for jury duty.
Those who had only one horse at the time of mobilization were called "Lófő" (heads of horses). This name was derived from the fact that when the men were lined up, it was the heads of the horses that were counted. The Székely infantrymen were called "darabont" (pixidarius) or Székely commoner.

According to social standing the betrothal gift, given by the groom to the bride, was precisely determined in the entire Székelyföld (1555):[6]

From a primor	24 Ft
From a lófő	12 Ft
From a darabont	6 Ft
From a peasant	3 Ft

Notes surviving from the 17-19th century record the existence of these social distinctions in everyday life. Thus, the children of a military wife were not allowed to play with the children of villeins. The soldiers sat in the pews on the right side of the aisle in church, the villeins sat on the left side.

There are written traces of the village ordinances regulating joint ownership from the 16th century. In these, the distribution of land and the management and preservation of the forests, pastures and orchards is regulated. The early ordinances of the Székely villages reflect a strong sense of community. The villages led a collective life, made rules for themselves and banned certain types of behavior. Usually the entire village voted voluntarily on these ordinances. In the 16th century frequent mention was made of the commonly held property of the village, the land that was handed over for use to individual families. The higher strata of village society frequently considered such distributed land as their own property, refused to return it and increased it by clearing additional land.

Religious freedom (ecclesiastic self-government)

Village ordinances pertaining to the congregation or to the pastor are known from as early as the 16th century. The ordinances determined the way in which the leaders and the office-holders of the church were elected, their duties and salary, the management of the assets of the Seat, the practice of attending services, the affairs of the schools and schoolmasters and the punishment for moral misdemeanors. Prince György Rákóczi I, wrote in 1640 that the members of the clergy did not depend on their bishops and prelates, but on the villages and on the laity. Thus the Székely Catholic parishes were administratively related to the village community and this peculiar Székely legal situation was not the result of the Reformation, although in the 16-17th century Calvinism and Unitarianism were spreading very rapidly among the Székely.

If there was a dispute about the use of a church, Prince Gábor Bethlen rendered his judgment and did not permit one denomination to lord it over any

---

[6] Albert Gondos: Az öreg hárs faggatása. (Interrogation of the old lime tree.) Csikszereda, 1994, Alutus Press. (Private publication)

other. He instructed the Udvarhely Seat to protect the Catholics of Betlenfalva since, as he wrote, he was trying to maintain and protect all denominations and would not tolerate any high-handed activity in his realm. Other letters make it plain that he was in favor of the communities electing their own clergyman of the denomination of their choice. In 1629, he elevated the Calvinist pastors and their descendants to the rank of nobility.

Their privileges

The Székelys could regulate their internal affairs independently at their National Assemblies. They did not pay taxes and the occasional gift of oxen (1/6 of the total herd) to the king served to feed the royal army. Székely property did not revert to the state if the owner died. In the absence of heirs, the property went to a neighbor. In general, the son inherited the real property and if there was no son, but there was a daughter, then the "male daughter" inherited everything. (As an example, Ilona Apor, the "male daughter" had two husbands and a son from each of them. They kept their mother's maiden name and were known as László Apor and Mihály Apor).[7]

It was only during the reign of Ulászló II that the Székelys asked that their ancient laws and customs be codified. This occurred after the Voivode, István Báthory, was forced by the Székelys, with the support of the Archbishop of Esztergom, to resign because of his cruelties. The Letter of Privileges, issued by the King in 1499, precisely delineated the military obligations both within the country and abroad. In exchange, "the Székelys, recognized by the glorious former kings of Hungary as noblemen, were free of all taxation and of all other impositions". The number of the Székelys going to war was determined by the Bailiff and the major Seats. "At the legal coronation of the king, every Székely Seat was obliged to give an ox. When the ox-tax was imposed, the Székelys had the right to take half of the herd for themselves and have the king's man select an ox for the king from the remaining half". The same thing happened when a crown prince was born and when the king was married for the first time. The Letter of Privileges determined the hierarchy of the courts and ordered that whenever anybody initiated anything against the common good of the Székelys, the affected Seat might call a general assembly (Diet), or the Captain of Udvarhelyszék could summon the three orders of the Székelys for them to rule on the issue with the decision being taken to Bailiff.

Some local divisive forces endeavored to turn the tripartite division of the country, in 1541, and the weakening of central authority to their advantage. Thus, the leading personalities crippled the Székelys' civil rights and increased the taxation. The dissatisfaction finally led to the 1562 uprising that was put down by János Zsigmond, the Prince of Transylvania. As punishment, it was decreed at the Segesvár National Assembly that henceforth the Székely commoners would become villeins.

Bloody battles and internal warfare ensued and it took more than forty years before they regained their old freedom. Prince István Bocskai urged the Székely Captain-in-Chief in several letters to protect the Székely commoners

---

[7] Ibid.

15

from the molestations of their own leadership and that the guilty parties should not be allowed to escape their legal punishment. Bocskai also elevated a large number of men from a low status to noble, lófő or free Székely status. Prince Gábor Bethlen realized that the Székely commoners were escaping from the excessive taxation into voluntary villeiny, since in that status they did not provide military service and did not participate in paying the taxes due to the Turkish Porte. Their number was estimated to be 10,000 and Bethlen discovered that, if this unfavorable trend were not stopped, the number of the cavalry forces, consisting of free Székelys, would be drastically reduced. Therefore, the 1622 National Assembly decreed that anyone making a free Székely into a villein would have to pay a fine of 400 Ft. and further, that the villeins had to pay the taxes as well. In his 1635 Letter of Liberation, Prince György Rákóczi I returned all the privileges that were taken from them by János Zsigmond. These included the privilege that, in the case of death where there was no heir, the estate would not revert to the king but would become the property of the community.

During the war of liberation against the Turks, Transylvania came into Habsburg hands in 1690 and its fate was decided in Vienna. It was taken from Hungary and established as a separate entity (gubernium). Their tax-free status was confirmed by Leopold I, Emperor of Austria (1640-1705) and King of Hungary (1657-1705) in the Diploma Leopoldinum, issued in 1691.

At the time of Queen Maria Theresa (1740-1780), a part of the Székelys were organized into frontier defense troops and their privileges were gradually curtailed. This led to a bloody accounting, the so-called Mádéfalva threat ("Siculicidium") in 1764, when general Buccow massacred the protesting Székelys at the village Mádéfalva. After this event, in 1763-1764, whole villages migrated mostly to Bukovina but also to Moldavia.

After the 1848-1849 War of Liberation, the Austrian administration first established military districts in the country. These were converted to civilian administration after 1854. In 1876, a unified system of civil administration was introduced nationwide and henceforth the autonomy of the Székely ceased to exist.

After the Compromise of 1867, interest in the Székelyföld increased and the unfavorable environmental conditions, the backward nature of the area and its economic immaturity were recognized. A number of corrective measures were initiated (railroads, education, protection of the small industries, farmers' unions, cooperative endeavors, preferential seed prices, etc.) and these improved the economic situation of the region. These efforts ultimately proved to be insufficient.

The Csángó-Hungarians living in Moldavia

The earliest Hungarian settlements in Moldavia were probably established at the time of the conquest when the original settlements along the Prut and Seret rivers were charged with the defense of the frontiers against the attacks of the Pechenegs and, later, of the Cumans from the East.

The first major move to this area occurred during the reign of András II and was continued by Béla IV who relocated Hungarians to the east of the Carpathians as a defense mechanism against the Tartars. During the subsequent stormy historic period the slow migration to the East increased. This Hungarian-speaking ethnic group that settled in the Middle Ages among the Romanians in Moldavia is known as Csángó, In the 12-13th centuries, the Hungarian settlements between the Seret and the Carpathians were much more numerous than those found in 1646 by Bandinus. The early settlements were established by the Hungarian kings as a continuous defense barrier from the Eastern line of the Carpathians to the Seret river.

A new wave of settlers arrived in Moldavia in the 14th century when the area again came under the authority of the Kings of Hungary for a short while. In the 15th century, their number was increased by the Hussites expelled from Hungary. These "Heretics", expelled by King Mátyás (Mathias) for following the teachings of John Hus, founded a city in Moldavia and called it Hus. The historians of King Mathias also report that the King was considering the repatriation of the Csángó to Hungary. The Székely, who left their homeland when the frontier defense perimeter was established, built a village named Pusztina in the large prairie of the Tatros district, not far from Háromszék and Csík. According to the Romanian historian N. Iorga, there existed a county named Secuieni (Székely) until the end of the 19th century in the present area of counties Buzau and Prahova. The spiritual care of the Catholics of Muntenia and Moldavia was entrusted until the 15th century to the Bishop of Milkó who was in charge not only of parts of Moldavia, but who had deaneries in the Székelyföld as well (Udvarhely, Seps, Marosszék). The Turkish armies devastated Moldavia in 1441 and destroyed the see of the Bishop of Milkó, whose lands were taken over by the Orthodox Vlachons. After 1525, the See entirely ceased to exist.

Priests for the numerous Hungarians in Moldavia were provided between 1592 and 1605 by the Bishopric of Bakó, established by Pope Clement VIII. The work of the Bishops of Bakó was greatly assisted by the Franciscans coming from Csiksomlyó.

During the following decades, the churches were alternately supported or destroyed by the Moldavian Princes, the Boyars and the Tartar marauders. The people were taxed heavily. In the 17-18th centuries, Italian and Polish Catholic priests were active in the Moldavian villages. They spoke no Hungarian but were supported by the prebendary of Lemberg (Lvov). Petrus Deodatus, the Vicar of Moldavia and Muntenia, traveled throughout Moldavia in 1641 assessing the situation of the congregations. He found that their priests were ignorant of both Hungarian and Romanian. The number of Csángó decreased gradually and the villages and towns became increasingly Romanian. It was in vain that they sent desperate, pleading letters to the Holy See, asking that no Italian or loose-living Polish missionaries be sent to Moldavia. (After the death of Bandinus, the Moldavian Hungarian Jesuit Houses were incorporated into the Polish diocese.) Between 1622 and 1812, none of the 54 missionary prefects sent to Moldavia by the Congregation for the Propagation of Faith spoke Hungarian. "...The missionary brothers whom Your Holiness and the Sacred College have sent ...are drunks, chasers after women, flirt and chat with them, lead a hideous dreadful life...We would rather join the Romanian's schism and listen to their bishop...than accept them", they wrote in the letter of complaints.[8]

Preservation of Csángó identity was made difficult in 19th century Romania by the fact that they did not have a single school where they could study in Hungarian. They lived in a situation without rights while the Transylvanian Romanians, subjects to the Austrian Emperor and Hungarian King, were under the protective wings of their ecclesiastic autonomy and could develop their independent system of institutions. All this is well illustrated by the case of János Rab.

According to the agreement reached at the 1856 Paris Congress, seven European powers (Great Britain, Austria, France, Russia, Prussia, Sardinia and Turkey) collectively supervised the preparation of an Interim National Assembly in Moldavia and the Havasalföld, called for the purpose of electing a prince. As a result of the elections held in Moldavia in 1857, János Rab, a Csángó, was chosen as representative in a Romanian county. The prefect and the Bishop declared that the election was invalid because János Rab had no right to represent the peasantry of the county, since he was not Orthodox and was not a Romanian. Although, referring to the above case, Kogălniceanu submitted a legislative proposal to the Interim National Assembly, called in 1857, requesting that all citizens be given equal rights (franchise), even if they were not Orthodox, since they paid taxes and served in the army, just like the Orthodox. The proposal was rejected.

The official 1859 census shows 37,869 Hungarians in Moldavia of whom 22,426 lived in County Bakó. (The 1930 census shows 20,964 Hungarian nationals in Moldavia and 23,894 who claimed Hungarian as their mother tongue. The inaccuracy of the census is revealed by the data on religion which show 109,253 Catholics and 1,402 Calvinists in Moldavia, although it is well known that the border between Eastern and Western Christianity coincides with the Eastern border of Transylvania. In Moldavia, the Catholics and Calvinists were, with few exceptions, of Hungarian descent. *Over the centuries in the absence of Hungarian schools and Hungarian preaching, only the church could preserve their sense of national identity.*

---

[8] Antal Horváth: A moldvai katolikusok ősei (Ancestors of the Moldavian Catholics). Történelmi Dokumentumok (Historical Documents), 1227-1702. Hölgyek Egyesülete 2001, Bp. 2000, p. 89. The Szabófalva Catholics and five neighboring Hungarian sent a joint letter to the Propaganda Fidei office at the Holy See on October I, 1671. The same type of information appears in all other reports as well. In his letter to the Vicar, Giovanni di Frata the Minorite Father, Paolo Bonnicio writes on April 24, 1930, from Galac, "Let his Holiness know that every day Catholics become Orthodox...The priests, ignorant of the Wallachian, Hungarian or German language, can accomplish nothing." Petru Parcevic followed Bandinus in the Bishop's Chair and in his letter, written in 1670, he confirms the problems and openly states about the missionaries that they are of no use in this area since they are unfamiliar with the language and have no permanent domicile. The people did not like the Poles and did not trust them (ibid. p. 85). The case of János Rab and the speech of Kogalniceanu are given in some detail by Lajos Demény: A csángó magyarok kérdése Moldva Ideiglenes Országgyűlésén.(The Question of the Csango Hungarians at the Interim Moldavian National Assembly). In Tűzcsiholó In honor of the 90 year-old Gábor Lükő. Ed. Péter Pozsgai. Táton bt. 1999, pp. 37-45.

The Pechenegs[9]

The slow migration of the Pechenegs (in Hung: "besenyők") into the Carpathian basin continued from the 10th to the beginning of the 12th century. The first group arrived around 955, under the leadership of Tonuzoba, followed by two or three other groups. Taksony assigned an area to them in the mid-Tisza region. Most of them were settled in widely scattered communities on the borders, in Western-Hungary, in the Felvidék (Upper-Hungary) and in Counties Tolna and Fejér. This was done so that they did not represent a potential danger to the central authority. One group was settled near Dévény to protect the western border. In these decisions, the Hungarian Monarchs were probably motivated by the memories of the fights prior to the settling of Hungary (the severe defeat at Etelköz in 894) and by the repeated hostile incursions of the Pechenegs in the 10th century. In the Felvidék and in the Mátraalja, there are Pecheneg village names dating from the 10-11th century, wedged in among Palóc and Slav villages, presumably of Kabar origin. Village names also prove that the Tomaj tribe settled next to Losonc.

The Kings wished to rely on the lightly armed, mobile mounted archers in the defense of the borders. *The 1224 Árpás Letter of Privileges informs us about the privileges granted to them.*

Their highest dignitary was the Nádorispán (Palatine bailiff) who was endowed with administrative and judicial authority. He appointed the Pecheneg bailiffs who led the warriors in case of war. The Pecheneg officials were:

The Nádorispán (Palatine bailiff)
The Ispán (Bailiff)
The Udvarispánok (Curial bailiffs: counselors and judges)
The leaders of the Villeins (iobbagiones)

Those who belonged to the community but were unfit for military service could redeem themselves for money. By the 15th century, the Pechenegs melded into the various layers of Hungarian society and gave up their traditional costume and separate status.

The Cumans and Jazygians[10]

Among the foreign groups settling in Hungary during the Árpád era were the Cumans, who spoke a Turkic language, and the Jazygians who spoke Iranian and who were descended from the Alani.

The Cumans were one of the Turkic people who came from Central Asia to Eastern Europe. Between the 11th and 13th century they established a huge empire in the area between Caspian Sea and the Carpathians. Their rule in southern Russia, lasting almost two centuries, was brought to an abrupt end in the beginning of the 13th century by the armies of the Mongolian Batu

[10] József Kiss: A Jászkúnok meghonosítása (Settlement of the Cuman-Jazygians). Historia, 1991, #2-3.
[9] Zoltán Kordé: Besenyők az Árpád-kori Magyarországon (The Pechenegs in Hungary in the Arpad Era.) Historia, 1991, #2-3, p. 8.

Khan. The fate of the westernmost Cuman tribes was settled in 1223 by Ghenghis Khan in the battle by the River Kalka. The Cumans and the Pechenegs formed one people and were the ruling group in Moldavia until 1239. Moldavia was known at this time as Cumania although the Hungarian Kings referred to it as Greater Wallachia, since the Wallachs of the area were living under the rule of the Cumans and Pechenegs and were intermingled with them. (From the 19th century on, the Wallachians were referred to as Romanians).

After the severe defeat of 1223, Kötöny Khan reorganized the nationalities and, together with other tribal fragments, moved to the Balkans from where they asked to be admitted to Hungary.

They did move in 1239, but there were continuous clashes between the foreign, nomadic settlers and the settled Hungarian landowners and villeins. Finally assailants murdered the Prince of the Cumans, Kötöny and his people left the country, pillaging and despoiling as they went.

After the Tartar invasion of 1246, Béla IV, King of Hungary, called the Cumans, who had left in 1241, back to Hungary and settled them between the Danube and the Tisza and in the area between Szolnok and Debrecen. These areas, depopulated during the Tartar invasion, being known later respectively as Nagykunság and Kiskunság (Greater Cumania and Lesser Cumania). The historian György Györffy estimates the number of the Cumans and Jazygians to have been about 10,000 families, i.e., 40,000 souls. According to István Mándoki Kongur, their number had to be somewhere between 40,000 and 68,000. Both written sources and archeological investigations attest to the marked economic and social stratification of the Cumans. According to the testimony of some charters, the most prominent classes among the Cumans in Hungary were the Capitaneus and the Dominus. There were seven tribes (Olás, Csertán, Kór, Borcsol, Kondám, Honcsuk and Jupogó). Originally Béla IV wanted to settle them in the Kőrös-Maros-Temes triangle, assuring them their traditional way of life. According to the agreement, *in exchange for military service they could retain their national framework in their new nettlements between the rivers Dunube and Tisza but the King did insist that they be settled permanently and convert to Christianity.*

In the format of a nomadic ceremony, the ten leaders of the Cumans took an oath, according to the customs of their people, that, "as servants of the King, they would protect the land of the Hungarians against the Tartars and against other people"(1246).[11]

For about a century and a half, the Cumans practiced a nomadic form of animal husbandry. They lived in felt-covered tents, tended their enormous herds of horses, cattle and sheep and frequently strayed onto the neighboring pastures and fields of the nobility. Their first settlements appeared in charters only in the middle of the 14th century. These were, in all probability, not real settlements but rather merely nomadic winter quarters as the settlements have no name and were referred to in the charters only by the name of a neighboring Hungarian village or town or by the name of a chieftain who owned the land where the settlement was located. The first settlements having their own name appear in the charters only at the end of the 14th century. Most

---

[11] Jenő Szűcs: MOK p. 36.

of these names are derived from the personal name of the owner of the land, with the suffix -settlement, -people, -seat or -house attached to the possessive form of the personal name. Several of these names can be identified with individuals who lived in the 13th or 14th century. Cumans with Christian names can be found in the charters from the 13th century on.

Their privileges

In 1279, László IV gave them land for **autonomous settlements** in the Temes-Maros-Kőrös triangle, in the area between the Danube and the Tisza and in Mezőföld. This was the reward **for military service.**

The Cumans were accompanied to Hungary by the Jazygians. They were of Alanian descent and settled in the area known later as Jászság (Jász is the Hungarian form of Jazygian. Tr.). **The 1323 charter of the Hungarian King, Károly Robert** (1308-1342), in which he granted the Jazygians autonomy and other privileges for military service is preserved. Although they lost their privileges repeatedly (1514, 1526, 1702), they later acquired new ones. After their linguistic and national assimilation, it was their regional autonomy, or rather the fight to reclaim that autonomy, that held together the inhabitants of the Jászság and gave them national consciousness.[12]

Self-government

By the beginning of the 14th century, the Cuman winter quarters were probably in a fixed location with permanent boundaries. By the end of the 14th and the beginning of the 15th century, there was a system of settled Cuman villages. The 15th and 16th century Cuman settlements and communities differed little from the contemporary Hungarian villages in their appearance, structure and economic life.

The Cuman and Jazygyan Seats evolved from the original settlements during the 15th century and were endowed with judicial responsibilities. It seems likely that the tribunals of the judges dispatched by the central authority were located where the centers of the Cuman and Jazygian Seats developed and the Seats were frequently named after the judge.[13] The Seats were organized into districts, known as Universitas. The Seats and settlements were led by Captains and above them stood the Palatine.

The leaders of the tribes and clans (settlement captains) endeavored to make the tribal lands into private property. By the 15th century, the position of the settlement captains became so identified with nobility that their daughters could be designated legal heirs in the absence of surviving sons.

In the system of estates, *the Cumans were the Queen's people and received certain privileges for services rendered.*[14]

By the middle of the 16th century, war and internal dissensions led to the disappearance of 55-60% of the former settlements and the Turkish occupa-

---

[12] Zoltán Ács: Nemzetiségek a törtenélmi Magyarországon (Nationalities in historic Hungary). Kossuth Publisher, Bp. 1986, pp. 88-89.

[13] Zoltán Ács: Ibid. p. 86.

[14] Tibor Bellon: Nagykúnság (Greater Cumania) Gondolat, Bp. 1979, pp. 16, 19, 25, 38, 43, 51, 55 - 56.

tion accelerated this process so that by the end of the 17th century, the older system of settlements had largely disappeared.

The beginning of the 18th century was the period of re-settlement. Families belonging to one clan or serving together in the army occupied individual villages or districts within the towns. The distribution of land was also made on a street-by-street basis. Cardinal Kollonich drew the Teutonic Order of Knights' attention to the Cumanian Triangle. The Knights did buy the area but those who were thus reduced to villeiny paid their taxes through a community-wide autonomous system. The contract between the Habsburg Court and the Teutonic Order despoiled the Cumanian Triangle from the privileges granted centuries earlier causing the Cumans to flock to the banners of Rákóczi.

The joint ownership of land and agriculture was preserved. No villein lands were created, which meant that no land was worked by individual families. Their autonomy at the beginning of the 18th century was enjoyed only as members of the community. The leadership, elected from among their own ranks, functioned as an economic and political organization. The Szatmár Peace Conference at the termination of the Rákóczi rebellion (1711) makes reference to the need for regularizing the legal situation of the Cumans. According to the Peace:

"The privileges of the Jazygians, Cumans, Heyducks and their cities, if recognized to be contrary to the laws of the land, shall be terminated by the national Assembly for all times."

Redemption / renewal of the autonomy

In the middle of the 1740s, the inhabitants of the Jászkunság petitioned to have their ancient rights restored and offered to pay any security pledges still outstanding. Empress **Maria Theresa approved the petition and, as the Queen of Hungary,** issued a Letter of Privileges in 1745 in which the legal status of the Cuman-Jazyigian Triangle was regulated and which determined the way of life for the inhabitants of this region for the next 150 years. The privileges included:

- Judges – The Palatine as Judge and Captain of the Cumans, and their own judges,
- Freedom of duties within the country,
- At the election of judges, the Palatine would appoint the Palatine Captain,
- The captains, assessors, district officers and the judges of the communities are elected by the respective communities under the supervision of the Palatine Captain,
- They would determine whom to accept as a member of the group in the division of the common tax burden,
- The privileges and advantages of the inhabitants of the Jászkún region were to be shared equally among all of the inhabitants, under the same stipulations, and they would enjoy the same privileges and freedoms.

By 1751, the Jászkunság paid off the security pledge. **Act XXV of 1751** initiated and guaranteed the privileges. Within the communities, all inhabitants participated, according to their ability, in generating the funds required to pay off the pledge. Those who were not able to contribute were left without land and many of them moved to the southern areas, recently recaptured from the Turks, in order to make a living.

The collective freedom gained by the people of the Nagykúnság by this "Redemption" was a hundred years ahead of general Hungarian conditions and of the emancipation of the villeins.

The Jazygian district came to and end in 1876 and was integrated into the county system.

Church, religion and native tongue

The conversion of the Cumans to Christianity was initiated by the Bishop of Milkó, beyond the Carpathians. This bishopric was repeatedly destroyed by the Tartars in the early centuries but was rebuilt each time by the Kings of Hungary. It is shown in papal documents that in 1227, young King Béla, who at the time was governing Transylvania, went to the land of the Cumans, accompanied by Robert, the Archbishop of Esztergom. During this visit, the Chieftain of the Cumans, Borics, and 15,000 of his followers converted to Christianity. Their persons and freedom was guaranteed by a solemn letter from Pope Gregory IX and by a Golden Bull from the young King Béla. Pope Gregory X, upon learning that there were people living in Moldavia who called themselves Wallachians and who, together with Csángó-Hungarians living in the same area, were converted by Greek Orthodox "False Bishops" (pseudoepiscopi), instructed the Catholic Bishop, Theodoric, to appoint a suitable Vicar from the people, who were ready to return to the fold of the Catholic Church.[15] The Jazygians who fled to Hungary were all following the Byzantine religion.[16] King Kun László (1272-1290) himself supported the spread of the Eastern Rites. When the conversion of the pagan Jazygians living beyond the Carpathians was completed by the 15th century, the Jazygians living with in the country also converted to the Latin Rites.[17]

The Cuman language was still alive at the time of the Turkish occupation and when the Reformation spread through the country. A 16th century Turkish traveler, Seyh Ali, who visited Hungary in 1558, wrote that they dressed in the Tartar fashion and that many of them were speaking the Tartar language. (The Ottoman-Turks called all Turkish people speaking a different language Tartars.) It is evident that the traveler spoke of the Cumanian dress and language. During the Turkish occupation, the Cumans became fugitives. Because of continuous harassment, many of them sought refuge in the swamps and reeds of the Kunság and of the surrounding areas. Others left their homeland and sought safety further afield. Their Hungarization was strongly supported by the Hungarians who were in hiding or in exile with them, who strongly assisted them after their return and who settled among and around them.

The Cumanian language died out in Hungary by the middle of the 17th century and its traces can only be found in geographic designations. The Cumans remain-

---

[15] István Pirinyi: A magyarországi görögkatolikusok története (History of the Greek Catholics in Hungary), Görög Katolikus Hittudományi Főiskola (Greek Catholic Theological University), Nyiregyháza, 1990.

[16] Ibid. p. 73.

[17] Ibid. p. 73.

ing in the Balkans forgot their own language even more rapidly than their brothers in Hungary. The widely scattered settlements and the lack of privileges made them into smaller and smaller minorities and after a short while they were assimilated into the Romanian or Bulgarian ethnicity. Only in the areas occupied by the Mongols did the Cumans preserve their mother tongue, but being under the auspices of the Golden Horde, they are being referred to as Crimean or Kazan Tartars. The Cuman language belongs to the Cuman-Kipcsak branch of Turkic languages. The language of the Pechenegs belongs to the same ancient linguistic group.

Linguistic records of the Cuman language in Hungary can be found in two areas: textual and scattered. Among the textual remnants, the most valuable is the Lord's Prayer in Cumanian that was used as a teaching text in schools in Kisujszállás and Karcag until 1948. The translation was probably prepared during the Reformation, or soon thereafter, and was first recorded at the end of the 17th or the beginning of the 18th century. The song of "Halas", a blessing, children's poems and sayings can be found in the museums in the Kunság region and also in the volume of essays by István Mándoky Kongur. The scattered remnants of the language include personal and family names recorded in charters, in the Register of Births of the cities in the Kunság, in geographic designations, the names of localities, regional dialect fragments and Cuman words taken over into Hungarian.[18]

The Transylvanian Saxons

After the borders were pushed further outward, permission was granted for settlement in Transylvania on royal lands that were formerly part of the border region. Once permission was granted, Saxon, i.e., German settlers arrived in three large waves as shown by the place names in three different areas. In the first wave, some of the settlements were given names ending in -németi, mostly in Szatmár, while after the second wave the names ending in -szász can be found, mostly in the Bihar region. The first wave settled in Szeben and its region, the second in the Barcaság and the third one in Beszterce and its region.

The Saxons in the Nagyszeben region were settled there by King Géza II (1141-1162). Their provenance is not entirely clear. In the 12-13th centuries, they were speaking a variety of dialects and are referred to as Flamands, Teutons and Saxons. It can be assumed that most came from the Rhein-Mosel region but a South-German origin can not be excluded.[19]

---

[18] István Mándoky Kongur: A kún nyelv magyarországi emlékei (Remnants of the Cuman Language in Hungary). Karcag város önkormányzata kiadásában, 1993, pp. 27-31. István Mándoky Kongur devoted his entire life to Cuman studies.

[19] Korai Magyar Történeti Lexicon (Encyclopedia of Early Hungarian History) Edited by: Gyula Kristó, Akadémia, Bp. 1994, pp. 618-619.; Lajos Hanzó: Az erdélyi szász önkormányzat kialakulása (Formation of the Transylvanian Saxon Self-Government) Értekezések a magyar királyi Horthy Miklós Tudományegyetem Magyar Történeti Intézetéből. (Essays from the Hungarian History Institute of the Royal Hungarian Miklós Horthy University), Szeged, 1941. pp. 18-29.

Later there was some intermingling with Walloons. Their task was to improve salt mining, to man the border fortresses, to strengthen the economy and to mine gold in the Transylvanian Érchegység.

King Endre II (1224) in his charter, Andreanum, granted autonomy and collective rights to the Saxons. The rights were granted to Szeben and its region and later the surrounding Saxon regions were granted the same rights. A Saxon University ("Universitas Nationis Saxonicae in Transylvania") was established and was first mentioned in 1486. It functioned until 1868.2

The rights

1. Szeben and its region constituted a single political entity under one judge. The Count of the Saxons was first appointed by the King but later was elected by the Royal Judges of the various districts. In 1402, King Zsigmond granted permission for the Bailiffs be elected to their office.
2. Only a person living in the region was eligible for a judgeship. The nobles were excluded.
3. They paid 500 silver Marks to the King each year and their markets were free of duty.
4. For military service within the country, they had to furnish 500 armor-clad cavalrymen. Outside of the country, if the King led the army personally, they had to furnish 100 men. During peacetime, 50 fighters had to be trained and available.
5. They could elect their own priests and tithed directly to them.
6. Only the King or his bailiff could render judgment over them if their own judge refused to do so. According to the immunity granted to them, they were not subject to "foreign", i.e., Hungarian County Courts. Their own Common Law (Der Sachsen in Siebenburgen Statua oder eigenes Landrecht) was in effect until 1853 when it was replaced by the Austrian Civil Law.
7. They could use the forests and the waters, even the King's or the Wallachians. Rights were later extended to matters of inheritance and the sale of meat and alcoholic beverages. The latter was on a community-by-community basis. They could hold markets freely and without being taxed.

Beginning at the end of the 13th century, the agricultural villages develop into the Saxon towns. In the 14th century, the Saxon Seats functioned as judicial entities with a Royal Judge in charge. The highest representative of the closed communities was the Royal Bailiff who was a member of the Transylvanian Voivode's (later prince) council. The full Saxon self-government evolved under King Mathias when it was given the right to elect the Royal Judge and the Transylvanian privileges were extended to all other Saxon regions. Thus the entire Saxon nationality constituted an administrative-political unit, with the "Count of the Saxons" at its head. This position was traditionally held by the mayor of Szeben.[20]

The peasant uprising under the leadership of Antal Budai Nagy in Transylvania, in 1437, could be defeated only by a union of the privileged classes, the Hungarian nobility organized on a county basis, the Székelys liv-

---

[20] Zoltán Szász: Szászok (The Saxons), MOK. p. 49.

25

ing in Seats and the Saxons also organized into Seats. This union remained a major power until 1848.

The Saxon laws were codified in 1583 by Albert Hutter, the Nagyszeben Royal Judge, and **this codex was endorsed by Prince István Báthory (1571-1586) and by the Emperor, Leopold I (1657-1705).**

The Body of Laws functioned as follows:[21]
The 22 representatives elected by the Saxon Seats and regions met annually in Nagyszeben under the chairmanship of the Saxon Count. Every Seat or region was under a supreme official (mayor or Royal Judge) who was in charge of the administration. In the free royal cities, the council assisted them in the administration. The Seats and regions also held annual meetings where the officials and the delegates to the National Assembly were elected. The towns and villages could also have meetings where the local officials and representatives were elected. The Saxon autonomy was dismantled in 1876 by the Dualist Hungarian State when a general bourgeois administration was introduced on the French model.

Ecclesiastic organization[22]
The fact that the Saxons could preserve their language and culture throughout the centuries was due not only to their administrative autonomy and to their parochial schools, but also to their ecclesiastic organization. Electing their pastor was the privilege of every Saxon community. Part of the tithing was kept by the pastor but the remainder was at the disposal of the community. Since the battle between the Transylvanian bishop and the Saxons over tithing was lost by the Saxons, they tried to maintain their religious independence from the Hungarian ecclesiastic organization by developing independent deaneries. Finally, at the time of the Reformation, most of them opted for the Lutheran religion that granted them organizational independence.

In Transylvania religious freedom was guaranteed ever since 1557 to the Catholics, the Calvinist county nobility, the Catholic and Calvinist Székelys, the Lutheran Saxons and the Unitarian towns people. All four religions were free and protected for all the classes and orders in Transylvania. (Decrees of the Torda National Assembly, 1557, 1564 and 1568). Two shields protected the Transylvanian Saxons: guaranteed religious freedom and the Saxon administrative privileges.

Developments at the turn of the century[23]
In the educational and ecclesiastic organizations evolving after 1867, the teachers worked very closely with the clergy, trained in German Universities, and were of great assistance to the peasantry trying to modernize their agriculture.

The nationality groups could consistently elect leaders from among themselves, frequently ministers or congregational elders, who preserved the micro-society and

---

[21] János Hunfalvy: Nagyszeben. A szászok alkotmánya (Nagyszeben. The Constitution of the Saxons), Magyarország és Erdély (Hungary and Transylvania) I-III. Darmstadt 1856, 1860, 1864, György Gusztáv Lange, pp. 60-61.
[22] Lajos Hanzó: Ibid. pp. 52-55.
[23] Zoltán Szász: Magyarok, románok, szászok (Hungarians, Romanians and Saxons). Historia, Bp. 1991, #2-3.; Annemie Schenk: Deutsche in Siebenbürgen, Ihre geschichte und Kultúr, München, Verlag C.H.Beck, 1992.

saw to it that the community was united in their external stance. It was thus that under the leadership of their intellectuals, the peasants could develop into citizens sensitive to the needs of economic modernization and into prosperous farmers.

By the end of the 19th century, their cottage industries developed into major Saxon industrial endeavors: salami production, breweries, distilleries and leather works.

The Saxon banks made major contributions to the development of cultural and educational activities and also had their own scientific, cultural and sporting associations. One of the outstanding representatives of this period was Karl Wolff, the president of the largest Szeben Bank, who was very active in urban development, in the organization of agricultural credit associations and in luring German capital for the industrialization of Transylvania.

The Saxons retained the leadership of the cities for themselves, in spite of the free entry of sizable Hungarian and Romanian groups. They also preserved the use of their own German language in all of their communities.

The Szepesség (Zips) Saxons

The Szepesség Saxons did not all settle at the same time. The first settlers arrived about the middle of the 12th century into the valley of the Poprád and Hernád. The second period of settlement took place after the Tartar invasion and was part of the purposeful settlement program of king Béla IV and his successors. The so-called Gründler settled in the mining district in the Lower Szepes region. The Kings gave the settlers huge forests and uncultivated land. Arrangements for the settlement of various groups, including the Saxons, were made by agriculturally knowledgeable land agents, soltész, who negotiated with the landowners.[24]

The Saxons came from a variety of German provinces and even from Flanders. Their origin is a matter of debate. According to Győző Bruckner, the dialect of Upper Szepes suggests a Silesian origin. The language spoken by the so-called Gründler in the mining districts of the Lower Szepes, who settled here after the Tartar invasion, suggests that this group came from Austria-Bavaria. They cultivated rye, flax and hops and introduced the manufacture of linen and brewing beer. They were expert in raising sheep and cattle.

At the middle of the 13th century, 24 Royal Parishes were established, initially as a cooperative to assist the local congregations. Later on, they were very helpful in the development of the Saxon villages.

At the head of the Szepes Saxons stood the Landgraf, who was known as the Count of the 24 Saxon towns.[25] **The charter issued by King Stephen V (1270-**

---

[24] Szűcs: Ibid. p. 37.

[25] Győző Bruckner: A szepesség multja és mai lakói. (History of the Szepesség and its present inhabitants) In János Loisch: A Szepesség Lajos Kókai Publication, Bp. 1926, pp. 10-13. The provenance of the Szepesség Saxons is debated. The Upper Szepesség dialect suggests a Silesian origin. The settlers who came after the Tartar invasion and settled in the mining district of Lower Szepesség probably came from Austria-Bavaria. According to the Korai Magyar Történeti Lexicon (Ed. Gyula Kristó, Akadémia, 1994, pp. 618-619), the first settlers came during the second half of the 12th c. from County Abauj. The settlers, who came during the 13th c., speak a dialect suggesting a German, perhaps Saxon, origin.

1272), in 1271, granted a special legal standing to the Saxon University " Universitas Saxonum" and also reinforced all the old privileges of the Szepes Saxons. They were made into an independent community. The Count of the Saxons was the representative of the region but was, to some extent, under the supervision of the Bailiff (Várispán). The Saxons were given privileges to hunt, fish, cut down forests and open mines and had full control of the sales of their products. These privileges were entirely independent of foreign judges. They could elect their own priests and collect tithes. In exchange for these privileges, they had to pay 300 silver Marks, as land taxes, on St. Martin's Day and they also had to pay chancellery revenues. In case of war, they had to furnish 50 lancers to the King's camp.

The charters of King Charles Robert (1308-1342), issued in 1312 and 1328, raised the land tax, but eliminated the military service obligations and payment of the chancellery revenue because of the heroism with which the Saxons fought in the battle of Rozgony. The development of towns got under way. In the 1370, they collected and codified their laws. This is not an independent legal system, but a slight modification of the Saxon law. The women, widows and children received more protection than that granted by the original Saxon law suggesting the influence of the Hungarian common law.[26]

In 1412, the Holy Roman Emperor, Sigismund (1387-1437), who was also King of Hungary, gave up 13 towns to the Poles as a security for debt. The Polish Kings and their agents slowly did away with the privileges and this led to the gradual decline of these towns.

Some respite was given by the directives of Maria Jozefa, Queen of Poland and wife of Agost III, King of Poland (1734-1763). One of these directives directed that Hungarian be taught in the schools. In the meantime, the use of the Magdeburg Law spread through the land but the mining towns, under the leadership of Gölnicbánya, became organized under the Gölnic Statutes.

The remaining 11 towns were unable to protect their privileges during the later centuries against the powerful Barons. In the middle of the 16th century, the Saxon University joined the Lutheran division of the Reformation and the Lutheran religion became the religion of the entire region. It was to protect their religious freedom that they joined in the rebellion of Imre Thököly. Prince Ferenc Rákóczi II issued a charter protection for the towns as recognition for the Saxon's participation in his fight for freedom (1703-1711).[27]

In 1772, Maria Theresa gained back the towns pawned by King Sigismund to Poland and in 1774 she organized the 16 towns into a district. She placed them administratively under the Palatine Council and in economic matters under the Royal Treasury.[28] The charter banned the use of the Saxon Law and made use of the Hungarian Law mandatory. Only Lőcse and Késmárk, lying outside this district, were able to preserve their freedom against the inroads of the great landowners.

At the time of Emperor and King Joseph II (1780-1790), the civil rights of the

[26] Ibid. pp. 10.
[27] János Hunfalvy: Nagyszeben. A szászok alkotmánya. (Nagyszeben, the Constitution of the Saxons). Magyarország és Erdély I-III (Hungary and Trannsylvania) Darmstadt 1856, 1860, 1864, pp. 60-61.
[28] József R. Hajnóczy: Szepes vármegye történeti változásai (The historical changes in county Szepes). In János Loisch: op.cit. pp. 34, 36.

Szepes Saxons were in danger, since the King *lifted the autonomy of the Free Royal Towns and made German the official language for the entire country.* In protest, the German-speaking Szepes Saxons, who were loyal Hungarians, kept all their official records in Latin until 1845. From 1845 to the end of World War I, they insisted on keeping these records in Hungarian.[29]

Following the Compromise of 1867, the Hungarian government re-established the previous self-government of County Szepes, of the 16 towns, of the 2 Free Royal Towns and of the mining district. In 1876, when a countrywide uniform administrative system was introduced, the government discontinued the independent civil rights systems in all areas and the Saxon region was merged administratively into County Szepes.

The Croats[30]

Prior to the Hungarian occupation of the Carpathian basin at the end of the 9th century, there were already Slavic people living along the southern tier of the area. These included the Slovenes, Croats, Bosnians, Serbs, Bulgarians and Macedonians. The Slovenes and the Croats embraced the Latin Church while all the others belonged to the Byzantine Orthodox church.

Croatia existed as an independent country since 822. After the Croatian dynasty became extinct in 1091, the widow of the last Croatian king petitioned King Saint László (1077-1195), her brother, to occupy Croatia, and **until 1918 this area was a part of Hungary and was considered a sister state of the Hungarian Kingdom.**

King Kálmán, the Learned, (1095-1116) occupied Dalmatia, which constituted the southern part of Croatia. Jointly with historic Slovenia, these territories were an integral part of Hungary until 1526. The territory of the Zagreb bishopric and perhaps counties Pozsega and Valkó belonged to the Slavonian Bánát.

It was probably Saint László who initiated the system of royal counties in Slavonia. The Croatian royal house, facing extinction, had so little land that there was no possibility for the institution of royal counties. The Dalmatian cities were acquired by Kálmán the Learned, but throughout the Árpád era they could be preserved only at the cost of continuous strife with Venice. By 1300, the Subic became so powerful that they could invite their own candidate, the Anjou Charles Robert, to fill the throne of Hungary, even though King András III was still alive. It was his son, Lajos the Great, who did much for this area by liberating some major Dalmatian cities from Venetian rule in 1358. Ragusa, an independent Dalmatian city-state, declared its independence from Venice and placed itself under Hungarian protection.

Lajos the Great even considered building a fleet to protect these cities from renewed Venetian attacks, but the Dalmatian cities did not make adequate contributions. Under the Rule of Zsigmond of Luxemburg, the Dalmatian cities were lost even though Zsigmond pawned the Szepes cities to Poland to raise money for the war against Venice. Without a fleet, this could not be successful.

---

[29] Ibid. p. 2.
[30] László Szarka: Horvátország és a horvátok (Croatia and the Croatians), MOK. p. 173.

Many southern nobles rose to high office. They included János Vitéz, Janus Pannonius and also the Thallóczys, Frater György, Antal Verancsics, the Zrínyis, etc. During the reign of King Mátyás (1458-1490), the united Hungarian and Croatian armies were successful, against heavy odds, in holding back the Turkish advance. It was Mátyás' famous army and diplomatic skill that prevented the Turks from overrunning Dalmatia and Croatia. At this time, Ragusa considered Hungary as its main protector and its ships flew the Royal Hungarian flag.

After Mátyás' death, the defenses collapsed and the Mohács disaster (1526) sealed Hungary's fate. After the Turkish occupation of Slavonia and most of Croatia, the Croats fled to Western Hungary and Southern-Austria. Huge areas were thus de-populated and were partly resettled by Orthodox Vlachs under Turkish protection. The attack of the Turks against Vienna in 1532 was stopped at Kőszeg by Miklós Jurisics, Croatian commander. Miklós Zrínyi died a hero's death at Szigetvár in 1566, while his great-grandson, Miklós Zrínyi, Croatian Viceroy, poet, military commander, and tactician proved that successful campaigns against the Turks were possible.

In the 17th century, the Zrínyis, the Frangepans and the Erdődys became involved in livestock trade and their interests clashed with Habsburg commercial policies. The peace of Vasvár (1664), bringing to an end the successful campaign against the Turks, was followed by an open confrontation with the Habsburgs. The Croat peers who participated in the conspiracy were sentenced to death and an attempt was made to separate Croatia from the Hungarian Crown.

The Croats living in Hungarian areas were separated from each other geographically and also represented different groups (Sokác, Bunyevác, etc.), which differed from each other not only in their dialect but also in their history.

At the turn of the 17th - 18th century, many of the Bunyevác undertook military service under the Habsburgs. They were given free border-guard status and several families were ennobled by Charles III for valor. Many of their people were engaged in manufacture and trade. At the time of the Turkish occupation, in the 15th and 17th century, Catholic Bosnian (Croat) artisans and merchants appeared in Buda, Pest, Pécs and Szeged. They had a significant role in the re-building of the cities after the Turkish destruction and there were appreciable numbers of them living in Buda, Pest, Baja, Szeged, Mohács, Kalocsa and Szigetvár. The Croatian artisans formed separate Croatian guilds and kept their records in Croatian. The Croat citizens participated in the governance of the cities and became members of the magistracy. In Baja, for instance, until 1765, *three nations, Croat, German and Serb, constituted the membership of the magistracy* but thereafter the Bunyevác in Baja were considered to be members of Hungarian Nation (Nation Hungarica). *In 1768 the newly elected judge took his oath in Croatian in the Franciscan church in Baja.*

Cultural awakening

The 15th century saw the first publication of an epic, a tragedy and a novel in Croatian and there were personalities who were considered outstanding members of both the Hungarian and Croat literary and scientific communities. The first Croatian grammar was published in 1604 and in 1669 the first Croatian establishment for higher education, the Zagreb Academy was founded. Peter Zrínyi translated his brother, Miklós Zrínyis's, epic the "Szigeti veszedelem" (The

Threat of Szigetvár). Faustus Verancsics published a dictionary for five languages in Venice. Renaissance painting and architecture spread rapidly in the 15th century and numerous Dalmatian stonemasons worked in Hungary in the new style.

The Buda Franciscan monastery was an important center of Croatian culture in kaj dialect during the 18th century. It was here that the entire bible was first translated into Croatian. Szentpéterfa belonged to the Zrínyis and was settled largely by Croatians. Numerous interesting documents were preserved here. In the surviving book of rituals ("De Sacramento Matrimonio"), the questions to be asked of the couple being married were to be asked in the language of the couple. The appropriate passage had parallel columns, in Slavic, Hungarian, German and Latin and the questions in Croatian were pasted over the ones in Slavic. This book of rituals was published in 1700 under the patronage of Imre Eszterházy (1663-1745), Archbishop of Esztergom. According to a canonical visitation report of 1848, the languages of instruction in Szentpéterfa were Croatian and German. While the Croatian regions were under the Roman Catholic bishopric of Zagreb, the Franciscan played a major role in the religious life of the Croats living in Hungary. With Papal permission, the Bosnian Franciscan Province extended its services in the 16th century over the entire area of Hungary under Turkish rule. The Franciscans had a dominant role in assuring the survival of the Croatian population in this region. In many Hungarian communities in the 16th century, the Croats represented the majority of Catholics. The Buda center of the Franciscan Province distributed many religious texts in Croatian, while prayer books were generally distributed by the Zagreb bishopric. When, in the middle of the 18th century, the Court deprived the Franciscans of their parishes, the Croatian nature of these parishes began to fade. Máriagyüd, near Siklós, was a famous pilgrimage site where mass was celebrated in Croatian. The activities of the Buda cultural circle were also due to the Franciscans. The various Croatian national groups (Bunyevác, Gradistye Croats, etc.) all engaged in independent cultural activities. They wrote textbooks, plays and published newspapers.

The Croatian national movement appearing among the increasingly bourgeois intelligentsia at the beginning of the 19th century made personal contact with the representatives of the Pan-Slav and Austro-Slav movements in the Monarchy. Ljudevit Gaj reformed Croatian spelling on the Czech model and his book was printed in Buda in 1830. A group in the Austrian government under Kollowrat supported the Croatian national endeavors. At this time, the Croatian regions (Istria, Dalmatia and the border regions) were either under Hungarian or under Habsburg control and spoke three different dialects. The Illyrian movement under Ljudevit Gaj wanted to make the "što" dialect the Croatian literary language and this movement also drafted the political aims of the Illyrian movement attempting to unite all the Slavic peoples. Illyrian literary circles were formed and in 1839 the first Croatian tragedy was staged. The first Croatian opera was performed in 1846.

In 1840, the Croatian parliament petitioned the king to allow the establishment of a Croat chair at the Zagreb Academy and to make the learning of Croatian mandatory in all middle schools.

Regional autonomy
Hungary and Croatia were linked by a union lasting for seven and a half centuries. During that time, Croatia preserved its regional independence in law. It was *a sep-*

arate "political nation" with territorial self-government and its own parliament. During the Middle Ages, the Croatian Bán (Warden) was one of the barons of the realm.

The kings of the House of Árpád linked Croatia to Hungary as a personal union and Croatia, Slavonia and Dalmatia were governed either by viceroys (wardens), representing the king, or were given to one of the royal princes as a dukedom. During the 13th century, the independent Slavonian and Croatian-Dalmatian viceregal principality was created. The Slavonian Warden stood over the Warden of the Littoral, unless a royal prince assumed the title of Duke of Slavonia. In the 13th century, there was a separate Slavonia silver coinage known as the Warden's coin.

Until the Turkish times, the Croatian-Dalmatian and the Slavonian territories had independent legal status, the administration being provided by separate territorial assemblies and the king's person being represented by the Warden. The judicial system (Warden's Court) was also independent from the Hungarian legal structure. Croatia did not send county representatives to the Pozsony National Assembly but delegated one representative to the Upper Chamber and two representatives to the Lower Chamber as national delegates. After the Royal Fiat was granted, **the laws enacted by the National Assembly were valid for Croatia as well, while the laws enacted by the Croatian territorial assembly were valid only for Croatia and again only after they had received the Royal Fiat.**

When Dalmatia and Venice were given to the Austrian Empire after the Peace of Campoformio with Napoleon (1797), General Rukovina, a native of Zagreb, made the territory submit itself to the rule of Francis I, King of Hungary. "I have assured the Dalmatians that the territory will be under Hungarian administration, just as their ancestors had been subjects of the Holy Crown. This is in accordance with His Majesty's rights and the people's wishes", he stated in his report. In Spalato, the Hungarian flag was flown from the castle. Had the territory been attached to Hungary, it would have meant the preservation of the ancient territorial independence vis-à-vis the Viennese centralization and such an arrangement was strongly supported by Cippico, the Archbishop of Spalato and by Blaskovics, the Bishop of Makarska. The proponents of this daring plan rapidly fell out of favor and the territory was attached to Austria. In his letter dated June 17, 1801, Archduke Joseph informed the Emperor that the attachment of Dalmatia to Hungary should only be rejected if the people of the territory so wished it or if such an attachment would have led to the loss of the ancient privileges...."The attachment of Croatia, Slavonia and earlier of Transylvania to Hungary has proven that the Hungarians have always respected the constitution and privileges of these regions" he wrote.[31]

The endeavor to establish a national identity, and particularly the debate about the official state language, divided the Croatian and Hungarian politicians during the 19th century. Under the influence of the French "enlightenment", the demand was raised in Hungary for the introduction of Hungarian into the administration and into education to replace the German hitherto used in administration and the Latin that was still prevalent in education. It was primarily in opposition to Joseph II's Germanizing edicts that National Assemblies from 1790-1791 until 1848 strove to

---

[31] Ernő Töttösy: Dalmácia. Mécses Publ., Bp. 1992, p. 103.

modernize the educational system administratively and so far as the use of Hungarian in instruction was concerned. The Assemblies wished to replace German in administration and Latin in secondary education. They also demanded that the deliberations of the National Assembly be conducted in Hungarian. The Croat delegates viewed this latter move as dangerous to their traditional independence in civil rights. They stated that, "One kingdom could not make rules for another kingdom." They also protested the introduction of the law into Croatia that guaranteed equal rights to Protestants to hold all offices. Yet, at that time it had not occurred to any of the Croat nobles to introduce Croatian as the official language of Croatia.

The Napoleonic wars affected Hungary only incidentally, but considerable parts of Croatia came under French rule as the so-called Illyrian Province of the French Empire. *It was at this time that Latin was replaced by Italian and Croatian in the schools. The Illyrian Province lost all its former privileges and all traces of self-government.* Fouché's spies and the guillotine became active. After the French were expelled, the Austrians organized an "Illyrian Kingdom" under their own control, a move bitterly resented by the Croatian nobility and other ranks. The "Illyrian Kingdom" established in 1813 was dissolved in 1822, at which time the Illyrian areas were incorporated into Austria as a hereditary province. It was in vain that the Hungarian National Assembly demanded that Dalmatia be returned to the Holy Crown.

Concerned about their independence, the Croatian Parliament had all the customary and traditional territorial rights published in 1827 and, at the same time, it agreed to the mandatory teaching of the Hungarian language in Croatian middle schools.

While, in opposition to the more liberal Hungarian nobility, the Croatian nobility insisted at the 1832-1836 Pozsony National Assembly that the deliberations of the Assembly continue to be conducted in Latin, an Illyrian movement was organized by the bourgeois circles. By 1841, two political parties appeared representing two different political directions. One was the Croatian-Hungarian Party that favored a very close sister-state relationship with Hungary and the Illyrian Party that wished to reform Croatian civil law and that, by 1848, demanded a complete separation from Hungary. During the 1848-1849 War for freedom, this latter party demanded recognition of the principle of self-determination and asked Hungary to cede the border regions, Dalmatia, Fiume and the Muraköz to an independent Croatia. Because of the divisive policies of the Viennese Court, no compromise was possible.

In the spring of 1848, the Croatians demanded national independence with a government responsible to the Croatian National Assembly and with only the most tenuous relationship with the Hungarian Crown. The Viennese Court supported the anti-Hungarian right wing of the Illyrian Party. With Ljudevit Gaj's support, the Sabor proposed Jellasics (Josip Jellačić or **Jellasics in Hungarian**) for the Croatian Wardenship. Jellasics was a colonel in the border guards and known for his loyalty to Vienna and for his pro-Illyrian sentiments. Jellasics supported the Serbian Patriarch of Karlóca and the Serbian insurgents.

The Batthyány government was willing to yield in the matter of Croatian autonomy but Jellačić, on the inspiration of Vienna, came up with a new set of demands. Accordingly, he demanded that the Hungarian government yield the economic and defense portfolio and recognize Serbian independence.

Kossuth was no longer opposed to the complete separation of Croatia but refused to yield any of the Hungarian autonomy that was delineated by the April 1848 Hungarian statutes. Thus, a confrontation became inevitable and Jellasics crossed the Dráva on September 11 in order to overthrow the Hungarian government.

Contrary to the Serbs, the Bunyevác, a Croatian group, living in the South of Hungary, remained loyal to the Hungarian revolution. Following the defeat of this revolution, the Viennese government dismissed the Croat parliament in 1850 and, in 1852, demoted the Warden's Council to a simple caretaker organization. The county system was discontinued and Croatia and Slavonia were divided into five districts. German was gradually introduced as the language of the administration.

German, Slovenian and Czech officials were appointed to most positions and German was introduced as the language of instruction in all secondary schools. Only in the elementary schools was Croatian the language of instruction. Jellasics was allowed to retain his title as Warden but his authority was curtailed. *Statute XXX of 1868 enacted that Hungary and Croatia were separate political entities having separate territorial jurisdiction.* As far as their internal matters were concerned, they had their own legislative and administrative powers. Complete independence was granted in internal administration, education, religion and the administration of justice and the Zagreb Parliament was independent in these matters. The Croatian Warden, appointed by the King, was in charge of the administration, conducted in Croatian. Defense, fiscal matters and the relatively poorly developed economic situation remained a joint Croatian-Hungarian activity. The Croatian portion of joint expenses was born largely by Hungary. All territorial matters, except Fiume, were settled and the Croatian-Hungarian agreement was exemplary in the autonomy it guaranteed. *This autonomy had many of the hallmarks of a completely independent country, including administration, language, flag and crest.* Some of the Croats were still not satisfied and wished to establish either an Austrian-Hungarian-Croatian tripartite country or be given complete and full independence. Other Croats were well satisfied with the arrangements. The Bunyevác of Szeged and Buda were completely assimilated into the Hungarian population by the end of the 19th century.

Between 1880 and 1910, of the total population of Hungary and Croatia, 8.78% were Croats and 0.42% were Bunyevác and Sokác.

Ecclesiastic Autonomy

With the exception of the Saxons, the nationality groups described in the previous chapter were given their privileges in exchange for military service but enjoyed regional autonomy and freedom of taxation as members of a community.

At the same time, the Serbs in the South, the Romanians and the Ruthenians, lived under a feudal system controlled by their own privileged leaders. Those who belonged to the leading class received the same privileges as the Hungarian nobility and received them on an individual basis. This nobility melded into the Hungarian nobility over the centuries.

The large settlements during the Turkish occupation and following the expulsion of the Turks led to the formation of large nationality groups along the borders of the country by the end of the 18th century. At this time, the ratio between the Hungarians and the nationalities was 45%-50%. The Habsburg rulers decided to repopulate the country, not only because of the depopulation during the Turkish occupation, but also because they hoped that all the different nationalities would help to curb the

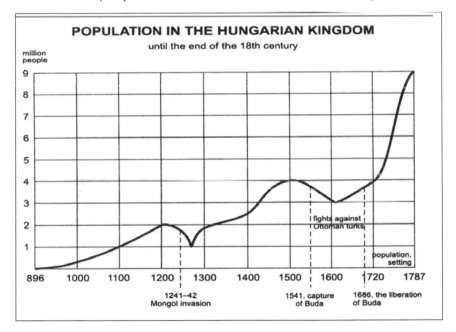

35

rebellious Hungarians. In the words of Cardinal Kollonich, they wished to settle people who were not tainted with Kuruc blood. At the time when the Temes Bánság was settled, Maria Theresa, who settled the Germans in this area and provided them with furnished houses, barns and cattle, admonished them that "different religions and nationalities should not intermingle". The same spirit pervades the Edict on the Regulation of Education (Ratio Educationis) that Maria Theresa issued in 1777 and that was re-issued in 1806. It emphatically supported the development of education in the native languages of the nationalities.

Act XXVII of 1791 declared that the rights previously granted to the Greek Orthodox regarding their establishments, educational system and the education of their youth remained in effect. This meant that they could manage their religious and educational affairs autonomously. The rights to self-government were administered by the Congress (Council) and the Serb Metropolitan Archbishop of Karlóca whose authority extended over the Orthodox Romanians as well. This eventually led to friction between the Serbs and Romanians. The Illyrian National Foundation and all other such establishments were led by an elected body of four members under the chairmanship of the Metropolitan of Karlóca. The edicts of the National Assembly affected only the Roman Catholic educational institutions (universities, academies, lyceums and high schools) since the foundations established to support these institutions were created by the leaders of the Catholic Church and were made possible by the edicts of Maria Theresa and Joseph II. Their authority did not extend to the elementary schools or to the Protestant and Greek Orthodox secondary and higher educational institutions, since *Act XXVI of 1791 guaranteed all Calvinist and Lutheran schools full religious educational authority in Hungary.*[32] This meant that while Catholic schools, high schools and universities were directly controlled by the Emperor, through the Viceregal Council (the selection of textbooks and the appointment of teachers), the control of Protestant education was exercised by the diocese. In the case of the Lutherans this was usually limited to supervision.

In any case, the Act of 1791 provided the legal framework for the German and Slovakian Lutherans in pursuit of their nationality and religious aspirations. It stimulated not only the maintenance of the existing schools but encouraged the foundation of new ones. The Act compelled the landowner to provide appropriate and adequate land for the construction of churches and schools. The Royal Ordinance of October 18, 1799 exempted the Protestants from the taxes ordinarily imposed on schools and on the land pertaining to them.

When national consciousness evolved, in the beginning of the 19th century, intellectual leadership was necessarily assumed by the Greek Catholic, Orthodox and Lutheran pastors, who institutionalized the ecclesiastic framework and who, under the protection of the laws, endeavored to increase and enlarge ecclesiastic autonomy. Within that autonomy they strove, in the parochial schools and cul-

---

[32] Miklós Bényei: Oktatáspolitikai törekvések a reformkori Magyarországon (Educational policy endeavors in Hungary during the Reform Era) Debrecen, Csokonai, 1994, p. 53, pp. 83-84, p. 106;

Tamás Katona: Nemzeti összeütközések 1848-49-ben (National conflicts in 1848-49) MOK, pp. 148-155;

Zoltán Szász: A nemzetiségek és a Magyar forradalom (The nationalities and the Hungarian revolution), In: Historia 1999/3, pp. 15-17.

tural societies, to foster the ideas of nationality and of unity within the nationality. Ecclesiastic autonomy evolved principally in the areas where solid blocks of nationalities lived together in a defined area. During the period when the achievement of a solid bourgeois status was the major driving force, the National Assemblies endeavored to control education, to establish a unified educational system and to modernize education. They wished to replace the Latin and German languages with Hungarian as the common language of education. This would explain why in the 1820s the representatives of the nationalities encouraged the teaching of Hungarian and it was only in the 1830s that in the nationality regions there was a strong movement that in the Catholic schools under state control, the language of instruction to replace Latin or German be other than Hungarian.

Act VII of 1792 mandated that Hungarian be included as one of the subjects regularly taught in school, but the Viceregal Council viewed it only as a secondary language, and it was only in 1819 that Hungarian became a regular and required subject. It was indicative of the situation that it was only in 1820 that the King required that reading and writing Hungarian be taught in the Orthodox Romanian and Serbian schools.

The Royal Manuscript of June 17, 1844, that became a Viceregal Council ordinance three days later, required that Hungarian be the language of instruction in all academies and universities. This was made possible, among other things, by the fact that the physicist Ányos Jedlik, a professor at the University of Budapest since 1840, created a Hungarian technical vocabulary in the physical sciences. Hungarian was the required language of instruction in the 44 schools located in the Hungarian-speaking regions, but in the 17 schools in the nationality regions Latin remained the language of instruction for the time being. *Act II of 1844 in essence confirmed this status quo since it affected only the Catholic Royal educational institutions but did not affect the elementary schools. The Calvinists had switched earlier to Hungarian as the language of instruction, the Lutherans preserved German as the language in a few schools in the Felvidék and the Greek Orthodox fought over Romanian or Serbian becoming the official language of Church and school.* The 1845 Ordinance of the Viceregal Council required that instruction be given in the mother tongue and that even in the nationality regions Hungarian had to be taught. It dealt separately with Croatia and related areas. There the issue was whether to make Hungarian a required subject or leave it as an elective.

The laws enacted on April 11, 1848 laid the groundwork for a bourgeois state with a representative National Assembly, franchise for all owners of land, universal taxation, emancipation of all villeins with governmental compensation, freedom of the press, elected city officials and a government responsible to Parliament. These laws also favored the individual nationalities. Shortly thereafter, however, the nationalities demanded that they be recognized as independent nations, and the recognition of the language of the majority in any county as the official language. In addition they demanded independent regional administration, i.e., territorial autonomy. The nationality assemblies also drafted legal demands that were already part of the governmental program and had already been ratified in the Pozsony statutes. These included such items as state salaries for pastors and teachers, emancipation of the villeins, equality before the laws, etc. The Hungarian government recognized the autonomy of Croatia but some of the Croats dreamed about an independent state, separate from Hungary, but still within the Habsburg Empire, to include Croatia, Fiume, Dalmatia and Slavonia. This idea was familiar to Kossuth since it was on his recommendation that the Hungarian Liberals advocated at the Pest County meeting in 1842, that Croatia be raised to an administratively and legislatively independent Kingdom under the auspices of the Hungarian Crown. Jellasics, however, was willing to negotiate only with the Viennese Court, which wished to utilize the anti-Hungarian Croatian National Party in trying to control the Hungarian reform endeavors of the 1840s. The Liberal nobility, forming the government in 1848, viewed the reconstitution of the country on a federal basis or the separation of the nationality regions as inevitably leading to the dissolution of the country and hence was opposed to it. The laws thus did not assure the use of their language to the nationalities, but did not invalidate the linguistic privileges of the autonomous churches.

The Declaration of Independence, accepted during the War of Freedom, on April 14, 1849, was followed by the government endeavoring to create a constitution that would have included the rights of the nationalities.

The July 14, 1849, Szeged Hungarian-Romanian "peace project" mandated that in counties having a Romanian majority, the minutes of county meetings had to be in both languages and guaranteed the use of Romanian in schools, courts of justice and in the National Guard. It further mandated that community matters be managed in the language of the majority of the population. This is the reason why the Romanian Orthodox Church was separated from the Serbian Church and was endowed with the same autonomy and privileges as those enjoyed by the Serbian Church. The most significant statement in this document was that, "the Romanians constituted a separate nationality". It was on this basis that **Act IX of 1849,** actually the Parliamentary statute of July 28, 1848, was promulgated. The **Statute guaranteed, "to every nationality its unhampered development", regulated the use of the official language and also dealt with ecclesiastic and educational matters.** In counties with a nationality majority the internal administration could be conducted in the principal language of the county and even where the nationalities represented a minority they could address formal meetings in their own language. It prescribed that, "in instruction, the language of the community or of the Church will be used". The military defeat of Hungary made the implementation of these statutes impossible.

In the period following the Compromise of 1867, the status of the minorities was given special legal recognition, even beyond the constitution. Hungary was unique in this in the Europe of the day. The minorities were not given identified areas or separate counties, however, and this led to considerable resentment on their part leading, in some cases, to the rejection of the law.

Even before enactment of the Nationality Act, Parliament enacted **Act IX of 1868** that resolved the ecclesiastic fight between the Romanians and Serbs by removing the Transylvanian Romanian Orthodox Church from under the authority of the Bishop of Karlovac and by elevating the bishopric to an archbishopric. **It guaranteed both churches and thus, implicitly, both nations the right to self-government.** According to this Act *they could manage their ecclesiastic, educational and foundational matters autonomously.*

Act XLIV of 1868 declared that all the citizens of Hungary constituted politically one nation, the homogenous Hungarian nation of which every citizen, regardless of nationality, was a full member with equal rights. The so-called minority recommendation, drafted by the nationalities was considerably more radical than the Act and stated:

"In Hungary the following historic nationalities, Romanians, Serbs, Slovakians, Russians and Germans are recognized as nations with equal rights for whom their national integrity and political autonomy is guaranteed within the general political framework and national security of the country by the fundamental laws of the land."

The nationalities were dissatisfied with the proposed Nationality Act that spoke of a politically unified country and did not guarantee that the regions where the nationality represented a majority would be granted a full and separate autonomy. Yet in European practice, this was the first instance where equal rights for all nationalities were declared by statute, which also *granted free use of their native tongue in local administration*, courts of justice and *primary and secondary education*. The statute also guaranteed the right to establish foundations and full autonomy in ecclesiastic and educational matters.

Even today, it is not easy to achieve a Nationality State as defined in the above quotation. The concept of a National State, as defined in the matter of the Corsican autonomy by the French legislature in 1991, may serve as an example. It stated that since the French Republic was based on the equal rights for all citizens, it did not recognize any individual differences and the term French People must designate the community of all citizens.

The Nationality Act guaranteed the possibility that beside the Hungarian language **the minority language could be used in official documents, administrative matters and in communications with the government wherever 1/5 of the representatives of the municipality demanded it.**

"Every citizen of this country has the right to prepare any submission to the local government, ecclesiastic authority or municipality in his/her own native tongue." The statute thus guaranteed the use of the minority language in the community and county political life, in the Church and in the courtroom. Anybody could establish educational, scientific or commercial organizations and selecting their language was the unquestioned prerogative of the founder. Every community, church or individual could establish and maintain schools using any language of his/her choice as the language of instruction.

The Minority Recommendations also stated that, "Every citizen of the country may use his own native tongue in any submission to the local or national government. In submissions to another community or jurisdiction, and their officials, the official language of the country, or one of the languages used in that community or jurisdiction for official communications may be used."

The Nationality Act did not touch the language used in sermons, in the registry of births or in official transactions and acted in the spirit of **Act IX of 1868,** "The parishes may decide, without offending the rights of the higher ecclesiastic authorities, what language shall be used in the registry of births, in the management of ecclesiastic affairs or in their schools, provided that this is done within the guidelines of the National Education Statute". *When it was made mandatory that national registries of birth be written in the official language of the country (1895), the parishes continued to have the right to keep the local registry of births in whatever language they chose*: The Calvinists, Unitarians and the majority of the

Catholics (in the diocese of Vác, Eger, Szatmár, Kalocsa, Nagyvárad and Pannonhalma) kept their records in Hungarian. Among the eight other Catholic dioceses, the language was Latin in 616 parishes. In the four Lutheran districts of Hungary, the records were kept in German in two locations, in Slovakian in 63 locations and in Latin in 2 locations. In three of the districts, the language was Hungarian, while in Transylvania, 263 Lutheran congregations kept their books in German. The Orthodox Serbs used the Ancient Slavic while the Greek Catholics and Greek Orthodox usually kept the records in the native language of the parish (Ruthenian, Romanian).[33]

The Public School Act (XXXVIII) of 1868 reinforced the above when it stated that, *"every student shall be taught in his native tongue"*. The same Act also made provisions for the establishment of public schools in all communities.

The representatives of the nationalities vehemently attacked the legislative proposal made by Ágoston Trefort, the Minister of Education, because it proposed to introduce the teaching of Hungarian, the official language of the country, into all public schools. *Act XVIII of 1879* mandated that *in the ecclesiastic teacher education schools*, where teaching was in a language other than Hungarian, *the official language had to be taught* in a concentration that assured that all graduates could read and write Hungarian adequately. It further mandated that three years after its enactment (teacher training was a three year course) "a teacher's certificate may not be issued to a person who is unable to teach Hungarian satisfactorily. Nor may such a person be employed as a regular teacher or as an assistant teacher". For those who were already teaching, the Act allowed six years for the acquisition of an adequate knowledge of the language. Those teachers who were over 50 years of age could petition the Minister to be excused from this requirement. These particular points were strongly attacked by the nationality politicians of the day and yet, it is worth mentioning that today, teaching a foreign language in elementary school, even at a basic level, requires a three-year training program. Also, the recent retraining of the teachers of Russian to teach some other foreign language was accomplished along very similar guidelines. Trefort felt that the mandatory teaching of the official language would decrease the likelihood of misunderstandings based on the inadequate knowledge of each other's language and minimize the dislike of each other escalating into hate. In his justification he writes, "As the instrument of contact and mutual understanding between all citizens of the country one of the languages used in the country must be chosen and this must be the language of the majority, namely Hungarian." Today, at the end of the 20th century, we can show several examples where one or more languages are used as official languages in one country. During the past, this could be implemented only in Switzerland. Trefort continued his justification thus, "As proven by the 1000 year history of Hungary, this country has never endeavored to assimilate the other nationalities or eliminate their language. Most recently, in the statute about the equal rights of the nationalities (XLIV, 1868) it permits, with the greatest liberality, and guarantees the use of their native tongue to all the nationalities living in the country."

---

[33] Gyula Vlassics, Minister of Religion and Public Education: Report on the Languages used by the Denominations, in Gábor Kemény: Iratok a nemzetiségi kérdés történetéhez Magyarországon a dualizmus korában. (Papers on the history of the nationalities in Hungary in the era of Dualism). II. Vol., Budapest, 1952, pp. 220-223.

Act XXVII of 1907, the so-called Apponyi Act about "the emoluments granted to the non-public elementary schools" stipulated that the teaching of Hungarian had to be introduced in all schools in order that the children write, speak, read Hungarian within 4 years. Accordingly the Ministry prepared a curriculum for the schools where the language of instruction was other than Hungarian. According to the number of the teaching staff, Hungarian had to be taught for 13-39 hours per week. In schools with only one teacher, 13 hours had to be taught per week, in schools with two teachers 21.5 hours and in schools with 6 teachers 39 hours. This meant that, on the average, 2 hours and 10 minutes (3 lessons per week) were spent teaching Hungarian per class per week. In exchange, elementary education was made free of charge and the salary of the teachers was increased. The Ministerial justification emphasized that this regulation was necessary since some ecclesiastic authorities demanded that the language of instruction in the parochial school under their control be different from both Hungarian and of the native tongue of the pupils. The purpose of the Act was that in all parochial or public schools the language of instruction should be either Hungarian or the native tongue of the children. Paragraph 20 prescribed that five subjects, Hungarian language, geography, history, mathematics and law, be taught according to a curriculum and with the use of textbooks approved by the Minister. Such approval was otherwise not required.

It must also be mentioned that *when the elementary schools were set up, instruction could be provided in the local dialect,* i.e., truly in the native tongue of the children and not in the artificial, literary language ordinarily used in the 20th century.

The above-described legal regulation of the nationalities was without precedent in Europe and, in practice, the financial assistance to the nationality institutions and to the minority press represented a form of "positive discrimination". It is a legitimate question to ask the reason for the determined anti-Hungarian sentiment of certain political groups within the nationalities. At the end of the 19th century, the franchise being tied to a high census, the gerrymandering of electoral districts in favor of the government party and the failure to institute land reform, created a common grievance among the Liberal opposition of the government (later the Social Democrats) and the radical nationality parties.

In 1876 the administration was unified and redrawn along bourgeois lines and the privileged regions of the nationalities were melded into the unified Hungarian administration according to the wishes of the modern, capitalistic bureaucracy. As part of this, the separate status of the Saxons was terminated, the remnants of the border region were erased and a unified system of counties was introduced in Transylvania. This was interpreted by the nationalities as an infringement of their autonomy and triggered vigorous protests. Similar ordinances were passed in most of Europe during the first half of the 19th century, but in Hungary such action could take place only after the Compromise of 1867 that made the bourgeois transformation along capitalist lines possible. At the same time, south of the country, the establishment of independent Balkan national states began, strongly supported by the Serbs and Romanians living in Hungary. Granting universal franchise could have increased the number of nationality representatives in the Hungarian parliament and could have made the reconstitution of the Hungarian counties along the Serb and Romanian border along ethnic lines more successful.

The Romanians

The Romanians appeared in Transylvania in large numbers only after the Tartar invasion. They were settled in the Southern Carpathians by the successors of Béla IV as "Royal Tribes".[34]

It was in vain that King András III (1290-1301) endeavored to reserve for himself the exclusive right of establishing settlements, since by the 14th century, the large landowners settled large groups of Romanians on their properties. During the 14-15th century, they were governed by Romanian common law.[35] This low-level autonomy was organized by village or by groups of villages and the leaders, the military *Kenéz*, were gradually absorbed into the Hungarian nobility by virtue of their privileges. A number of them established historically eminent families such as the Josika, Kendeffi, Majláth and Hunyadi.

After 150 years of Turkish rule, the number of Romanians was very small and hence new settlements were established in the areas abandoned by the Hungarians who had moved toward the central part of the country. The settlers on "free lands" came from beyond the Carpathians. Consequently, the percentage of Hungarians in these areas, 80% prior to the Turkish occupation, decreased to 45%. For the first time, the Romanians represented a majority in Transylvania vis-à-vis the Hungarians, Saxons and Székelys.

Queen Maria Theresa began to organize the Transylvanian border defense region. This was well received by the Romanians since the acquisition of land and the military pay strengthened their economy and it was also to this new organization that they owed the new and stronger system of education.

The development of the Church, schools and mother tongue until the beginning of the 19th century

The Romanians were, without exception, Greek Orthodox. At the time of their original settlement, they had bishops, but with the death of the bishops, the bishoprics came to an end. The Protestant magnates and the Princes tried to convert the Romanians to Protestantism. The Saxons tried to convert them to the Lutheran religion but soon realized the failure of these endeavors and discontinued all such efforts. The Transylvanian Princes first wished to convert them to Calvinism, hoping that the new religion would also raise their level of education. Prince János Zsigmond (1541-1571) prescribed that the language used in the Romanian churches be changed from the previous liturgical Slavic to contemporary Romanian. There were a number of ordinances in the 17th century that survive and that advised the Romanian bishops to abandon the "foreign" language and substitute the national one. They also advocated the support of Romanian publications and Romanian schools. *György Rákóczi I*, appointing Ábrahám Burdánfalvi to the Romanian bishopric of Bihar in 1641, instructed him *to preach in Romanian and make his priests preach in Romanian as well,*

---

[34] Zoltán Szász: Románok a középkorban (Romanians in the Middle Ages) MOK. p. 49.
[35] Jenő Szűcs, op.cit. p. 17.

so that, "the poor Romanians could listen to their own native tongue and thus daily improve in their search for salvation and daily wend their way from the darkness of superstitions to the light of truth"

The first Romanian publication, printed in Latin characters appeared at this time. It was the Psalter of Gergely Szegedi and it was followed first by an Old Testament and later by a New Testament. The first Romanian textbook was printed in Gyulafehervár and the first Romanian public schools were opened, by order of the Prince, in 1669.

Prince János Zsigmond was willing to accept only a Protestant Romanian church, but the Catholic Báthorys re-established the Greek Orthodox Church and since 1634, the Calvinist bishop was titled the "Bishop of the Orthodox Wallachians". This was an honorary title since the Orthodox Church was actually governed by the *Vladica* or Metropolitan, sitting in Gyulafehervár. Of the 50 contemporary Protestant synods, 40 were under the management of the Metropolitan while the others were directly under the Calvinist Superintendent. This relationship was a peculiarly Transylvanian phenomenon and did not exist anywhere else in the world. After 1628, the Transylvanian Princes set some conditions for the appointment of the Metropolitan. He had to preach in Romanian and conduct the entire service in that language. After 1640, the Calvinist catechism, printed in Romanian, had to be used. "The Wallachians live at the level of animals," wrote Prince Gábor Bethlen to the Patriarch of Constantinople. The priests had very little learning and could barely read and write or sing the liturgical songs. It was for this reason that the Princes insisted that schools be established where teaching was primarily in Romanian, but where some Latin and Greek could also be taught. In 1624, Bethlen issued an edict mandating that the landowners refrain from keeping the sons of villeins from attending the schools, under a penalty of 300 Forint. The wife of the ruling Prince, Zsuzsanna Lorántffy, established a Romanian school in Fogaras.

Until the arrival of Protestantism, the Romanian priests were villeins and it was only after this time that they were released from the payment of tithes. Bethlen was endorsing the edict of Gábor Báthory when, in 1614, he endowed the Wallachian priests of Bihar, Kraszna and Középszolnok with the privileges enjoyed by the Hungarian priests.[36]

Prince Mihály Apafi ordered that the Metropolitan Szaicz establish a new Romanian printing establishment to replace the one destroyed during the troubled times following the unfortunate end of the Polish war. It was the existence of the Transylvanian Wallachian printing establishment that explained the cultural effects of Transylvania on Moldavia and on the Havasalföld. János Kemény, the ambassador of György Rakóczi, took books printed in Romanian to the Havasalföld. At the same time, the Transylvanian Romanian Church was in active contact with Moldavia and the Havasalföld and received substantial support from them in the form of liturgical vessels, money, books, etc. The Imperial troops liberating Hungary from the Turkish occupation in 1690 put an end to the independence of Transylvania.

---

[36] Pál Péter Domokos: Rendületlenül (Steadfastly), Eötvös-Szent Gellért, pp. 20-21.; Marianne Székely: A protestáns erdélyi fejedelmek hatása a román kultúra fejlődésére. (The Influence of the Protestant Transylvanian Princes on the Development of Romanian Culture) Tiszántúli Könyv és Lapkiadó Rt., Debrecen 1935, pp. 6-19 and 27.

The Charter of King Leopold I (1657-1705), the Diploma Leopoldinum, regulated the situation of Transylvania. The region was taken away from Hungary and placed under a separate Chancellery in Vienna, guaranteeing religious freedom. In a decree issued a year later, he granted the Orthodox Churches the same privileges enjoyed by the Catholics, provided that they recognized the supreme authority of the Pope. Following the unifying synod of 1699, Leopold I, in 1701, regulated the legal status of the new Greek Catholic, or Unitus, Church. Accordingly the Unitus Church was entitled to the same privileges as the Latin Church. These included:

- The Unitus priests paid no taxes on their own property and no tithes after income from Church property,
- Romanian schools would be established in Gyulafehérvár, Hatszeg and Fogaras,
- The Bishop would be selected by the King from a slate of three names submitted by the clergy. The King would pay the bishop's salary,
- Henceforth, Romanian Unitus youths would receive their secondary education at the Jesuit High School in Kolozsvár.[37]

In 1791, an Act guaranteed the freedom of the Orthodox religion under the bishops appointed by the King. This was done in order to end the Slavic or Greek control of the Church. The gifts of the Tsarina Elizabeth, which implied Russian support, also motivated the above act.

It was decided in Vienna in 1758 to establish an Orthodox Bishopric.[38] It was with the support of the Treasury that the priests and teachers of the Greek Catholic and Greek Orthodox Churches stimulated Romanian national consciousness and the theory of Daco-Romanian continuity. The 1848 Romanian movement was largely directed by the priests of these two Churches and the same priests laid the groundwork for Romanian public instruction in 1849-1867.

Ecclesiastic self-government

In accordance with a Papal Bull, "Ecclesiam Christi" of Pius IX (1853), the leadership of the Hungarian Roman Catholic Church recognized the independence of the Greek Catholic Archbishopric of Gyulafehérvár-Fogaras. Thus these bishops could fully support the interests of the Romanians. After 1868, the Romanian Greek Catholic Church in essence elected its own leader from among the three names submitted, since the King always nominated the one who had received the most votes at the synod and whose name appeared in first place among the three. At that time the Hungarian Catholic bishops were appointed by the King, evidently discriminating in favor of the Romanians.[39] *In 1868 the Hungarian Parliament legally recognized the independence and self-government of the Romanian Greek Orthodox Church as the Romanian "National" Church.* The charter of the organization was prepared by well-known politicians according to "Protestant" principles.

In all synods, whether of the higher clergy, bishops, archbishops and even at the national ecclesiastic congress, the lay members represented 2/3 of the member-

[37] Pirigyi, op.cit. pp. 100, 101, 104, 107, 108.
[38] Pál Péter Domonkos, op.cit. p. 32.
[39] Sándor Biró: Kisebbségben és többségben – Romanians and Hungarians, 1867-1944. (In Minority and Majority), Europai Magyar Protestáns Egyetem, Bern, 1989, pp. 107-108.

ship and the clergy only 1/3. The officers were elected. They could make all decisions on their own in all matters pertaining to the Church, to education and to the foundations. Thus the Romanian intelligentsia, jointly with the clergy, had almost complete control within the Orthodox Church. According to chapter 5 of the by-laws, the body meeting every three years was in full control of the elections and of the ecclesiastic, educational and foundation matters. The first issues discussed were educational and nationality matters.[40] Vasile Lucaciu, a Greek Catholic priest of the Szamosujvár diocese, was also the Secretary General of the Romanian National Committee and thus one of the leaders of the Romanian national movement.

In 1892, the Romanian National Committee prepared a memorandum in which it lists the complaints of the Romanian people. The memorandum was taken to Vienna by a delegation of 300 members. The King did not receive them and the Royal Cabinet Office forwarded the memorandum to the Hungarian government. Since it was not addressed to the Hungarian government, it was returned, unopened, to Joan Rat, the president of the Committee. Upon this, the Committee published the memorandum in four languages. This led to the indictment of the leaders of the Committee. In 1894, 30 foreign correspondents informed all European nations of the events before the tribunal. It was particularly the French, Italian and Belgian press that was preoccupied with the situation of the Romanians. This trial was very detrimental to Hungary. The leaders were sentenced to prison, with Lucaciu being sentenced to five years of imprisonment but the King pardoned the entire group in September 1895. Yet, as a consequence of this affair, Hungary was viewed by European public opinion as the oppressor of the minorities.

The Economic Situation of the Romanian Churches[41]

CHURCH	LAND OWNED IN 1900	LAND OWNED IN 1917-1918
Romanian Greek Catholic Church	208,746 cadastral yoke	226,582 cadastral yoke
Romanian Greek Orthodox Church	60,000 cadastral yoke	89,838 cadastral yoke

Neither the income from the land, nor the collections and gifts were sufficient to defray the costs of the Romanian Churches. The Hungarian State paid for the operation of the Romanian Church offices, the training of priests, the building and maintenance of churches and the emergency expenditures of the clergy from the Religious Fund, consisting of Roman Catholic assets, and from the General Funds of the country.

The expenses of the Szamosujvár Romanian seminary were covered at an annual cost of 14,800 Forints. The sum given to assist in the construction of buildings for the diocese amounted to 600,000 Korona in 1911 (100 Korona was the equivalent of $ 20.26 US). The central administrative organization of the Romanian Greek Orthodox Church, its parishes and seminaries, survived only because of government subsidies. In this way, the Hungarian government assured the existence of more than 3,500 priests and their families. In 1914, there were 1,943 Greek Orthodox priests and more than 1,500 Greek Catholic priests in the country, divided among 1,457 major and 1,600 minor congregations.

---

[40] Ibid. p. 113.
[41] Biró, op.cit. pp. 132-143.

Use of the Romanian language[42]

The Nagyszeben Tribunal wrote in 1885, *"Our public education, under the protective shield of our Church, was free of any government interference. In our villages Romanian was used as the official language. In the courts, Romanian men found people who understood the language, knew their customs and their needs and who were well intentioned toward them. Any submission was accepted and decisions were issued in Romanian. In the Romanian villages, we had an army of Romanian officials to whom we could turn with complete confidence and there was nobody who questioned our right to use our mother tongue in all official business. Even in the Court of Appeal, in the High Court and in the Ministries we had our people who could give us precise information about any and all matters and who could act on our behalf with the greatest good-will"*.[43] Where the members of the community council determined that the official language of the village was going to be Romanian, the issue of language was usually resolved permanently.

In a number of places, however, record keeping in two languages became burdensome and for the sake of convenience, people switched to Hungarian.[44] Where a village was assigned a town clerk who was not Romanian, he had to be familiar with the language of the population, as demanded by the regulations governing the examination of the clerk. The candidate had to pass this exam before a board consisting of the deputy lord lieutenant of the county, the county prosecutor, the chairman of the orphans' board and the tax assessor. The oral examination was conducted in public.

In the counties having a Romanian majority, the right to submit requests in Romanian was generally recognized. In 1906, the Deputy Lieutenant Governor of County Temes started a course of instruction in Romanian for forty county officials. Until the turn of the century, appeals and requests to the Ministries in Budapest could be submitted in Romanian.

From 1867 to 1918, the majority of the schools were under ecclesiastic control and hence in these schools the language of instruction was always Romanian. The so-called Apponyi legislation, passed in 1907, increased the number of hours in which Hungarian had to be taught but did not interfere with Romanian as the language of instruction. The school records, the minutes of staff meetings and all documents relating to the activities of the school were always kept in Romanian alone. It never even occurred to the Hungarian authorities to introduce a parallel, bilingual Hungarian-Romanian keeping of documents in order to simplify governmental supervision.[45]

In the regions of the country inhabited by several nationalities, place names frequently appeared in different languages (Kolozsvár = Klausenburg = Cluj). There were thus numerous communities that appeared in public documents in various forms causing considerable confusion, particularly to the postal system. Act IV of 1898 decreed that every community could have only one official name that had to be used in all official correspondence. It did allow, however, that the alternate name could appear in parentheses after the official name. In

---

[42] Biró, op.cit. pp. 72-85.
[43] Ibid. p .73.
[44] Ibid. p. 78.
[45] Biró, op.cit. p. 98.

46

deciding the official name for the community, the decision had to be made with the approval of a general meeting of the citizens of the community. This law was not fully enforced until the coming of world war one.

In practice, the Romanian names were used for mail, for seals, in documents and certificates without any restrictions and without indicating the parallel Hungarian name. At the turn of the century, the Romanian intellectuals did not attend county meetings and generally ignored public affairs. It is for this reason that the Szászváros weekly *Libertatea*, wrote: "We have lost large parts of our rights and privileges in the county and in the communities still guaranteed by the law through our own negligence."[46]

Instruction at the turn of the century

In 1914 there were only 2,901 schools where the language of instruction was Romanian. There were not quite 3 million Romanians living in Hungary and thus there was one such school per 1016 Romanians. At the same time, in Romania, with 6.9 million Romanian inhabitants, there was only one school per 1,418 inhabitants. Clearly, the Romanians in Hungary were better supplied with schools than the Romanians in Romania. It appears that in 1900, only 19.6% of the Romanians in Romania could read or write, while in Hungary at the same time, 41.4% of the men and 24.6% of the women were literate.[47] The biggest tempest was caused by the so-called Lex Apponyi, discussed above.

Economic independence at the turn of the century

At the end of the 19th century, there was a marked increase in Romanian banks in Transylvania. The new Romanian bourgeoisie developed among the banking bourgeoisie, which in turn evolved from the landed gentry. As a result of the emancipation of the villeins in 1848, the Romanians became the owners of 600,000 acres of land in Transylvania. Through very clever banking maneuvers, about 8% of all land in this region came into Romanian hands. Almost all the political leaders also had an interest in the financial institutions.

Excluding Croatia, the Romanians represented 16.18% of the population of Hungary between 1880 and 1918.

The Serbs

There is little archeological evidence for their presence at the time of the Hungarian occupation of the Carpathian basin and the first major settlements seem to have taken place along the Száva in the Szerémség, in the 12-14th century. It was the spread of the Turkish population in the Balkans, beginning in the 14th century, that led to a significant increase in the Serb settlements.[48] In 1389 Lazar, the Prince of the Serbs, was defeated by the Sultan Murad in the bat-

---

[46] Biró, op.cit. p. 82.

[47] Ernő Raffay: A vajdagazdaságoktól a birodalomig (From the voivodeship to empire.) History of Modern Romania, JATE, Szeged 1989, pp. 125 and 171.

[48] Lajos Arday: A mai Vajdaság (a történelmi Bács-Bodrog, Torontál, Szerém vármegyék) rövid története. (A Short History of the Vajdaság.) Manuscript; Ferenc Szakály: Szerbek a középkori Magyarországon. (Serbs in medieval Hungary.) Historia, 1991, #2-3. pp. 15-17.

tle of Rigómező and was beheaded after the defeat. King Zsigmond (1387-1437) donated huge tracts of land to Stefan Lazarević, the son of Prince Lazar, in order for Stefan to help protect the exposed regions against the Turkish threat.

Twelve years before this entire area was conquered by the Turks, the King, fearing increased Turkish attacks, took back the fortresses of the Macsó Bánság as well as Belgrade, compensating Stefan's heir, Djordje Brancović, with estates in Hungary. The Serb ruler settled Serbian peasants on these estates and these settlers included numerous free soldiers. Serbian settlements were established along the Danube as far north as Esztergom, Komárom and Győr.

In 1456, János Hunyadi defeated the Turks at Nándorfehérvár (Belgrade) and until 1521, Belgrade remained a strong bulwark against the Turkish flag. It is noteworthy that the ringing of all the church bells at noon, still widely practiced all over the world, was instituted by the Pope to celebrate the victory of Nándorfehérvár.

The first wave of Serbian settlers was followed, after the occupation of Serbia in 1459, by a much larger one. The family of the Serb ruler found refuge in Hungary after a brief sojourn in Turkey, Italy, Albania and Austria. King Mátyás (1458-1490) and his successors, the Jagellonians, gave large estates to the Serb and other Balkan refugee nobles, trying to integrate them into Hungary. Consequently, there was a spontaneous migration from the Serb border regions during the 15th and 16th centuries. The Hungarian National Assembly, in 1481 and 1495, exempted the Serb settlers from paying the tithe due to the Hungarian clergy. In exchange for the estates, the Hungarian Kings expected military service from the new settlers.[49] In the famous "Black Army" of King Mátyás, the Danubian vessels were staffed mostly with Serb sailors and officers. At the same time, numerous Orthodox Serbs fought in the service of the Turkish Sultan. *In 1440, King Ulászló I (1440-1444) settled Serbs from the Keve region along the lower Danube to what is now Ráckeve and granted them substantial privileges.*

The Serbian nobles participated in the deliberations of the Hungarian National Assembly and there is no evidence that they were treated differently from any other citizen of the country. Their troops were used not only in the South but also in Austria and Bohemia. They differed from the other national troops only in their greater ferocity and cruelty[50].

The Serb rulers continued to hope that they could return to Serbia. The nobles endeavored to marry only within their own small group. After the death of the last member of the ruling Brankovics family (1502), the Hungarian kings appointed other Serb rulers who were accepted by the Serbs in Hungary as their chieftains.

In the occupied Serbia, the Pravoslav (Orthodox) Church became the symbol of the nation's political unity. Thus, the court of the Serb rulers, which had fled to Hungary, was regulated by the holidays of the Greek Orthodox Church. These rulers established Serb monasteries and the bishops residing in these monasteries strengthened the national self-esteem of the Serbs and were the instrumental in promoting their national development.

Even though the idea of a military border zone was first raised in 1699, it was only in 1702 that the Vienna Military Command separated the area from

---

[49] Glatz: Szerbek (The Serbs) MOK, p. 87.
[50] Szakaly: op.cit. p. 17.

the border of Transylvania, along the Maros and Tisza as far as Titel and assigned it to the Serbs of Arsenije Čarnojević. The entire area was considered a "new acquisition" and thus, according to them, the Hungarians had no say in the matter. The neighboring counties were coerced to contribute their taxes to the support of the Serb divisions. At the outbreak of the Rákóczi rebellion in 1703, the Privy Council recommended to the Court that until a sufficient number of German soldiers could be moved in, the Croats and Serbs should be mobilized against Hungary. Prince Eugene of Savoy repeatedly stated during the rebellion that, "the dislike of the Hungarians by the Serbs should be encouraged and fomented". It was for the same reasons that, during the reign of Maria Theresa, Count Kollowrat made it a guiding principle that the protection of the Serbian Nation was the prerogative of Austria and that these people were part of the patrimony of the Austrian ruling house and that they should not be considered as subjects of Hungary.[51]

Serbian ecclesiastic autonomy and education in the mother tongue

The Pravoslav Serb archbishopric of Buda was probably established under the Serb ruler István Lazarevics, during the reign of King Zsigmond. The Serb bishop's chair was established in Buda in 1557 and was the northernmost religious center for the Serbs living in Hungary.

The Serb community in Buda must have been reasonably well-to-do even during the Turkish occupation, since the Turkish traveler, Evlija Cselebi, mentions that they had three churches. They had a bishop and a metropolitan, as shown by a letter from the Orthodox Patriarch of Jerusalem, written in 1640, in which he asks for additional contribution for the Holy Sepulcher.

After the re-occupation of Buda in 1686, the imperial troops advanced as far as Nis and Sarajevo. Following the Turkish counter attack, approximately 35,000 Serb families fled to Hungary and Croatia under the leadership of Arsenije Čarnojević, the Patriarch of Ipek.

The independent Serb Pravoslav Church, renewed in the 16th century, was under the leadership of the Patriarch of Ipek. The move of the Patriarch to Hungary promoted the development of Serb national consciousness. In the Délvidek, the role of Ipek was assumed by Karlóca and all the Greek Orthodox bishoprics in Hungary came under the control of the Metropolitan of Karlóca. During the coming years, four bishops of Buda were elevated to the Metropolitan See of Karlóca.

Leopold I (1657-1705) Emperor of Austria and King of Hungary issued two charters to the Serbs (1690 and 1691) in which he *guaranteed a military-noble social structure and ecclesiastic (cultural) autonomy.* They could elect their Patriarch freely and the Greek Orthodox Canon Law was the law under which the Patriarch functioned.

He removed them from under the administrative authority of the newly liberated Hungarian regions and set up a separate military border zone governed directly from Vienna. From time to time, they could hold their own National Assembly, that was to deal with ecclesiastic affairs only, but inevitably became the source of political demands. Since no Bailiff was elected, the Patriarch became not only the religious leader but the administrative leader as well.

---

[51] Hóman-Szekfü: Magyar történet, vol. IV (Hungarian History) Királyi Egyetemi Nyomda, Bp. 1935, pp. 261, 262, 288, 433.

Taking advantage of the authority granted to him, the Patriarch established 16 bishoprics in the interior regions of the country and initiated a relentless battle against the Unionist Greek Orthodox Churches and their membership, who abandoned the "Old Faith" and joined the Roman Catholic Church.[52] The Church was a determinant factor in the life of the communities and it was around the Orthodox rites that their traditional way of life was practiced and their native language was maintained. The Imperial manifestos guaranteed the autonomy of their communities and they also enjoyed their own administration. Even though, technically, they were subject to the City Magistrates, the Serbs in Buda had their own elected Serb council, chairman, judge, jurors and the right to make community decisions. Their mandate went into effect on the Day of St. George and was for one year. Administration was in the Serb language. In 1730, their school in Buda had 70 pupils and the children of the poor and of widows were exempted from paying tuition.[53] Since these privileges placed the Serbs into a favorable position vis-à-vis the Hungarian villeins whose taxes had been raised and who were subject to having soldiers quartered with them, they fought on the side of the Habsburgs, during the freedom fight led by Ferenc Rákóczi.

In order to prevent the rapid spread of the religion, King Charles III (1711-1740) withdrew some of these privileges. The Serb bishops were henceforth (1729, 1732 and 1734) appointed by the King and not by the Metropolitan, albeit from a panel of three names submitted by the Metropolitan. The complaints of the Serbs against the Hungarians were still presented to the King by the Metropolitan[54]

Instruction in their native tongue began in the 17-18th century. In the regulations laid down for the Tisza and Danube area military border zone, the Vienna Royal Military Council decreed that by 1703, every village in these areas had to have a parish and a school. In every village, a lot (25-30 hectares) was set aside for the teachers. The languages of instruction were Serb and German and the teachers were appointed from among the non-commissioned officers of the border guard and from among the Greek Orthodox cantors.

There is a document in the archives of the Archbishop of Kalocsa, dated 1765, that refers to a Sokác-Latin elementary school. It is mentioned again in 1774 as an Illyrian-Hungarian school with the language of instruction being Croatian and Hungarian. A memorandum exists from 1778, in which the superintendent of the Pécs region urges the city of Ujvidék to establish Hungarian, German and Serb elementary schools in conformance with the mandate of Queen Maria Theresa. In its answer, the city indicated that it needed not only elementary schools but secondary schools as well. The administration also mentioned that they would like to pay the two teachers of the Serb elementary schools from the general funds of the city. At this time, the Greek Orthodox dioceses were assigned individual school superintendents in the person of Abraham Mrazovics and his assistant, Mate Rudics. The appointments hastened the development of Serb schools in Hungarian regions. It may be assumed that there was a Greek Orthodox Serb school in Zenta, in the heart of the military district, as early as 1697, and it is

---

[52] Pirigyi, op.cit. pp. 31, 92-93.
[53] Sztojan Vujicsics: Szerbek Pest-Budán (The Serbs in Pest-Buda), Főpolgármesteri Hivatal és Szerb Fővárosi Önkormányzat, Bp. 1997, pp. 14-15.
[54] Pirigyi, op.cit. p. 94.

known to have been in continuous operation from 1797 until 1900. The minutes of the county meetings of County Bács-Bodrog reveal that matters pertaining to the schools took a prominent place in their deliberations from the 18th century on. The assembly could demand that a given community build and maintain a school, repair the Greek Orthodox schools, pay the salary owed to the teachers, gather contributions for the schools, etc. The Royal Governor's office was responsible for the establishment and continued support of Catholic and other parochial schools, scholarships, the engagement, salary and continued education of teachers and the selection of textbooks.

After the death of Joseph II in 1790, an ecclesiastic synod met in Temesvár and drafted the following political demands:

- An independent Serb region,
- Serb elementary schools,
- 8 middle schools,
- 10 teacher education schools,
- Equal rights of employment,
- Appointment of Serb city counselors.[55]

The uniform implementation of the 1868 Nationality Acts achieved undeniable results even though they did not fully satisfy the most radical Serb politicians. The August 10, 1868 Special Ordinance, issued as a supplement to Act IX of 1869 mentioned above, gave full autonomy to the Greek Orthodox Church, not only in ecclesiastic matters, but also in the affairs of the Serb schools, foundations and monastic properties. It also mandated that all children had to attend school between ages 7 and 12, and that every community had to establish a school and retain a teacher if there were 50 children of school age in the community. The books for religious instruction were approved by the bishops' council, while all other textbooks were approved by the government on recommendation of the highest ecclesiastic authorities. The ordinance declared that, "In Serb schools, the language of instruction shall be Serb". There is no mention of teaching the "official language". The income from the so-called "Clerical Fund" was used to defray the costs of the secondary schools, religious schools and graduate schools, while the "inalienable national fund" served the direct ecclesiastic needs. Since the Greek Orthodox Serb Ecclesiastic Assembly was in charge of all matters pertaining to the autonomy of the Serbs (church, school, cultural and eleemosynary), it functioned essentially as the Parliament of the Serbian population in Hungary. Two thirds of the representatives were laymen. These nationality laws produced significant results, naturally with the assistance of the intellectuals who were active in the matters of the Church.

The statistics of instruction in native tongues in 1875, in County Bács-Bodrog that had the largest percentage of Serbs anywhere in the country indi-

[55] Arday, op.cit. p. 12.; Ács, op.cit. pp. 248 and 262; László Bíró: A szerbek és 1848 (The Serbs and 1848) Historia 1998/3, pp. 23-25;

Bács-Bodrog vármegye egyetemes monográfiája (Complete monograph of county Bács-Bodrog). It relates the history of the Catholic and other denominational elementary and middle schools organized in the county, pp. 331, 336-337;

Péter Tóth: Felekezeti elemi iskolák Zentán (Denominational elementary schools in Zenta). Data to the history of the Zenta Public Schools. Gy. Dudás Múzeum és Levélbarátok Egyesülete, Zenta, 1979.

cate that of 120,338 children of school age 42% were Hungarian, 29.6% were German, 18.4% were Serb and Croat, 4.2% Slovak, 3.4% Bunyevác and 1.7% Ruthenian.

Of the 359 elementary schools, the language of instruction was Hungarian in 263 (73%), Serb in 64 (17.8%), the local Slovak dialect in 10 (2,7%) and German in 8 (2%). There was one each of Bunyevác, Ruthenian and Bunyevác-German schools. Most of the local German population sent their children to Hungarian schools. With the exception of the Calvinist, Lutheran and a few Hebrew schools, all schools were supported by special taxes assessed on the communities and from the general funds of the Government. Act XXXVIII of 1868 required that in every community 1,747 hectares and 297 square meters of grazing land be devoted to the maintenance of the school. This was supplemented from educational and instructional funds derived from the moneys allotted to the military border zone (240,882 Korona). There was a teacher training school in Zombor, both for males and females. There was also a regular school in Zombor and a secondary school in Ujvidék. After the enrollment of Serb students dropped to one quarter of its previous level in the Zombor high school, the language of instruction was changed to Hungarian but the teaching of the Serb language and literature was maintained.

Cultural development[56]
Since the Turkish authorities prevented their independent economic and cultural developments, it was the framework of the Habsburg Empire that gave the Serbs an opportunity for national renewal. Vienna became their first cultural center and it was here that the first Serb daily paper was published in 1791. When censorship was tightened in Vienna, the Serb cultural center moved to Buda and to Pest and flourished here at the beginning of the 19th century. After the demise of the Vienna papers, Serb daily and weekly papers were published in Pest beginning in the 1830s.

The first Serb high school was established in Karlóca in 1790-1792, the Szentendre teacher college was started in 1812 and the Ujvidék high school was opened in 1816.

The members of the nascent Serb literary groups (Vuk Stefanović Karadžić and others) met at the beginning of the 19th century in the home of the attorney Sima Ignjatović, who was the notary-in-chief of the City of Buda. There were extensive debates about revising the language but these meetings were also attended, under the slogan of Slavic solidarity, by Fran Kurelac, the Croatian linguist and Jan Kollár, the Slovak Evangelical Minister, one of the enthusiastic promoters of the Pan-Slavic idea. In addition to the Serb writers, the home of Mihály Vitkovics, in Pest, was also visited by Berzsenyi, Kölcsey and Vörösmarty.

The necessity of converting Hungarian into a literary language led to the establishment of the Hungarian Scientific Society in 1825 and this concept stimulated the Serbs as well. They realized that it would be most beneficial to establish the Serb Academy for the development of Serb literature and culture and for the continued publication of the Serb annual. The *Matica Srpska* became the scientific association of the Serbs living on the right side of the Danube.

---

[56] Sztojan, op.cit. pp. 18-21 and 56-58.

The conditions were favorable. There were prosperous Serb citizens, merchants, artisans and officials, there were young Serb intellectuals studying at the University and there was a Serb printing press active in Buda castle. After participating in the defeat of the Hungarian revolution of 1848-1849 and being disappointed in the promises of Austrian benefits, the orientation of the Serb political leaders underwent a change and the Academy moved in 1864 from Pest to Ujvidék, closer to Karlóca and old Serbia.

In 1838, Szava Popović Thököly, a landowner nobleman from Arad, the Maecenas of the domestic Serbs, established a foundation to assist the poor but talented students in pursuing their university studies. The College became known as the Thökölyanum and the foundation came under the control of the Greek Orthodox Serb diocese after the death of the founder and was supervised after 1902 by the Patriarch of Karlovác. With its assistance, more than 400 Serb students obtained a degree at the Budapest Universities and institutions of higher learning.

There were two other foundations established to assist Serb students. A foundation was established by Naum Bozda and his wife in 1870, to assist the Serb merchants, artisans and technicians in Pest-Buda and Szentendre at the beginning of their careers. Bozda was the scion of a wealthy merchant family who operated the pontoon bridge across the Danube prior to the construction of the Lánchid. The other foundation was established by the Women's Association of the Saint Angelina Greek Orthodox Educational Corporation to assist the young women enrolled in the professional schools in the capital through a college it endowed in 1904.

In 1848, Teodor Pavlović proclaimed a Yugoslav program for the rights of the Serbs and Croats in Hungary and for the national liberation Serbia, Bosnia and Bulgaria.

Initially, the publishing of Serb books in Pest-Buda was linked to the press of the Pest University that, since 1795, published textbooks, liturgical material, literature, scientific, historical and linguistic works under an Imperial Charter. Until the middle of the 19th century, the University Press published almost a thousand Serb works. In addition to publishing activities, the *Matica Srpska* sold Croat, German and Polish works in its store.

Serb theatrical activity was linked to the very first Hungarian theatrical troupe, under the leadership of László Kelemen. A young Hungarian actor, István Balog wrote a play, "György Czerny" commemorating the Serb uprising of 1804. The play was performed in Serb translation in Szeged and Ujvidék (Novi Sad) in a Serb theater as early as 1815. It was also performed in Serbia but at a much later time. The translator, Joakim Vujiæ, was assisted by Hungarian actors in obtaining the Palatine Joseph' permission in 1813 to organize the first Serb theatrical presentation anywhere.

The new promoters of Serb culture and its most outstanding representatives were living in Hungary. The National Theater in Belgrade was created by actors from újvidék and the *Matica Srpska* functioned from Ujvidék. The majority of the intellectuals and officials of Serbia and Montenegro were graduates of the Karlóca and Újvidék high school and the Zombor Teachers' College.

Economic growth

The Serb community grew significantly in 1690 during the great immigration following the Turkish occupation. Their being granted imperial privileges encouraged this move. In Buda, the community had a well-organized administration and its elected officials were responsible for gathering taxes and administering justice. Emperor Leopold I issued an edict granting the Serbs citizenship. The Serbs at this time had 88 mercantile establishments and their artisans worked in a large number of workshops. They were entitled to purchase property and the first such deed was dated in 1702.

In the 1706-1708 census, 484 Serb taxpayers were listed for Buda. The Serbs in Buda and Pest had their most prosperous years in the 18th and early 19th centuries. It was this flourishing economic existence that made it possible for Pest and Buda to become one of the sources of modern Serb culture and education.

At the turn of the 19-20th century, the majority of the great landowners, small farmers, agricultural tenants and agrarian workers were Hungarian. The owners of mid-size farms were mostly Germans, Serbs and Bunyevác. Their banks, savings banks and the cooperatives organized by the Radical Party promoted the purchase of land for political reasons. In this, the situation was very similar to that arranged by ASTRA, the cultural organization in Transylvania for the Romanians.

Politics[57]

The Serb National Program (Načertanije) proposed in 1844 by Ilja Garašanin and demanding that all Serb and Yugoslav regions be liberated and united into a single Serb state, clearly had a markedly radicalizing effect on the intellectuals who grew up and became vocal within the framework of the Greek Orthodox Church in Hungary. Garašanin was a minister in the Serb Vassal Principality that gained increased autonomy within the Turkish Empire at the beginning of the 1830s.

The members of the congregation gathered first in the Thökölyanum in Pest on March 17-19, 1848 and then in Ujvidék on the 27th, to formulate their demands. *At the April 14, 1848 meeting in Karlóca they demanded territorial autonomy.* They demanded that, on the basis of their ancient rights, they be permitted to elect their own Voivode who would be the head of a Serb Vajdaság (Voivodina) consisting of the Szerémség, Bánát, Bácska and Baranya. In addition, they demanded that a Serb National Assembly meet annually. In lieu of the ecclesiastic council, summoned by the Hungarian government for May 27, the Serbs in Hungary called for a National Assembly on May 13-15 at which two Serbian Imperial Counselors participated. The majority of the participants at this meeting wished to carve out a Serb Vajdaság from the regions of Southern Hungary and the Szerémség. It was to continue under Habsburg rule. In the proposed area of this Vajdaság, the Serbs would have represented the largest ethnic group but would have been barely one third of the entire population. This issue became one of the major reasons for antagonism between Serbs and Hungarians, since the Hungarian Parliament wished to maintain the noted territory under the Hungarian county system.

---

[57] Arday, op.cit. pp. 18-19; D. Sokcsevits, I. Szilágyi, K. Szilágyi: Déli szomszédaink története (History of our southern neighbours), Népek Hazája Sorozat, Bereményi Kiadó, Bp.; Emil Palotás: Occupacio-annexio 1878-1908. (Occupation-Annexation), Historia 1996/5-6, pp. 25-28.

The appearance of the Serbs in the political life of the country was clearly helped by the autonomy of their ecclesiastic organizations. It was this autonomy that gave a framework for their political aspirations and it was in the parochial schools that the intellectual leadership of the nationality minority was educated.

In the 1848-1849 Hungarian War for Freedom, Serbs fought on both sides. On the request of Djordje Stratimirović, supreme leader of the Serbs living in Hungary, Sándor, the Prince of Serbia, sent money and arms to the insurgents and, in August, permitted an army of volunteers to cross the Danube under the command of Kničanin, a former State Councilor. In December, the Serb National Council voted a large subsidy of 20,000 ducats and Prince Sándor gave 12,000 ducats of his own money. While the volunteers supported from abroad crossed the Hungarian border, Peter Čarnejović, State Councilor, General Damjanich, one colonel, five lieutenant colonels, seven majors, many line officers and more than a thousand Serb soldiers fought for the common freedom and shouldered the retributions and even the martyrdom that followed the war. The most popular general in this war was Joseph Damjanich. He was of Serb origin and was executed in 1849.

The Serbs were the most active minority in Hungary at the time of the Compromise. They had great influence in the county and city councils in the regions where they were in a majority, such as Torontál, Kikinda, Zombor and Újvidék. In these places, the official language was Serb until the end of the 1870s. One of their demands was that Torontál should be divided and that a totally Serb-speaking county be created with Kikinda as its center. This same Serb intellectual group watched the fate of Serbia under Turkish control.

Serbia had gained considerable autonomy at the beginning of the 19th century but was unable to exist without assistance from abroad. The Turks, marching toward Belgrade, were stopped by a Russian protest. The Balkan states could regain their independence following the Russian-Turkish war of 1877-1878 but this also markedly increased the Russian influence in this area.

The Serb Liberal opposition began to take shape under the leadership of Miletić Svetozar and Mihajlo Polit-Desančić at the 1861 annual ecclesiastic congress. They formed a party in 1869 and demanded that the counties be redrawn along nationality lines and that the language of the majority be the only official language in that county. In order to help their brethren in Serbia in promoting the union of all the Serbs, they instructed the representatives of the party to oppose any foreign policy that favored Turkey or wished to conquer any of the Balkan people. They also took a strong stand against the annexation of Bosnia and Herzegovina. The lack of success in these national endeavors motivated the more conservative elements to accept the Compromise and to find a way toward a peaceful arrangement with the Hungarians.

These political debates led to the formation of the Liberal and Radical Parties at the end of the 1880s. Their antagonism led to tragedy. Jaša Tomić acquired the *Zastava* daily paper for the Radicals by marriage. He was accused by the editor-in-chief of the Liberal Paper *Branik*, Misa Dimitrijević, that he had made a marriage of convenience. Because of this, Tomic killed Dimitrijević with a knife on January 3, 1890.

The scene of the Serb internal warfare shifted increasingly to the meetings of the National Ecclesiastic Congress where decisions were made over the use of substantial sums of money. It was also suggested that some Serb politicians in Hungary might have had a hand in the assassination of, the King of Serbia, Sándor Obrenović. In any case, the new King, Peter Karadjordjević, chose a new foreign policy and exchanged his former Austrian orientation with a Russian one, considering himself as a protégé of the Tsar.

Following the change of government in Turkey in 1908, Vienna announced the annexation of Bosnia since it was greatly concerned that Turkey now wished to re-establish its sovereignty over Bosnia. Consequently, Serbia mobilized its army and demanded territorial compensation. It was only because Russia was not prepared to go to war and pressured Serbia to desist, that the latter agreed to the annexation in 1909. The domestic Serbs naturally identified themselves with Serbia and protested.

From the 1880s onward, the focus of the Serb social and economic life shifted increasingly to Croatia. The Croat Bailiff, Khuen-Héderváry, increasingly used them as a buttress against the growing Croat National Movement. It was here that the center of the National Church, Karlóca, was located, it was here that the majority of the prosperous Serb merchant-bourgeois lived and it was here that the strongest banks and cooperatives were established. The Radicals made an agreement with the opposition and in 1906 two of their representatives were elected to the Parliament. Later on, a dozen or more landowners and officials sat on the government benches. The Serbs represented 5.3% of the combined populations of Croatia and Hungary.

The Slovaks

According to the available sources, the Slavs appeared at the rim of the Carpathian basin after the break-up of the Avar Khanates in the 8-9th century and, over the next few centuries, they were completely assimilated into the original inhabitants of that area.

During the 13th century, while the population density in the central parts of Hungary was 20 people per square kilometer, the enormous forests at the foot of the Carpathians, the territory of the Royal Forest Bailiffs, were almost entirely uninhabited. Almost half of the population perished during the Tartar invasion in 1241-1242. This induced King Béla IV and his successors, primarily the Anjous, to send their representatives to the far side of the Carpathians and recruit a variety of people, Moravian, Czech, Polish and Ruthenian, to settle in Hungary in exchange for a variety of privileges. Freedom from taxation, during the years of clearing the forests, single payments at a later time to the landowners, etc.[58]

After the Turkish occupation, the country was divided into three regions. The northern parts of Hungary escaped the Turkish occupation and there the medieval Slavic population of about 300-500,000 increased by the end of the 17th century to an ethnic block of more than a million. The large-scale Slovak settlements began after 1720. Bartenstein, Maria Theresa's counselor, advised her in 1755 that, "It would be dangerous to have disgruntled people living at the edges of the Monarchy. The insurrections under Báthory, Bocskay, Gábor

---

[58] Jenő Szűcs: op.cit. MOK. pp. 36-37.

56

Bethlen, György Rákoczi and Thököly caused concern for the Ruling House and this could happen again". The rights of the new settlers were determined by contract. They were granted free practice of their religion, that is, they could worship according to the Lutheran creed and could hold the services in Slovak. They had to pay no taxes, provide no free labor for one or two years and their emoluments were determined precisely.[59] Consequently large numbers settled in the Alföld as well.

As a result of the settlements, the southern border of the Slovak settlements had moved further south by 10-40 km. by the end of the 18th century. An area with a previously mixed population became entirely Slovak. The Hungarian population, destroyed or decimated at the time of the Turkish and Kuruc-Labanc wars, was also largely replaced by Slavic settlers. This state of affairs was recorded in the census data collected on orders of Maria Theresa and published as the *Lexicon Universorum Regni Hungariae locorum populosorum*. In contrast to the Croats, Saxons and Serbs, the Slovaks enjoyed no privileges of any kind. They not only lacked a national self-government but they were also without a neighboring motherland they could depend upon. Consequently the Czech contacts became increasingly important, particularly since this also meant a commonality of religion.

The change in generations in the 18-19th century was preceded by the Counter Reformation, conducted in the national language, and by the increasing growth of the independent Lutheran Church. *The ecclesiastic organizations using the Evangelical national language (Slovak) were the buttresses of national self-consciousness and the intellectuals trained in their schools became the front-line fighters in the battle for national aspirations.* It is well known that one of the demands of the Reformation was that the Gospel be preached in the native tongue of the congregation. In the Nagyszombat Catholic seminary, established after the synod of Trident (1542-1563), it was required that the teachers be familiar with Hungarian, Slovak and German.

Péter Pázmány, the Archbishop of Esztergom and one of the leaders of the re-catholicization in Hungary, demanded that in the Slav, and later Slovak, villages in the Felvidék, the Sunday sermon be preached in Slovak. He also insisted that the students sent abroad to study always include some Slovaks and he also translated all his religious polemic writings into Slovakian. The Nagyszombat University Press issued its publications in various languages for the same reason. These endeavors were greatly facilitated by the publication in 1848 of the first Hungarian-Latin-Slavic (Slovak) dictionary. Pázmány chose the dialect used in the area around Nagyszombat as his literary model. This so-called "Jesuit Slovak" was the language used by Anton Bernolák and his literary circle and liturgical texts and hymnals were published in it. It was only later that Štur and his group established the unified Slovak language, based on the Central-Slovak dialect. It might be more accurate to use the term of Northern Hungarian Slavs for "Slovak" or speak of the precursors of the Slovaks since, other than in a very narrow intellectual group, this term was not used and the true Slovak ethno-genesis did not take place until the establishment of the first Slovak Republic (1939-1944). The term "Slovensko", for the area inhabited by

[59] László Szarka: Szlovákok (The Slovaks), MOK. p. 112.; Ács, op.cit. p. 151; János Ölvedi: Napfogyatkozás. Magyarok Szlovákiában (Eclipse of the Sun. The Hungarians in Slovakia). Püski, New York, 1985, p. 23.

Slovaks, appeared only at the beginning of the 19th century and in the 1809 dictionary of Anton Bernolák it meant both Slovakia and Slavonia. The Lutheran Slovaks used the medieval Czech language and received both support and funds from the Czechs. Thus, many people followed Jan Kollar, the pastor of the Pest Slovak Lutheran congregation who had good relations with the Czech movement, rather than Bernolák who was written off as "Catholic and Hungarophile".

From the 1840s on, the center of the Slovak National Movement shifted to Pozsony (Bratislava) where Ludovit Štur was teaching in the Czech Department associated with the Lutheran Lyceum. He welcomed the March 1848 Hungarian revolution but doubted that this bourgeois event would be beneficial for the Slovak nation since most of the Slovak population lived in villages and had practically no intellectual component. On May 10, 1848, at Liptószentmiklós, the Slovak politicians, Štur, Hurban and Hodža drafted their petition in which they demanded a Parliament in which all nationalities were represented, a separate Slovak regional assembly, the Slovak language as the official language in the counties with a Slovak majority, the identification of a Slovak region, the establishment of Slovak nationality schools, the use of the red and white Slovak flag and a universal and secret franchise. They, in fact, asked for territorial autonomy in the modern sense with a decentralized administration, and they asked for this before the new revolutionary Hungarian government could even become stable.[60] This government was struggling for recognition from the Austrian government and was trying to introduce the ideals of the French revolution with the 1848 bourgeois revolt. It did not understand why the emancipation of the villeins and equality before the law was not sufficient for the nationalities who all made demands for autonomy and for their particular individual rights. The Slovak memorandum was considered an exaggerated and hostile document and the Minister of the Interior, Szemere, issued an arrest warrant against the authors Professor Ludovit Štur, the representative of County Zólyom at the 1848 National Assembly, Jozef Miloslav Hurban and Michal Miloslav Hodža, Lutheran ministers. The three men escaped to the Prague and there, at the Slav Congress Hurban declared, "We must act, Slovakia must be taken away from Hungary". Štur had already spoken against the Hungarians at the Vienna Slavic deliberations at the beginning of April, when he asked the Bailiff Jellasics to permit the Slovaks to fight against the Hungarians in the first line of the battle. Štur also received a considerable sum of money from Miloš Obrenović, the Serb Prince, who had fled to Croatia from Serbia. The Štur group also received a promissory note for 900 good quality rifles from the Vienna rifle factory but events in Vienna prevented the delivery of the weapons. Štur then traveled to Olomouc (Olmutz) to see the Emperor and suggested that a Slovak Grand Duchy be established in the Felvidék. In Belgrade, Hurban was promised that they would be given both money and arms if the negotiations with the Hungarians proved unsuccessful. Hurban urged the Slovaks in the South to support the struggle of the Serbs. During the month of August, the first Slovak volunteer regiment was established in Vienna, consisting of 8% Slovaks with the majority made up of Czechs and Viennese riffraff. One of the initiators of the insurrection, Hodza, received finan-

---

[60] István Káfer: A miénk és az övék (Ours and theirs), Magvető, Bp. 1991, pp. 12-13, 16; Dusan Skvarna: A Szlovák nemzeti mozgalom (The Slovak national movement) Historia, 1998 No.3, pp. 14-17.; Zoltán Balassa: "El kell ragadni a magyaroktól Szlovákiat" (One must wrench away Slovakia from Hungary) Trianon Kalendárium (Trianon Calendar) 2000, Trianon Társaság, Bp. 1999.

cial support from the Czech representatives. It became evident from the declaration of the three leaders, Hurban, Štur and Hodža, published in Bohemia, that the insurgents would fight for the King, for the unification of the Empire, for the National Liberation of the Slovaks and "for equality before the law". This led to the formation of the Slovak National Council and to an armed insurrection. It remained an isolated instance since about 100,000 Slovaks fought on the side of the Hungarians against the Austrians. An agreement was reached nevertheless and the Austrian government, in order to curtail the Hungarian striving for independence, made contact with the independence movement of all of the nationalities. By inciting them against Hungary, Austria wished to further its own imperial interests. It obviously could not suspect at this time how this artificially fostered hate ultimately led to the dissolution of the entire empire. In the constitution imposed on March 4, the Court declared that Hungary's hegemony had come to an end and declared that Transylvania, Croatia, Slavonia, the Adriatic littoral, the military border zone and the Serb Vajdaság created from the Bácska and the Temesköz, had become totally autonomous territories, entirely independent of Hungary. This seemingly satisfied the demands of the nationalities but, in fact, the autonomy of the territories would have been very limited.

In their petition of March 19, 1849 addressed to Emperor Franz Joseph, the Slovak National Council referred to the activities of the Slovak armed units in the war against Hungary and, in the name of the "3 million strong Slovak nation", demanded the identification of a separate national territory, equal rights with the other nationalities of the Empire, an autonomous regional administration and Slovak as the official language. Jan Kollar, a Lutheran pastor in Pest and a confidant of the Court, spoke of more than 2 million Slav inhabitants in the Carpathian basin, in his submission of March 22, 1849. According to the Imperial Statistical data gathered at this time, there were only 1,822,730 Slovaks living in Hungary.

Subsequent to the defeat of the 1848-1849 Hungarian revolution, the nationalities relied on earlier promises and expected that they would be granted independent territories separate from Hungary and under direct Habsburg rule. In 1848-1849, several Slovak leaders committed to the cause of the Court were given judgeships, educational administrative and civil administration positions. It was this group that, in the second half of the century, furnished the leaders who stood at the helm of the nationality politics. One of these was Viliam Pauliny-Tóth, the future president of the Slovak National Party. When the Hungarian county system was reestablished in 1860, they were disappointed in their expectations and would have been satisfied with an autonomous territory within Hungary.

In the Memorandum drafted at the Turócszentmárton meeting in 1861, they asked for territorial autonomy, namely a Slovak territory in Upper-Hungary created by the readjustment of the county lines according to nationality populations. They also raised the legitimate demand that in the upper chamber of a two-tier legislature the nationalities be represented according to the percentage of their nationality in the entire population.[61]

---

[61] Z. Ács, op.cit.p. 269; László Szarka: Felső-Magyarország, Csehszlvákia, Szlovákia (Upper-Hungary, Czechoslvakia and Slovakia), Historia 1992/8 p. 4; László Szarka: A szlovákok története (History of the Slovaks), Bereményi Kiadó, Bp., 1996. pp. 97-109; Gábor Kemény: Iratok a nemzetiségi kérdés történetéhez Magyarországon a dualizms korában (Papers on the history of the nationality question in Hungary during the Dualism) Bp., 1952. p. 34.

The Church, teaching in the mother tongue and politics

The Church represented a cohesive force in the cultural life of the Slovaks in the Felvidék, even though in this area there was no real national church such as the Greek Orthodox Church in Romania or Serbia. It was not a coincidence that along with the Catholic Church and the Greek Orthodox Church, the Lutheran Church gave the Felvidék the leading Slovak politicians.[62]

Three reasons for this are worthy of mention:

1. The Lutheran Churches could organize local congregations much more freely than the more rigid Catholic and Orthodox Churches. In fact they could function as autonomous religious communities.
2. The Lutheran Slovaks generally lived in a contiguous territory (Árva, Liptó, Turóc, Zólyom, Nógrád and Gömör). The Slovak political intellectuals were mainly ministers and teachers. The leading politicians came from the five contiguous Lutheran dioceses.[63]
3. 80% of the teachers taught in parochial schools.

The "first generation" of politicians in the era of dualism received their start either during the Slovak insurgence of 1848-1849 or at the 1861 Turócszentmárton National Congress. Jan Francisci's biography is typical (1822-1905). He participated in the Slovak uprising in 1848-1849. After 1850, he was a county official. Between 1861 and 1863, he was the editor of the *Pest'budinske Vedomosti* Slovak political paper. He presided over the 1861 Turócszentmárton Na-tional Congress. In 1863 he was appointed a gubernatorial councilor. In 1864, he was the Lord Lieutenant of County Liptó. After the Compromise, he was pensioned off and became the president of the Board of Trustees of the Nagyrőce Slovak Lutheran Gymnasium. Later, he was the director of the Turócszentmárton Press of the Matica. He was also the vice president of the Matica Slovenska.

At this time, most of the schools had their own curricula, were under ecclesiastic control and used the nationality language in instruction. It is understandable, therefore, that they were fighting against the state schools with a single lesson plan, even if they were bilingual or teaching in Slovakian. They were concerned that their identity, based on a historical perspective quite different from the Hungarian, may be in danger. The schools were under the protection of the churches and were maintained by them, usually with some additional state funds. It was for this reason that the politicians struggled so hard against ecclesiastic reform, including the introduction of the civil marriage ceremony. The ordinance of Kálmán Tisza, closing the three Slovak high schools in the Felvidék in 1874 for spreading Pan-Slav propaganda, is debated to this day.

Starting in the 15th century, Czech Hussites and other Slavs moved in large numbers to Nagyrőce and thus, by the 19th century, the city lost its German character and had a Lutheran Slovak majority. The Board of the new high school, the so-called *patronatus* gathering, consisted of the men who established and funded the school. The Nagyrőce Lutheran Slovak high school was in operation for only 12 years. Its teachers were active participants in the Slovak national movement. They initiated and engaged in numerous debates even

---

[62] Imre Polányi: A szlovák társadalom és polgári nemzeti mozgalom a századfordulón. (Slovak society and national movement at the turn of the century), Akademia, Bp. 1987. pp. 23, 34-34.
[63] Ibid. pp. 40-41 and 123.

beyond the diocese. In 1868, the school issued its diplomas in Slovak only and, without the permission of the diocesan congress, started a teacher-training course. It had 138 applicants in the first year but only 115 in the third. It issued its first diplomas in 1871. The diocesan congress of 1868 and several Lutheran general assemblies (1870, 1871 and 1872) protested against the diplomas being written in Slovak only. The patronatus was unwilling to accept the compromise suggested by István Czékus, the senior Canon, that at least the subjects and the grades be recorded in Hungarian. Since the school refused to submit to the decisions of the General Assembly and since there were numerous other complaints, the entire matter was submitted to Ágoston Trefort, the Minister of Religious Matters and Education. Trefort asked Czékus to appoint a commission consisting of church dignitaries to investigate the activities of the school.

The report on the activities of the Nagyrőcze Lutheran School of Higher Education contained the following comments[64]:

- The director dismissed the janitor because he did not vote for a Slovak teacher at the election of the staff. The director also instructed the students not to salute citizens who were friendly to Hungary,
- Teacher Csulik, told students that Hungarian was only for draymen and that he would prefer to teach Mongolian to this miserable Hungarian,
- Teacher Zoch, "praised Russia and urged the students to cultivate the Slovak national sentiment. He expressed his hopes that the land that belonged to no one else but the Slovak nation would be wrested away from the selfish ones". At one school he forbade Hungarian talk or dances,
- ...One teacher ripped the Hungarian tricolor ribbon from the lapel of a student because those were not the Slovak colors. Another teacher, after attending a funeral conducted in Hungarian said, "I have to go and rinse my mouth. It reeks of Hungarian words".

The report reflected on the unfortunate state of affairs that led to continuous arguments and even fights between the Slav and Hungarian parties and "something, unheard of before the establishment of this school, father fights with son, brother with brother, relative with relative, and they hate each other because one has Slav sentiments in his bosom and the other Hungarian ones".

The commission, consisting of the leaders of the Lutheran diocese, completed their investigation of the school and of the problems in the city, submitted its report to the diocesan council and recommended that "all support be withdrawn from the school and that the school should be declared to be abolished". In the mean time the citizens of Nagyrőcze submitted a request to County Gömör asking that this school be closed and that a technical high school be established. At the same time, the Slovak press was screaming. The County Gömör Assembly (Pelsőc, 1874), in its submission to the Minister (No. 4700), requested that the school be closed and that a state technical high school be established that "would not exclude the teaching of the Slovak language". The Lutheran diocese of the Tisza region held its general meeting on July 30, 1874 and supported the closure of the school, with one dissenting vote. A government edict closed the school on August 25, 1874.

[64] László Ruttkay: A felvidéki szlovák iskolák megszűntetése 1874-ben (Closure of the Slovak schools in the Felvidék in 1874), Felvidéki Tudományos Társaság Kiadványa, Pécsi Egyetemi Könyvkiadó, Pécs, 1939, pp. 92-96 and 121-123.

It must be remembered that at this time local instruction was under the control of the ecclesiastic authorities, that there was no centrally determined, mandated curriculum, no strict regulations, no injunction against inciting hatred and no parliamentary debates about "teachers' neutrality".

Overt political agitation was forbidden in the schools and today it would lead to the dismissal of the teacher. It was only prior to 1989 that it was not only permitted but also required that "Marxist education" be used to create the "Socialist type". Schools are occasionally closed today and the justification is usually the inadequate level of instruction. It seems likely that instead of closing the three Slovak schools for such, and similar, faults it would have been better to dismiss the director and some of the teachers. Unfortunately, the Ministry chose not to do this.

On the request of County Zólyom, an investigation was started against the Turócszentmárton junior high school. The investigation revealed that the nobility of County Túróc established a school in the 1840s in the ancient seat of the Justh family, in Necpál. It was called the "*Nacionale Institutum Hungaricum*". Its purpose was to teach Hungarian noble youth in the Hungarian language in a Slovak environment. It was transferred to Túrócszentmárton because there the Lutheran Church donated land that permitted the erection of a much more modern school. During the Bach period (1849-1859), the German and Czech officials banished the Hungarian language from this school which led to its gradual decline. In 1868, the Trans-Danubian diocesan congress agreed to the request of the *patronatus* that the diocese take the school and its assets under its own supervision without consulting the group that established the school. The school opened in 1879 with both qualified and unqualified teachers and with 90-100 students per class. The staff included some of the leaders of the Slovak national movement, as well as some members *of Matica* and some who were also on the staff of Slovak newspapers.

The superintendent, Lajos Geduly, did not accept the responsibility of taking charge of the investigation and, therefore, Trefort entrusted it to Baron Gábor Prónay, superintendent of general education. His reports made it clear that the Lutheran Church was just one of the members of the *patronatus*, with only 12 votes of 220. Its assets were handled separately from the Túróc diocese, instruction was entirely without religious supervision, the formal invitations lacked the seal and signature of the diocese and the entire system operated like a "privately owned corporation". The students were induced to nurture their Slovak culture with a variety of activities such as choirs, plays, etc. The report considered that the teaching of geography and history was partisan and referred to the known prejudices of Frantisek Sasin who taught at the school. The students were taken as a group to demonstrations and fanaticism was carried to the point that students, who came from Hungarian areas and who spoke Hungarian at home, claimed to be Slovaks. In view of the fact that the Znio and Nagyrőcze gymnasiums were closed, causing considerable popular unrest, the commission did not recommend the closure of this school, since then the 100,000 Lutheran Slovaks, living in the central part of the Felvidék, would be left without a school. They recommended that it be completely restructured, by eliminating the *patronatus* and by integrating the school fully into the organization of the Lutheran diocese.

Márton Szentiványi, a landowner in County Liptó and superintendent of the Trans-Danubian Lutheran diocese, was asked by the Minister of Culture to comment on the situation. He wrote, "When County Zólyom claims that in the three gymnasia under review, the youth is taught in an unpatriotic and hostile spirit, it says nothing new and only expresses a strong conviction that all of us share". He recommended that the government set up schools where the instruction was in Slovakian but whose teachers were selected and supervised directly by the Ministry. The government recommended to Franz Joseph that the school be closed and in 1875 this, in fact, took place.

The Ministry of Religion and Education endeavored at the end of the 19th century to open as many public schools as possible. Its primary educational aim was to supervise the quality and level of instruction, both through the school superintendents and also through the ecclesiastic authorities who helped support the schools. Interference into education by the government was a very touchy problem, since it could be construed as an anti-nationality activity that the foreign press would be pleased to broadcast worldwide. At the same time, the shortage in Slovak secondary schools made continued education very difficult. In the absence of good secondary education in the students' mother tongue, the development of Slovak intellectuals was made difficult and they were clearly handicapped in achieving intellectual careers. Between 1875 and 1908, the number of Slovak public schools decreased by 75%. According to Slovak critics, the reason for this decline was the establishment of new state public schools. In fact, the majority of these new schools were established at the linguistic borders in order to salvage the isolated Hungarian islands and the Hungarian villages that heretofore had no schools of any kind. At the same time, there is documentation provided by the Ministry and by pedagogic journals showing that in about 1,000 schools the education was not only necessarily bilingual but was largely Slovak, with Hungarian being taught as a second language. *It is certainly true that if the Hungarization of the schools had been successful, more than only 7% of the Slovak population would have had more than a smattering of Hungarian by the turn of the century.*

There are a number of examples in the 20th century showing that in less than 30 years, more than 90% of the population having a different native language can be made to speak the official language, if the pressures brought are forceful enough. When the Lutheran National Assembly changed the diocesan boundaries in 1893, this was done largely so that the ecclesiastic structure could not be used for the purposes of Slovak nationality endeavors. Those who protested against the new diocesan arrangement threatened to leave the Hungarian Lutheran Church and establish their own Slovak Lutheran diocese unless their demands were met. They considered the defense of their ecclesiastic autonomy identical with the defense of their nationality.

It is evident that the Hungarian political circles were frightened by the changes that characterized the nationalities in the 1880s. Even the press reflected very clearly the nationalities' desire to ally themselves with a foreign power, beyond the borders of the Monarchy, to leave the Monarchy and so to seek a way to develop their identity. Actually, some Serb and Romanian leaders were moving in this direction ever since the 1840s.

As far as the Slovaks were concerned, this endeavor went well beyond a common cause with the Czechs and clearly indicated their desire to seek the patronage of the Tsar.

In their discussions, beginning in 1893, the Slovak, Serb and Romanian leaders set as their goals:

- The fight against the Nationality Act,
- The Revision of the Franchise, and
- Protest against the civil wedding.

Instead of the latter, and clearly in conjunction with it, they emphasized their demands for ecclesiastic autonomy.

In addition to the above, they demanded, at the 1895 Congress in Budapest, that the county lines be modified according to language lines and that their interests be represented in the government by a separate minister, just as in the case of Croatia.[65]

As far as the change of the Bánffy government's feelings vis-à-vis the nationalities was concerned, it was caused by the government's fear of the separatist movement and by the anti-Hungarian demonstrations of the nationalities at the time of the millennial celebrations of the foundation of Hungary in 1896.

The jointly issued "Protest" called the occupation of the Carpathian basin a "humbug" and doubted the truth of the historic traditions relative to the Hungarian past.[66]

Economic growth at the turn of the century[67]

After Budapest, the most important industrial region was the Felvidék, particularly the valleys of the Garam, the Sajó, the Hernád and the Ipoly rivers. This was the most important area for mining and for lumber, textile, building materials and food production. Pozsony and the area around Kassa were the two most important industrial areas in the country.

The increasing Slovak bourgeoisie was more interested in banking. At the turn of the century, there were 22 Slovak financial institutions and 127 non-Slovak ones. The Czech investments pouring into this area were handled primarily by the Slovak financial institutions. Slovak capital played only an insignificant role in industry, but its participation increased with the increasing influence of the Czech capital. The same Slovak names appearing in the banking industry and in the leadership of other industries as among the leaders of the Slovak nationality movement and the control of the Slovak political newspapers.

Assimilation

Nationally, the ratio of the Slovaks versus the Hungarians shifted in favor of the Hungarians (63%-37%), while in the Felvidék, the shift was in the opposite direction (53%-47%). István Révay compared the 1773 data, published in the "Lexicon", with the census data of 1918 and found that there had been a shift in language and that more villages shifted their language away from Hungarian than toward it.[68] It is a clear indication of the failure of the much-criticized educational policy that, at the turn of the century, only about 7% of the Slovaks spoke some Hungarian.

The gains made by the Slovaks against the Germans, and particularly against the Ruthenians, in the Felvidék were impressive. Concerning assimila-

---

[65] Polányi op.cit pp. 109-111.
[66] Polanyi. op.cit,. pp. 116-117.
[67] Ibid. pp. 28 and 33-35.
[68] Ibid. pp. 46, 92; Révay's work is cited by Olvedi: op.cit. p.24. See also: pp. 24-31 on the decrease of the Hungarian population.

tion, it may be worthy of mention that between 1840 and 1910, the Slovak population in Hungary increased by 16% and at the latter date they represented 10.68% of the entire population. During the 70 years between 1921 and 1991, the number of Hungarians in Czechoslovakia decreased by 13% while the number of the Slovaks increased 2.5 fold.[69]

The Ruthenians

The Ruthenian population of the Kárpátalja came originally from the Eastern branch of the Slav linguistic group. In addition to their Slav origins, they incorporated Romanian, Slovak, Serb, German and Hungarian ethnic elements.

As the royal domains and private large landholdings expanded toward the forests of the Carpathian Mountains, new nationalities appeared in the Carpathian basin. The migration and settlement of the Ruthenians began in the 13th and lasted until the end of the 17th century. After the terrible devastation of the Tartar invasion, Béla IV had a number of fortresses erected along the border and distributed large tracts of the former royal forests among his faithful followers. It was thus that in the Northwest the Makovic, Sztropko, Sicsva, Homonna, Ungvár, Munkács-Szentmiklós and Huszt-Ronaszek estates were established. The landowner made a contract with the tribal leaders who were willing to arrange for settlers. A written agreement specified the rights and duties of the villeins to be settled. They were usually exempt for a period of 6, 8 or 10 years from paying the landowner any dues or services.[70]

The leaders became the judges of the settlements they established. They were villeins themselves but were exempted from all villein obligations. The Ruthenians came primarily from the Halics Principality. Because of internal strife, this principality came under Polish control in 1340, which led to an intolerable increase in the burdens imposed on the villeins. The Ruthenian settlement practices were similar to those of the Romanians and hence they were handled under the same law, the *"Ius Valachium"*.[71]

Act 45 of 1495 mentions the Ruthenians alongside the Romanians and Serbs and states, *"According to their custom...they are settled on the invitation of His Royal Majesty, the Voivode, Bailiffs and other national dignitaries and live under their guarantees"*. The so-called Dolisnyak settled in the plains. Initially, they were pastoral but soon settled down and took up agriculture. The so-called Lemak settled in the Nagyberezna and Perecsény districts, along the valleys of the rivers and engaged in pastoral activities, agriculture and, later, trade. They built characteristic wooden churches and houses. The Hungarian National Assemblies of 1464 and 1495 relieved the Ruthenians, Serbs and Wallachians of paying tithes. During the Turkish era, and in order to generate more income from these areas, Emperor Maximilian (1564-1576) requested the Assembly in 1572 to rescind this law, saying that it was very odd that foreigners who had settled relatively recently in the country had to pay less in taxes than the Hungarians, who, in addition

---

[69] Zoltán Balassa: Hogyan változik tájaink nemzetiségi összetétele (How the nationality composition changes in our regions) Szabad Ujság, July 25, 1992.
[70] Pirigyi: op.cit. p. 64.
[71] Jenő Szűcs: op.cit. p. 39.

65

to their taxes, had many other heavy obligations in the defense of the country. His request was denied by the National Assembly. In 1567, Maximilian set up the *Kamara* (Chamber) of Szepes to regulate the finances. This *Kamara* sent a committee to the areas inhabited by the Ruthenians and reported that as soon as the period of tax exemption was about to expire, the Ruthenians moved to a new area and started the tax-free period all over again.

At the time of the war that expelled the Turks from Hungary (1686-1699), the imperial troops invading the Kárpátalja caused such devastation that entire villages disappeared forever.

The mountaineer Huculs arrived in small groups from Galicia and Bukovina from the 15th century on and this migration increased appreciably in the 16th century. The Bojko came during the 15-18th centuries, first surreptitiously and later, at the invitation of the Munkács-Beregszentmiklós estate, in large numbers. They engaged in animal husbandry and agriculture. Since much of the Kárpátalja was owned by the Rákóczis in the 17th century, large numbers of the Ruthenian villeins joined the flag of the insurrection in hope of the promised liberty. According to Ferenc Rákóczi II, László Bige and "a Russian priest" came to see him in 1703, when he was staying in Brezan castle in Poland. They came to tell him about the miserable state of the people under the Habsburg rule. Rákóczi writes about his reception as follows: "...the news of my arrival in the Munkács principality spread like wildfire and it is impossible to credit the diligence and pleasure with which the people were attracted to me. They came in droves, bringing bread and meat and all other necessary foodstuffs. These people came with wife and children and when they espied me from afar, they knelt and made the sign of the cross in the Russian fashion. They copiously shed their tears of joy...."[72]

The Prince called the Ruthenians his most loyal subjects (*Gens fidelissima*). After the defeat of the Rákóczi rebellion (1703-1711), Vienna confiscated the estates of the "rebellious" landowners and gave them to Germans or retained them for the Crown. These Germans came mostly from Bavaria, Swabia and Lower-Austria. It was from them that the Huculs learned about forest management and lumbering. The miseries of the villeins were alleviated only by Maria Theresa's ordinances.

The political aims of the Ruthenianas were first drafted in the spring of 1848 when a Ruthenian Council was established and a separate Ruthenian Crown Territory was demanded. Contrary to the Serb and Romanian Greek Catholic Church, the Ruthenian one backed the 1848 revolution and the War for Freedom. In this, a major part was played by Pál Vasvári, the scion of a Greek Catholic priestly family and one of the drafters of the "12 Points", demanded by the young revolutionaries on the 15th March, 1848. He and his company of irregulars were captured by Avram Iancu and Vasvári was beheaded. On call from the leaders of the diocese, about 51 seminarians joined the rebellious forces as volunteers. The priests preached and prayed in the churches on behalf of the revolution and asked the faithful to fast for this noble reason. In the spring of 1850, 30 wagonloads of prisoners were taken from there to the prisons in Olmütz and Kufstein.

There was only a tiny minority of the Ruthenian Catholic intelligentsia, such as Adolf Dobranszky, who was a Russophile and who opposed the Hungarian revolution and war from the very beginning.

---

[72] Ferenc Rákóczi II: Emlékiratok (Recollections) Szépirodalmi Könyvkiadó, Bp. 1985. p. 60.

It caused concern, particularly during the second half of the century, that the intelligentsia, evolving from the ranks of the priesthood, followed the traditions of the ancient Slavic-Russian liturgical language and also came under the influence of the well-developed Russian literature. This, in turn, led them to the use of the Russian language and linked them emotionally to the Russian politicians, just as the use of the Czech language had linked the Slovaks to the Czech politicians. The Pest University Press was publishing books printed with the Cyrillic alphabet in the middle of the 19th century and Russian books were readily available from Russia.

The Russophile trend was strengthened not only by the Russian troops that invaded Hungary to crush the revolution but also by the activities of the Pravoslav priest of the Russian embassy in Vienna, Mihail Rajevskij, who was working for the Tsarist secret service. It was one of his duties to keep an eye on the changes in the conditions of the Poles, Ukrainians, Czechs, Slovaks, Ruthenians, Croats, Serbs, Slovenes and Bulgarians living in the Monarchy and report to St. Petersburg from time to time. He distributed money and books received from Russia, assisted in establishing contacts between publishing houses in the Monarchy and in Russia, provided a cover for those who had to flee the country and assisted them to emigrate to Russia and also provided substantial financial assistance to the Slavic movements in the Monarchy. The anti-Hungarian Habsburg policies of the 1850s strongly encouraged the nationalities to formulate their demands, even territorial ones, and therefore the Austrian-Hungarian Compromise of 1867 caused these nationalities a major disappointment. The Russophile Adolf Dobrzansky, as Lord Lieutenant of four counties in the Kárpátalja, inhabited by Ruthenians, endeavored to make Russian the official language and when the Russophile Saint Basil Society was founded, he became its president.

The turn of the century

Since the Kárpátalja was the most backward part of Hungary, there was a significant emigration at the turn of the century and there was considerable voluntary assimilation there as well. The spread of the Slovak linguistic area, at the cost of the Ruthenian one, was remarkable. This was particularly significant in Counties Sáros, Zemplén and Ung, in the valleys of the Tapoly, Ondova and Laborc rivers. At the time of the ever-increasing anti-Hungarian nationality fights, following the Compromise, the Ruthenians attempted to reach an agreement with the Hungarians. This endeavor was largely the consequence of the vigorous activities of the Greek Catholic bishop of Munkács, Gyula Firczák.

The bishop, who devoted almost his entire income for the common good; e.g.- benevolences, establishment of the Ungvár Greek Catholic Teacher College and the creation of high school dormitories and scholarships, found a basis for agreement with the Bánffy government in 1896. They agreed that the ecclesiastic buildings would be repaired with government grants, that an economic program would be worked out to raise the standard of living of the Ruthenian people and that they would be appropriately represented in the administration. The government program, called the Hegyvidék Action, was initiated at a conference in the Hungarian parliament in 1897, attended by the bishop and by the parliamentary representatives of the involved counties.

These representatives then formed expert committees and advised the ministries about actions to be taken. The application to the Ministry of Agriculture describes the situation thus:

"One of the principal reasons for the intolerable poverty of the people of this area, for whom agriculture is the only means of livelihood, was the enormous influx of immigrants from Galicia (mainly Jews) which coincided with restrictions in using the large sylvan and mountainous grazing areas for animal husbandry. These two processes led to the indisputable situation where, with few exceptions, the people of Counties Máramaros, Bereg, Ung and Ugocsa were completely unable to support themselves.[73]

As a solution, they recommended, among other things, that the pasture technique successful in other mountainous areas be introduced, that one or two model agricultural estates be created, that the mountain villages be given land and animals, that any outstanding debt of more than five years be canceled and that the Treasury grant loans to the farmers.

The Ministry of Agriculture had attempted to remedy the situation even prior to receiving the memorandum. Thus, in County Ung, it ordered that the forested areas owned by the crown be rented out. The Minister of the Interior promised to limit the influx of very large groups of Jews who were expelled from Russia and who came from Galicia where their activities were limited to commercial enterprises. It was said that one of the main reasons for the spread of poverty was the "excessive presence of usury". Ignác Darányi, the Minister of Agriculture, entrusted the implementation of the program to the economist Ede Egan, who was of Irish descent. He saw some of the reasons for the problem in the poorly executed 1853 regulation of socage, i.e., distribution of land to the villeins, in the absence of industry and mining, and in the 30% usurious interest rate subsequent to the Galician immigration. As a consequence of the latter, more than half of the land and livestock of the mid-size landowners was taken over by the usurers.

The government took 12,622 hectares from the Schönborn-Buckheim estate in Munkács-Szentmiklós, the former Rákóczi estate, on a 25-year rental basis, to sublet it to Ruthenian villages or to give it to individuals on a sharecropping basis. In order to rid the Ruthenians from the burden of usurious interests, credit companies were formed and large nurseries were set up to promote the cultivation of fruit. Breeding stock was distributed among the farmers, storage facilities were set up, craft cooperatives were established and free legal assistance was provided. Courses in basic economics were attended by large numbers of the rural intelligentsia and priesthood. Twenty-five new Ruthenian public schools were started. The implementation of the program was not easy since the bishop was accused of conspiracy with the government against the Ruthenians, and Ede Egan, who provided land even for Jewish farmers, was accused of anti-Semitism. His house was set on fire several times and finally he was murdered by unknown assailants. Before his death, Egan actually worked out a solution for the Transylvanian problems as well, but the outbreak of World War I did not permit its implementation.

---

[73] József Botlik: Hármas kereszt alatt (Under the triple cross). Hatodik Sip Alapitványa. Új Mandátum Kiadó, Bp. 1997, p. 123.

It was apparent, however, that the solution of the Ruthenian problem was worked out by the Bánffy government, a government that was accused so vigorously by the nationalities for being overbearing and for forcefully Hungarizing.

The "Hegyvidék Action" was made successful by the fact that the Ruthenian priestly intelligentsia, together with their bishop, did everything to make the Action a success and sought an agreement with the government rather than engaging in active or passive resistance. This honest endeavor received full governmental support.

Ecclesiastic life

The priests came from their old home, today's Galicia, the Przemysl Pravoslav diocese. They were not subject, however, to the bishop of Przemysl, but to their new landowners who viewed the Ruthenian priests as their own villeins.

It was in, or about, 1396 that Theodor Koriatovics, Prince of Podolia settled with his Ruthenian people in the Kárpátalja. King Zsigmond gave him the castle of Munkács with the lands pertaining thereto. Monks established a monastery in Csernekhegy, near Munkács, and dedicated it to Saint Nicholas. *The first legitimate charter of the Munkács Greek Orthodox bishopric was issued by King Mátyás in 1458.*[74]

In a letter to Rome, Lippay, the Archbishop of Esztergom, wrote in 1654 that these priests were untaught and ignorant. Since the foundation of the bishopric was not justifiable on the basis of ecclesiastical law, the landowners ruled over the Ruthenian priests just as over their own villeins and, in fact, demanded the same services from them. After the Peace of Vienna in 1606, following the anti-Habsburg struggle of István Bocskai, Prince of Transylvania, most of the area of the Munkács diocese was transferred to Transylvania and the Munkács castle became the private property of the Princes of Transylvania. Gábor Bethlen and György Rákóczi, although Protestant Princes, recognized the rights of the bishop of Munkács. Unfortunately, this did not resolve the ecclesiastical legal conundrum and thus did not solve the problem. It was not an accident that on the 100 year old Polish model, a Union movement got under way in Kárpátalja at the end of the 17th century, since for the priesthood this would have meant the end of their being treated as villeins. The fact that, after the Brest Union was established in 1596, the situation of the Ruthenian priests in Poland underwent a marked improvement, was a strong incentive. Not only could the Polish Ruthenian priests now partake of Catholic continuing education but they could even serve in the National Assembly. In the Kárpátalja, it was after the peace of Linz, in 1645, that the opportunity arose for the Greek Catholics to join Rome, mainly because at this time County Bereg was returned to Hungary. In order to facilitate the creation of the Union, Rome permitted the continuation of the Ancient Slavic and Romanian languages in the liturgy in the Union (Greek Catholic) Church. In addition to the Ruthenians, there were also a large number of Slovak and Hungarian Greek Catholics but for them the use of Hungarian in the liturgy was forbidden until the 20th century with the justification that the liturgical language of the Roman Catholic Church was Latin. This led to the absurd situation that in the Nagyvárad diocese, Romanian was used as the liturgical language in Hungarian churches, because the Hungarians could understand it much better than Latin. It is not surprising that the Hungarian islands among the Ruthenians

[74] Pirigyi, op.cit. pp. 71, 77.

and Romanians slowly disappeared. The Hajdúdorog Hungarian diocese was established only in 1912 and protesting Romanians sent letter bombs to Church officials that killed three of them.

The settlement of Greek Orthodox Ruthenians, Greeks, Serbs, Macedonians and Romanians in the second half of the 18th century led to the expansion of the bishopric to 13 counties. In the 17th century, Russian Paravoslavism turned increasingly in this direction. It was for this reason that the Austrian government supported the Union movement that recognized the authority of the Pope and abandoned any attachment toward the East. *A Charter of Leopold I, in 1692, guaranteed the inviolable nature of the Eastern rites and ordered that the bishops should be elected by the priesthood of the diocese.* The Union clergy received all the same privileges granted to the Roman Catholic priests.[75] The King also ordered the landowners to provide land for the Union dioceses, schools and cemeteries.

The first counties to convert to Greek Catholicism from the Greek Orthodox (Pravoslav) religion were Sáros, Zemplén, Szepes, Ung and Kalocsa. They were followed shortly by Counties Máramaros and Bereg.

After the Union of Ungvár was established, the Holy See reached the conclusion that the Munkács bishopric had never been legally established and hence it did not recognize its existence. In its place, the Holy See organized an Apostolic Vicarage for the Ruthenians and appointed an Apostolic Vicar to lead it and placed him under the authority of the bishop of Eger. At the time of the Rákóczi uprising, Joseph I appointed József Hodemarszky, the choice of the diocesan priesthood. Rákóczi appointed his own man to the Ruthenian Union bishopric while the Holy See entrusted yet a third person, the bishop of Przemysl, György Vinniczky, with the leadership of the Vicarage. The priests protested saying that Vinniczky lived in a foreign country where both the language and the coinage was different. Polish Ruthenian was apparently different from Kárpátalja Ruthenian. The Holy See excused Vinniczky and henceforth appointed only Hungarian priests as Apostolic Vicars.

On the initiative of Maria Theresa, the Pope established the independent Munkács diocese in 1771 and thus the Greek Catholics were no longer subjects of the Eger bishopric. This was a distinct advantage since as long as they were under the rule of the bishop of Eger, he had issued a series of directives limiting the rights of the Greek Catholics in an area with a mixed population.

In the 18th century, bishop Mihály Manuel Olsavszky had a bilingual, Hungarian and Old Slavic textbook published in Kolozsvár and later a bilingual, Latin-Old Slavic primer. András Bacsinszky was an outstanding Ruthenian intellectual in the 18th century, responsible for the establishment of an Episcopal library, archives and teachers training-college at Ungvár. With the assistance of Maria Theresa, he established a seminary and obtained state support in the form of scholarships and salaries for the teachers. At both the Munkács and Ungvár seminaries, the language of instruction was Ruthenian and this was the first step leading to the development of a Ruthenian literary language. He strongly supported schooling for the Ruthenians and in order to further it, had primers published in Buda. Between 1699 and 1804, 12 books were published in Ruthenian in Buda.

The evolution of the Ruthenians as a nation began in the middle of the 19th century and there were three distinct linguistic branches:

[75] Pirigyi, op.cit. pp. 99, 144.

- The Ruthenian branch whose representatives, the Greek Catholic priests, wished to create a literary language from the Kárpátalja dialects.
- The Greater Russian branch that considered the Ruthenians and the Russians to be one people.
- The Ukrainian branch that appeared at the turn of the century and claimed that the Ruthenians and the Ukrainians were one people.[76]

The Hungarian government endeavored to counteract the Pravoslav tendencies and the Russian encroachments with the establishment of Hungarian public schools, with higher levels of education and by raising the standards of living.

Between 1880 and 1910, the Ruthenians represented 2.55% of the population of Hungary.

The Greeks

The slow seepage of Greeks into Hungary began in the 16th century when, in a country torn into three pieces, Hungarian commerce declined. Hungarians were replaced by Greek, Jewish and Armenian traders. The Greek colony in Brassó and Nagyszeben played a key role in the trade between the Balkans and East and Central Europe as early as the time of the Turkish occupation. It is not easy to determine exactly who belonged to the Greek colony since many traders coming from Bulgaria, Serbia, Bosnia or Macedonia called themselves Greeks. The term apparently was associated primarily with the profession rather than with the ethnic group. The historians also have difficulty in identifying certain family names as being of Greek or Serbian origin. Thus the catchall term of "Balkan traders" is frequently encountered.

The Albanian and Turkish invasions into the Balkans in the 17th century also started a new wave of refugees in a northerly direction and in 1662, for instance, a large number of refugees settle in Kecskemét. The Turkish invasion led to the destruction of a number of communities and the refugees felt considerably more secure in their new home than under Turkish sovereignty.

At the beginning of the 17th century, the Greeks took over the management of most of the commercial activities in the Turkish Empire, the Turks being fully occupied with fighting. In this, they had the full support of the Turkish authorities. During the 1688 war between the Turks and the Austrians, the Greeks, who sided with the Austrians, had to flee when the Austrians had to retreat. When Belgrade came into Turkish hands in 1690, a new wave of refugees started north and the Greek traders preferred to settle in the Free Royal cities. According to a 1735 report, 24 of the 29 traders in Buda were Greeks. The Greek settlers assumed a leading role in commerce in Hungary at the beginning of the 18th century. By the end of the 18th century, 70% of the mercantile establishments in Pest were in Balkan hands, organized into 25 associations. The "Greek" influence in Hungarian commerce continued to grow and in 1743 they were in full charge of all the trade with the Turkish Empire. Charles III, recognizing their importance, wished to grant them a privileged status but this

---

[76] Pirigyi, op.cit. pp. 59-60.

was blocked by the Austrian manufacturing and trading interests. Nevertheless, they were granted a very favorable 3% customs tariff. Since the citizens of the Habsburg Empire had to pay an income duty of 30-60%, this represented a very unfair advantage between the trading groups and also led to a decline in state revenues. Many of the Greek merchants, interested primarily in long distance trading activities, also took an active and even dominant participation in local merchandising, thereby seriously affecting the interests of German and Austrian merchants. Unfortunately, however, so long as the French-Turkish-Prussian alliance tied the hands of the Habsburgs, there was nothing they could do to eliminate the privileged position of the Greek merchants.

The situation changed only after the 1737 Turkish war. In 1714, Maria Theresa forbade the Greek, Jewish and Armenian participation in the wine trade. It is of interest to note that, when the customs officers attempted to confiscate the Greek goods, the Hungarian county officials rose to the defense of the Greeks, occasionally even with arms, as shown in a case in 1745. A study in 1776, submitted to Maria Theresa indicated that the Greeks caused a loss of 2 million Forints to the Treasury. When the Queen suggested that the Greek merchants should be urged to settle in the large cities and pay their taxes, the Committee opposed it because it was concerned that the Austrian merchants would not be able to compete with the lower priced Greek merchandise.

The prevailing conditions were thus preserved. The Germans were in charge in the large cities, the Greeks were in charge in Western Hungary and in the commercial towns and the Jews in the in the villages. Further immigration was forbidden.

The 1768-1774 war with Turkey led to Turkey's defeat and now Maria Theresa took advantage of the opportunity. The Palatine Council demanded an oath of allegiance of the Greek subjects of the Sultan. This led to the loss of their Turkish citizenship and, therefore, also to the loss of the duty privileges they had enjoyed ever since the Turks had obtained them for the merchants at the Peace of Pozserovác. The authorities banned the import of wool and cotton and also of some manufactured goods. The emigration of the Greeks from Hungary began although family settlements flourished. In 1790, Emperor Leopold II authorized the purchase of real estate and of the holding of offices for the Greeks. Many of them purchased land and a patent of nobility. They engaged in money lending but, because of Austrian commercial policies, could not invest their capital in industrial enterprises.

At the time of 1848-1849 Hungarian War for Freedom, the Lord Mayor of Pest was a Greek, Tersis Konstantinos, who was an enthusiastic supporter of the Hungarian cause.

Culture and the Church without ecclesiastic autonomy
The Spiritual focus of the Greek Diaspora in Hungary was Pest and, later, Buda. Many churches were built, priests and teachers were prepared and hundreds of books and pamphlets were published, all testifying to the cultural and educational endeavours of the Greeks in Hungary. At the same time, they also supported causes in their distant homeland and György Sína, for instance, made a major contribution toward the building of the Academy and of the observatory in Athens. He also gave 500,000 English Pounds for the building

of the Chain Bridge and supported the Hungarian Scientific Academy and the Danube Steamship Navigation Company. In the second half of the 18th century, the Greeks had 30 dioceses and 26 schools. Following the Edict of Tolerance of Joseph II, they started building a number of churches and, shortly thereafter, under the leadership of Dionisios, the bishop of Buda, the Buda Greek Pedagogical Academy was established.

Assimilation

Because of their commercial activities, they did not live in a tight group and very quickly learned Hungarian. When their commercial activities were curtailed, their numbers decreased and their assimilation became more rapid. This process was assisted by the fact that they had no ecclesiastic autonomy and thus practiced their religion within the Orthodox Serb Church. Consequently many of them became assimilated into the Serb communities as, for instance, in Ráckeve.

They were most numerous in 1770 and even at that time they numbered only about 10,000 and many of them were temporary residents in Hungary, living there only for a few years. By comparison, the Jewish merchants numbered 12,000 in 1735 and this number increased to 80,000 by 1787. The number of Greeks was never large and German-Greek confrontations were not unusual. When they occurred the Hungarian county authorities always went to their assistance.

The Habsburgs opposed Greek mercantilism for economic reasons and the Greeks became assimilated when they lost their privileged status and local commerce came into the hands of the Germans and the Jews.

The Armenians

Armenia lies on the border between Europe and Asia and at the crossroads where the North-South and East-West trade routes meet. It was a bone of contention ever since the 5th century. The Armenians living there had to defend themselves against all comers, but when they became the goal of a program of planned genocide many of them left their homeland and today they are scattered all over the world.

The first Armenians to reach Hungary presumably came from the Balkans in the 10 - 11th century. The existence of a colony of Armenians in Esztergom is shown by a charter issued by Béla IV that granted them land and a monastery. Several place names of the period attest to the presence of Armenians. These include Örményes, Örményszékes and Mezőörményes (Örmény is Armenian in Hungarian. Tr.) Archival documents show that in the 15th century an Armenus Egidius was a magistrate in Pest and that in the 16th century, a certain Stephanus Ermeni was chief judge of the City of Buda. Larger groups arrived in the 17th century to settle in Transylvania under the rule of Prince Mihály Apafi.

According to their own sources, they left their city of Ani after a Turkish invasion in the 11th century and again after the Tartar invasion in the 13th century. They moved first to the Caucasus, then to the Crimea and finally, after a long period of wandering, they settled in Moldavia. Their life under the

Moldavian princes was a very tenuous one, because of the high taxes and because they persisted in their Catholic religion. Prince Stefan V attacked the village of Vaslui in 1526 and Stefan VII ordered in 1551 that, "Whoever does not convert to the Greek Orthodox religion will be destroyed, his goods will be confiscated and his church will be demolished". In 1668, internecine wars broke out in Moldavia and fear of a Turkish invasion impelled the Armenians to abandon seven Moldavian cities and seek asylum in Transylvania. It is likely that the Armenian leadership was involved in the rebellion that broke out against the Romanian ruling Prince, Gheorghe Duca, in 1671. The first colonies in Transylvania developed near the Transylvania-Moldavia border (Beszterce, Gyergyószentmiklós, Görgényszentimre, Felfalu, Petele and Csíkszépvíz). Ebesfalva was the only settlement further inside the country. According to contemporary data, the number of the immigrants was about 8,000.

They were not allowed to purchase property and could only lease land. The situation was different in the south of Hungary, where, after the expulsion of the Turks, they could buy land left unpopulated and were also allowed to drain swamps and cultivate the land so reclaimed.

Neither Charles III, nor Maria Theresa allowed them to take a government position. They worked as merchants, carpet weavers, leather workers and tanners. They had to pay 100 Ft. tax per annum for the privilege of engaging in trade and in three years they also had to pay one thirtieth in duties. By the end of the 18th century, one quarter of all Transylvanian trade and industry was in Armenian hands. Needless to say that this competition was viewed with great disfavor by the Transylvanian Saxons. In Beszterce, this antagonism led to serious disturbances and the Armenians were forced to leave the city.

The expelled merchants settled in Szamosújvár, later in Erzsébetváros and Gyergyószentmiklós. Szamosújvár was incorporated in 1700 but gained its privileges only gradually. Charles III sold them some Crown land for 120,000 Ft. for the purpose of building a city and the Armenians took until 1758 to pay off this debt. Thirty to forty years after settling here, they could show appreciable progress. They had some Letters of Patent that allowed them to trade freely anywhere in the country. The Armenian merchants gathered wealth quite rapidly, mostly from cattle and also from leather. Instead of temporary dwellings, they erected large stone houses and built churches in their communities. Since, under the feudal system, land could be bought only by those having a Patent of Nobility, a number of Armenian families used their wealth to purchase such a Patent. A number of others were granted a Patent of Nobility by the Ruler for services rendered and these families, by marrying into Hungarian noble families, gradually became Hungarians. In 1790, Erzsébetváros and Szamosújvár became Free Royal Cities. In 1800, a Szamosújvár delegation petitioned the Crown for permission to use the Hungarian language in the administration of the city. At the same time, the assimilation of the Armenians got under way. The Armenian merchants had to deal with the Hungarians and hence had to learn to speak Hungarian. By 1900, the only Armenian spoken was the liturgical language of the Armenian Catholic Church.

Education

Ever since their settlement, there were elementary schools in Szamosújvár, Erzsébetváros, Csíkszépvíz and Gyergyószentmiklós where the teaching was done by priests and nuns. Until the middle of the 19th century, the language of instruction was Armenian. Later on, even in the Hungarian schools, Armenian was taught as a second language. In Erzsébetváros, there were three elementary schools: Hungarian, Armenian and German. Since the level of instruction was particularly high in the Armenian school, it was attended even by non-Armenians in the early 19th century. The first middle school was established in Szamosújvár in the 18th century and by the 19th century there were complete secondary schools in both Szamosújvár and Erzsébetváros. They were supported by the Church, the parents and wealthy citizens. In 1909, an Armenian Museum was established in Szamosújvár on the instigation of Kristóf Szongott, the editor of the Armenian daily paper.

Independent ecclesiastic organization

The seal of Talmács village, in County Szeben, indicates that there was an Armenian bishopric and an Armenian bishop as early as 1343. In the 18th century, Lemberg became the religious center for the Bukovina Armenians.

An exceptionally prominent personality and religious leader, Verzar Oxendius, took on the responsibility to act as an intermediary between the Armenian minority and the civil power structure. He realized that the strengthening of the Habsburg position would inevitably increase the political power of the Catholic Church. It was for this reason that he urged the creation of a religious union between the Armenians and the Catholic Church, while preserving Armenian as the liturgical language. He managed to convince Bishop Minasz of the necessity for a union and, in 1686, the bishop takes the oath of union at Lemberg. The right to elect the bishop remained with the diocese and required only confirmation from the Austrian Emperor.

Being urged to do so by Leopold I, in Bukovina the union with the Armenians was implemented between 1684 and 1690. The Armenian Church at that time numbered about 5,000. After Minasz' death, Verzar became the bishop of the Armenians. He used his ecclesiastic-political power to regularize the position of the Armenians. The permission to incorporate Szamosújvár was also due to his efforts. After Verzar's death, the Armenians could not agree on his successor and therefore Maria Theresa placed the Armenian Church under the authority of the Catholic bishop of Transylvania. The Hungarian Catholic bishop was appointed by the Pope on the recommendation of the Austrian Emperor. *The Armenian Church gained its autonomy only after the enactment of Act IX of 1868.*

Politics

The Armenians were invited to the Transylvanian National Assembly in 1725 and in 1791 Leopold II gave them citizenship. They endorsed the recommendations made by István Széchenyi at the 1825-1827 National Assembly concerning the improvement of the Hungarian language and subscribed 4,000 Forint toward the foundation of the Hungarian Scientific Society. The 1840 National Assembly recognized them as full citizens but it was only in 1848 that they gained full equality. In the 1848-1849 War for Freedom, about 1,200 men and 70 higher officers fought on the Hungarian side. Of the 13 Arad martyrs two, Vilmos Lázár and Ernő Kis, were of Armenian extraction. As punishment for their actions, the Imperial government canceled the privileges of Erzsébetváros and Szamosújvár.

By the end of the 19th century, the voluntary assimilation was almost complete and by that time men and women of Armenian extraction assumed important positions in all walks of life.

The Germans and Swabians

In the spirit of the mercantile economic policies of the 18th century, and the population pressures of the 19th century, very large numbers of Germans settled in Hungary. In 1773, their number is estimated at slightly above 500,000 but by 1880 this number rose to 2 million.

They came in the 18th century from various states of the Holy Roman Empire, including Austria, Swabia, the Rheinland, Hessen, Pfalz and Alsace. Most of them were farmers and village artisans and they were all identified by the name of Swabians. About 80% were farmers but large numbers also settled in the towns and cities and engaged in trade and manufacture. The industrial revolution during the second half of the 19th century attracted German capital and German skilled workers.

The Austrian Emperor encouraged immigration from the German Principalities by granting the immigrants a number of privileges. The artisans were tax-exempt for 15 years and the farmers were given full freedom of mobility and were exempt for several years from all state taxes and socage. Those who settled on Crown lands were given particularly favorable consideration. In the Bánság of Temes, devastated by the Turkish occupation, Maria Theresa settled the immigrants in housing designed by architects and they were given complete farming equipment, draught animals, seed and credit. On several occasions, the original inhabitants were moved out to make room for the newcomers. *While the Saxons in the Felvidék and the Transylvanian Saxons enjoyed territorial autonomy and could thus preserve their full identity, the villages of the later immigrants nestled among the Hungarian communities.* The settlers elected their own priests and judges and had a certain degree of local autonomy. Among their villages, the ones around Buda preserved their language and national character until 1945, but those who left the villages were lost to the community.

Assimilation was particularly pronounced among the urban dwellers engaged in trade and manufacture which was quite different from the original intent, according to which these German settlements were supposed to isolate the "rebellious" Hungarians.

In the 19th century, Germans fought on the Hungarian side during the Age of Reforms. In 1849, Haynau executed several German-speaking generals who fought for Hungarian freedom. Architects and artists of German extraction were instrumental in the modernization of Budapest and wrote a new chapter of Hungarian cultural history.

Between 1880 and 1910, the German population (Saxons, Swabians and others) of Hungary made up approximately 10.44% of the total population.

European Minority Policies and Practices in the Past

Comparing the motives of the European minority policies of the past and comparing the way nationality issues were handled, there are several similarities:

1. The majority group approached the problem from a concern about the threat to its territorial integrity.
2. Because of the maturity of the culture and social structure of the majority and awareness of its "superior civilization", the minority was forced to study the language and culture of the majority in the schools and was forbidden to use its own language or adhere to its traditions which were considered barbaric.
3. According to medieval practice, the centralization of the country could be achieved only if the regions with a population having a different culture and language were integrated into the majority population and were assimilated linguistically and culturally, leaving them only a certain degree of economic independence. In a feudal system, privileged social groups could exist only on the basis of their contributions and never on an ethnic basis. It is of interest to note that the Hungarian civil law practice differed from this universal European approach.
4. The integration of separate ethnic areas into a centralized unit was achieved with the same methods that were used during the colonization of distant lands in the 18th – 19th centuries.

To assimilate ethnic groups, the following methods were commonly used:

1. The ruler or the government forced the ethnic group to exchange its language and customs for the language and traditions of the majority nation.
2. The ruler did away with the ecclesiastic organizations of the minority nationality or the government made the functioning of such organizations very difficult. From this perspective, the religious wars can be viewed either as a fight between different nations and cultures or as an endeavor to create larger and more homogenous economic and political units.
3. The ruling government changed the administrative system, and gerrymandered the districts inhabited by the minority nationality.
4. The government replaced the locally elected leaders with judges appointed from the majority and replaced the local legal system with a national one.
5. The ruler forced a complete assimilation with the enactment of a union between the nationalities, e.g.- in Great Britain.
6. The king or the government used settlers to change the percentage of the oppressed people in a certain area. This was a common practice in Europe from Northern Ireland to Eastern Europe.

France

Population (1995): 58,027,000 (French - 93.6%).
Ethnic groups: Flemish – 80,000, Alsatian-German – 1,300,000, Breton – 600,000,
Provençal – 1,500,000, Basque – 80,000, Catalan – 100,000, Corsican – 70,000

Medieval France was fragmented both linguistically and territorially. The area north of the Loire, where the so-called Carolingian (Frank) culture flourished, was considered France. It included Paris, Orleans and the area around Tours where the so-called *langue d'oil* was spoken. The area south of the Loire, the Provence or Midi was characterized since the 10th century by the language known as *langue d'oc*. In this southern region, the Roman urban traditions survived longer and it was here that the Provençal literature developed. Aquitaine was the domain of the Counts of Toulouse that later also included some Aragonese and Catalan territories.

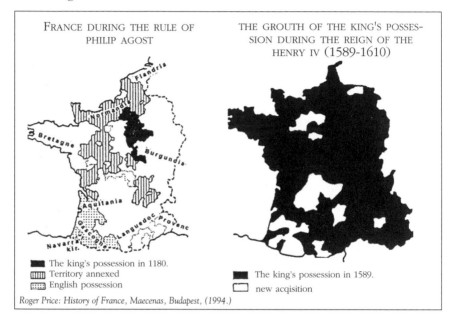

FRANCE DURING THE RULE OF PHILIP AGOST

THE GROUTH OF THE KING'S POSSESSION DURING THE REIGN OF THE HENRY IV (1589-1610)

■ The king's possession in 1180.
▦ Territory annexed
▤ English possession

■ The king's possession in 1589.
▢ new acqisition

Roger Price: History of France, Maecenas, Budapest, (1994.)

The dynastic wars of the Kingdom of France against the Plantagenets of England were intensified under Philippe Auguste II (1180-1223) and were instrumental in the linguistic and territorial unification of the area. The same purpose was served in the South of France by the war against the Albigensians in the 13th century. The centralizing wars of Philip Auguste II led to his control over Artois, Normandy, Anjou and Poitiers. At the beginning of the 13th century, Savoy and Provence were still independent principalities but the activities of the Inquisition and the persecution of the heretics led to a shift in the leadership of these areas with French noblemen replacing many of the local dignitaries. In 1246, Provence was incorporated into France. The Hundred Year War also led to the disappearance of a number of regional autonomies and in the 14th – 15th centuries

78

Aquitaine and Occitania were also incorporated into France. Even the religious wars of the 16th – 17th centuries were largely due to local nobles endeavoring to gain some degree of autonomy from the centralizing Catholic power.

Bretagne was inhabited by a Breton population. In consequence of the Norman occupation (907-937), Frenchification began. Because of the English-French rivalry, it could maintain its relative independence and its own autonomous administration from the 10th to the 16th century when Francis I by marriage, and some coercion, incorporated it into France (1532). According to the Act of Union, Bretagne now legally became a part of France, although it had its own General Assembly (Etats) that ratified its laws and also maintained its own legal administrative system. It lost its English markets and, until 1789, could develop its commercial activities only within France. Linguistic assimilation among the Breton nobles and bourgeois began in the 16th century. When Colbert enacted new taxes on tobacco and on charters in the 17th century, the nobles became rebellious and disturbances broke out. When, during Richelieu's administration, parliamentary powers were curtailed and a new system of regional units under royal intendants was imposed on the old territories, the central authority gained full dominion over the former regional bodies. *The centralizing endeavors of the French Revolution of 1789 were manifested by the complete eradication of all the old territorial boundaries and their replacement with an entirely artificial, national county system (Departments).* These arrangements broke up all the old regional units, including Bretagne. The Departments had very little independent autonomy and *the principal task of the prefects heading the Departments was to see that the orders of the central government were implemented.*

The Breton national consciousness, culture and history had a revival in the 19th century. *In the 1880s, the laws of Jules Ferry initiated the fight against the local religion and against the use of the Breton language.* The purpose of setting up community public schools was Frenchification. According to the Superintendent of Education, Carré, the coarse Breton language, lacking orthography and literature, had to be extirpated in order to put a stop to separatism and to the power of the priests. We learn from the lines of the Breton poet, abbé Jacques LeMarechal, that a wooden shoe was hung around the neck of every child who spoke Breton in class. In 1911, the first attempt was made to organize a Breton National Party. The Party, organized in 1927 under the name of *Strollad Emrenerien Vrezon*, was fighting for an autonomous Bretagne. It joined hands with the Alsatian and Corsican autonomy parties and formed a single organization for the protection of the three nationalities (*Comité Central des Minorités Nationales de France*). Theoretical arguments about the precise meaning of Breton autonomy destroyed the Party but a splinter group organized a new Breton National Party, the *Strollad Broadel Breiz*.

On August 7, 1932, when the 400th anniversary of the union of Bretagne and France was celebrated in Paris, an explosion took place in Rennes, the Breton capital, destroying the large statue symbolizing the union. In October 1932, Herriot declared, "The government will not tolerate even the slightest interference with the integrity of and indivisibility of the Republic and of

France."[77] The lower priesthood supported the linguistic struggle from the beginning, but there were few of Breton extraction among the bishops. Under abbé Perrot's leadership, a movement was started in ecclesiastical circles, in 1905, to cultivate the Breton language and the Breton traditions. The 50-year struggle for the Breton language bore fruit in 1930 when Adolf Duparc, Bishop of Quimper-Leon ordered that Breton be taught in the parochial elementary schools. In the 1930s, social organizations and clubs promoting the teaching of Breton came into being and became strong enough to force the local community administrations to endorse the teaching of Breton in the community public schools. In the 1936 National elections, the Breton National Party nominated 45 representatives of whom 15 were actually elected. In the battles for the Breton language, the similar struggles of related nationalities were followed with great interest. In 1900, the "Breton bards" had assumed responsibility for the maintenance of the Breton language and on the 20th anniversary of the Irish Easter Revolt in 1936, bombs were exploded in five Breton prefectural offices.

ALSACE

The original inhabitants of Alsace were Celts and Germans. It was an independent principality from 630 on and was divided into two dukedoms in 750. In 961, Otto I incorporated it into the Holy Roman Empire where it remained until the 17th century. During the Hundred Year War, its importance increased because the closure of the north-south trade routes shifted commerce to the Rhine valley. At the termination of the Thirty Year War, the Peace of Westphalia assigned Alsace to France, with the exception of Strasbourg. Strasbourg became a part of France only in 1681, when Louis XIV occupied it. Louis XIV forbade the Catholics to convert to the Protestant religion but granted a three-year tax exemption to all Protestants who converted to Catholicism. He obviously used Catholicism as a means of Frenchification. Alsace would preserve her own customs regulations and old administrative system until the French Revolution. After *the Union with France*, the German language and culture were maintained in Alsace and only the higher strata of society were bilingual.

The use of language
So far as the use of language was concerned, Francis I made French, as spoken in the Paris area, the official language for all legal documents and for legislative actions. French had to be used in the courtrooms and in the offices. Valid testaments could be written only in French. The representatives of the central government spoke only French, the local nobility gradually became Frenchified. The attractions of French literature and art were significant and after the 17th century the language of instruction in the schools was changed from Latin to French. Colbert sent French-speaking teachers to the districts where other languages were native and, as shown above, the Catholic religion was also used as a tool in the Frenchification process. The process came to a conclusion when the unifying force of *the French Revolution forbade the use of the*

---

[77] Miklós Párdányi: A breton kérdés (The Bretagne question), Balatonfüred Nyomda, Bp. 1937, p. 188.

Breton, Basque, German, Italian and Flemish languages. In 1792, the first laws of the Convention declared that "the French Republic is one and indivisible". The Convention debated a report in 1792, which admitted that the Alsatian Germans had the same rights as the French but regarded the local language "a remnant of the barbarism of past centuries" and stated that "all means had to be employed to make these remnants disappear as quickly as possible".[78] The Jacobin Education Act (1793) continued the requirement of its predecessors that French be used as the language of instruction in all public schools.

In the nationality regions, Bretagne and the South of France, illiteracy was rampant in the 18th century, although it largely disappeared by 1875, while at the same time the use of the nationality languages also decreased. Yet, linguistically, France was not homogenous and in 1863 about 10% of the public school students spoke no French. The language of instruction was French everywhere and, in the schools, the use of the local languages was most strongly discouraged. In Bretagne and elsewhere, if the teachers caught a student speaking in the native language, the culprit had to wear a wooden shoe tied around the neck or had a wooden ball pushed in his/her mouth. The student could escape this punishment only by reporting a classmate for a similar offense.[79] Industrialization and technical instruction accelerated the linguistic assimilation and in the Third Republic it was Jules Ferry who was responsible for the organization of the centralized, secularized and republican system of education. (1881-1882).

The Wilsonian principles, proclaimed at the end of World War I, raised hopes in the heart of the minorities in France. In 1919, a Breton delegation met with President Wilson and asked his support in implementing his 14 points in France. Their request was submitted to the delegates at the League of Nations - without effect. In the French Parliament, the issue of teaching the languages of the minorities was first debated in 1922. In Alsace-Lorraine, returned to France after the war, resistance grew against the minority policies of France and, in 1927, a Party seeking autonomy was formed. The events in Alsace naturally had a stimulating effect on the other minorities, including the Bretons and, in 1929, the parliament in Paris discusses the "sins" of the Alsatians and Bretons seeking autonomy. Poincaré and his Minister of Justice, Barthou, who in 1919 had attacked Hungary's minority policies, submitted a legislative proposal according to which any act of propaganda suggesting that any area of the country be removed from French sovereignty be punishable with a prison sentence of 1-5 years, a fine and banishment. This proposal was never enacted. *Parliament enacted a statute about regional languages in 1951 that permitted the teaching of Breton, Basque, Catalan and Provençal on an elective basis and at the discretion of individual teachers.* The law permitted the regional language to be taught for one hour per week, but nobody took this law seriously, no implementing legislation was ever passed and no effort was made to educate teachers to teach these languages. Real opportunities were created only by the new educational directives issued in 1964 - 1965 when the hours that could be devoted to the teaching of the regional languages were increased. Another step was taken in 1974 when Corsican Italian was included among the languages that could be taught and when integrated teacher education curricula included courses in the regional languages, literature and art.

---

[78] L. Karsay: A nemzetiségi kérdés Franciaországban (The nationality question in France) Kossuth Kiadó, Bp., 1983, pp. 51, 53.
[79] Ibid. p. 77.

In the 1980s, the Socialist governments diverged from the rigid, centralizing traditions of French administration and moved toward regional autonomy and strengthened regional self-government. The coalition taking over the government in 1986 reversed this trend and endeavored to protect the French language in the face of increased immigration.

When *the Constitution was amended in 1992*, the first amendment contained only one sentence: *"The language of the republic is French"*. In 1994, a statute was enacted concerning the French language, according to which French was the language of instruction, labor, commerce and public services. Only the schools specifically designed to teach foreign and regional languages were exempted from this rule and, in special situations, the appropriate Ministries were allowed to make exceptions (Paragraph 11). The Constitutional Court recommended several amendments to this statute since some provisions were found to be contrary to the French Constitution and to International Agreements. At the end of December 1994, 44 representatives submitted a legislative proposal on the "teaching of regional languages and cultures". These representatives alleged that the 1994 Act on instruction was discriminatory, since it granted constitutional privileges to one language without making any mention of the status of other languages. Mention was made of the fact that, while it was permitted to administer the baccalaureate exam in the Basque, Breton, Catalan Corsican, Gallic, Provençal, Alsatian and Moselle languages, there were insufficient teachers to do so. France, to this day, has failed to ratify the Charter of the European Council dealing with regional and minority languages. In 1993, 1% of the elementary school pupils spoke some minority language.

CORSICA

After the expulsion of the Moors, Corsica was controlled by either Pisa or Genoa. Excessive taxation led to the expulsion of the Genoese at the beginning of the 18th century. In 1755, Corsica became independent under the leadership of Pascal Paoli who introduced equality before the law and universal franchise for males. French occupation in 1769 put an end to this brief period of independence. Fighting in the French army in the First World War caused the loss of almost two thirds of its male population. The survivors became enthusiastic nationalists. Following World War II, the island became even more impoverished and in the 50s and 60s the average income of the Corsican males was one fourth of the average income on the mainland. The "Regional Action Program for Corsica", announced in 1957, pumped 350 million Francs into Corsica between 1957 and 1975, in order to improve the island's economy.

The likelihood of ethnic conflict was increased after France withdrew from Algiers in 1962 and several hundred thousand Algerian French (Blacklegs) settled in Corsica where they acquired a significant percentage of the land. The training area for the French Foreign Legion had been relocated to Corsica and this also led to the accentuation of the French-Corsican disagreements. After 1970, a number of autonomist organizations appeared. Starting in 1973, there were demonstrations in the street, strikes and bombings, and in 1976 the Corsican National Liberation Front was established. It organized and implemented terrorist activities with most of the terror attacks and bank robberies occurring in 1980. Finally, Paris relented and the island was given *territorial autonomy in 1982* with an elected regional assembly and regional council charged with education, environmental protection, agriculture, economic development, cultural affairs and urban development.

Yet, the serious Corsican economic problems (lack of employment opportunities, emigration and purchase of land by foreigners), combined with a lackadaisical implementation of the 1982 decentralization plans, led to the continuation of the tensions and to terrorist activities by the organizations demanding independence.

The first real step forward was made in 1991 *when a law was enacted to grant the Island a limited autonomy.* A Territorial Assembly was elected by a two-stage electoral system and an Executive Council with quasi-governmental powers was established. The latter was responsible for economic and social development, cultural and educational affairs, environmental protection and re-districting. It was also charged with improving agriculture, water supplies, tourism and transportation. Its activities were somewhat limited by the Prefect who was nominally in charge of local institutions and who supervised the legality of all ordinances. It is of great interest to view the debate on the 1991 Corsica Act. The representatives objected particularly to Paragraph 1. that states, "The French Republic guarantees to the Corsican people, who are a component of the French people and that who represent a vivid historical and cultural unit, the right to preserve their cultural identity and exercise their specific economic and social interests". The Constitutional Court rejected this paragraph in 1991, stating that, "...the legislature speaking of the Corsican people as part of the French people acted contrary to the Constitution. The Constitution recognizes only the French people, composed by the totality of the citizens without regard of origin, race or creed."

Evidently, the French conception of the national state is still alive today and is concerned lest the autonomy granted to Corsica be emulated by others and lead to some form of federalism. After all, the example of Corsica could be followed by the Bretons, the Basques, the Normans, the Alsatians, etc...

It was also evident that it was a fear of setting a precedent that led to the rejection of teaching of the Corsican language, which was finally permitted on an elective basis and only after a ruling by a Constitutional Court.[80]

Spain

Population (1995): 39,188,000
Ethnic Groups: Castilian - 73%, Catalan - 18%, Galician - 6%, Basque - 1.5%, Gypsy (?).
Official language: Spanish.

At the Departmental level, the other ethnic languages are official except the gypsy.

Formerly part of the Roman Empire, the Iberian Peninsula was occupied in 711 by the Berbers (Moors) under the leadership of Tarik. Counterattacks, under the reign of Charlemagne, established a border zone around Barcelona where the Christian and Muslim cultures remained in contact. After the death of Charlemagne, several semi-independent dukedoms were created in this area that ultimately became known as Catalonia.

---

[80] Béla Faragó: Van-e korzikai nép? (Is there a Corsican people?) Régió kissebségi szemle, 1992/2, pp. 36-58.

83

About the same time (9th century), the Basques, defending themselves successfully against both the Moors and the Franks, established the Kingdom of Navarre.

Aragon, the third of the Christian Dominions became a kingdom in the 11th century.

Simultaneously, with the birth of the northern Christian kingdoms, the southern part of the peninsula, ruled by the Moors, separated into a number of independent regions. This Muslim Spain was highly urbanized and took an active part in Mediterranean commerce.

The central part of the peninsula was referred to as **Castilia (Castille)** for the first time in the year 800. Its central position made it a buffer zone between Christian and Moor and, other than a short period under Navarre, it was independent from about 1000 A.D.

In the 15th century, Castille took a leadership role among the five Iberian states (Granada, Navarre, Portugal, Castille and Aragon) and when the heiress of Castille, Isabella, married the crown prince of Aragon, Ferdinand in 1469, the Iberian Peninsula slowly became an administrative unit. Granada was occupied in 1492 and Navarre in 1515. Except for a brief period under Philip II, Portugal remained independent.

Aragon, Catalonia and Valencia enjoyed considerable autonomous legislation, economy and military until the middle of the 17th century, but Philip IV, taking advantage of the Thirty Year War abolished the privileges of Catalonia. An uprising of Catalan nobles, in 1640, was supported by French troops and Catalonia was under French control until 1652. The Catalan nobles realized that French control was harsher than the Spanish one and thus, the southern part of the province reverted to Spain in 1659, while the northern part, Rousillion, became officially a part of France.

The Spanish War of Succession (1701-1714) became a civil war when the anti-Bourbon forces gained the support of Portugal, Valencia and Catalonia. When the grandson of Louis XIV, Philippe Anjou, renounced the French throne and became King of Spain, he made the rebellious areas into Castilian provinces. This happened to Valencia (1707), Aragon (1711), Mallorca (1716) and Catalonia (1717) and these provinces were governed by Castilian laws and procedures, abolishing all their earlier autonomies.[81] The use of the Catalan language was banned in all official communications. Navarre and the Basque country were rewarded for their loyalty and could preserve their autonomy for a while.

The Basque nation is divided by the Spanish-French border. The area inhabited today by the Basques is the former Kingdom of Navarre that was independent until the 16th century. The larger portion was conquered by Spain in 1512 and the northern part was attached to France when Henry of Navarre was crowned King of France as Henry IV. The Basque province could preserve its administrative, legislative and tax systems for a long period of time and these efforts were strengthened by the ethnic distinctions. The Basque provinces (Vizcaya, Guipuzcoa and Alava) had a peculiar guardianship role protecting Spain against France and against the sea and this assured them certain privileges. The adult male population of these provinces could not be forcibly enrolled into the military.[82] They paid taxes only to support the local administration and militia. Their development was greatly assisted by their duty-free status, the duty being paid at the Basque-Castilian border and not at the point of entry at the coast. In order to preserve their privileges, they supported Philip V in the Spanish War of Succession. Following the Napoleonic intermezzo and the restoration of 1814, their rights were again guaranteed and this was done again in 1823 when Charles IV ascended the throne.

The centralization of Spain began in the 18th century and continued in the 19th century with the development of a single commercial system for entire country. The Catalan commercial code and the Catalan maritime practice and laws were abolished. The independent status of the Basque Provinces came to an end during the first half of the 19th century.

Toward the end of the 19th century, the progression of the Galician, Basque and Catalan people toward becoming independent nations made great strides. The Galician national trend assumed a cultural aspect. The publication of folk tales, stories and legends, the appearance of Galician newspapers, periodicals and historical works, as well as the establishment of the Galician Library were major signposts along this road.

The development of the Basques and the Catalans as nations rested on the dynamic growth of capital in those areas. The Renaissance Movement, established in the 1830s, financed publications and strongly furthered the trend toward autonomy. In the 1870s, the first Catalan political parties appeared and then the Basque national Party was formed.

The Catalan Parties took full advantage of the elections and in 1906-1907, all the Catalan political organizations merged, resulting in the acquisition of 41 of the 44 Catalan seats in the National Assembly.

The beginning of the 20th century represented a new segment in the evolution of the national movements since through their organized political parties they could wrest representation for themselves in the Cortes in Madrid.

---

[81] Ádám Anderle: Megosztott Hispania. Államfejlődés és nemzeti mozgalmak Spanyolországban (Divided Spain. Evolution of the state and of the nationality movements in Spain). Kossuth, Bp. 1985. p. 72.
[82] Ibid, p. 97.

At the end of World War I, the nationality movements accelerated everywhere and the minorities "presented their bill" to the majority nationality for losses of life suffered during the war. The Russian Lenin in the East and the American President Wilson in the West both proclaimed the principles of self-government and thus contributed to the dissolution of the large multi-nationality empires. In Catalonia, autonomy was demanded in meetings and in violent demonstrations in the streets.

In 1922 an organization known as the Catalan State demanded an independent Catalonian republic.

The Basque National Party was successful at the elections and in 1918 it was able to seat 8 representatives in the Cortes in Madrid.

Between 1920 and 1923, these national movements were joined by movements in Andalusia and Aragon, demanding regional independence and by the labor movement, fighting for liberal and social aspirations. Thus, in opposition to the centralist Spanish government, there were increasing numbers of people who saw the future of Spain in a federal republic.

In 1931, the republican group was joined not only by the radical and left wing parties, but by the parties of the nationalities as well. These latter included the Catalan Left, the Catalan State, the Galician Autonomist Regional Organization and the Basque National Party. The 1931 constitution of the Second Republic divided Spain into regions without making any mention of the three small nationalities. The Popular Front was victorious at the 1936 elections and it re-established the constitution of Catalonia and also created the Basque Autonomous Province, the precursor of today's Basque Country.[83]

This development was stopped at the end of the Spanish Civil War when General Franco became the leader of Spain. He endeavored to create a strong, centralized state by forceful centralization, by doing away with the nationality movements and their institutions (e.g.- Basque University, Basque Academy) and by forbidding the use of the local languages, including the use of Basque during Mass. In practice, this meant the total disappearance of autonomy. As part of the centralization of power, the country was divided into eight regions, the elected regional officials were dismissed and replaced by officials sent from Castille. The Catalan resistance groups regrouped in neighboring France. In 1962, the outlawed Basque National Party reached an agreement with the Spanish Socialist Workers' Party and was promised the re-establishment of Basque autonomy. The radical, young members of the national movement established the ETA, the Basque separatist military organization in 1952 and this organization set as its goal the liberation of the Basque nation. Soon major disagreements erupted between this group and the more conservative leaders of the Basque movement and this disagreement led in 1959 to a split with the ETA becoming fully independent. It started a campaign of terror in 1961, organized and supported from France.

Until 1968, the ETA activities were not directed against individuals but this changed after Franco's National Guard killed one of its members. It was due primarily to the Franco terror that the ETA, at that time, enjoyed considerable popularity not only among the Basque population but among the Catalans as well.

[83] Balázs Gerencsér and Albin Juhász: Működő Autonómiák (Functioning Autonomies) 2 Vol. Bp. 1998. Manuscript, pp. 10, 16-17.

In 1971, the Catalan opposition groups joined forces in the Catalan Assembly and demanded amnesty, the reestablishment of political civil rights and the return of the autonomy.

Popular opinion changed in 1974 when, after the reestablishment of Basque autonomy, many questioned the legitimacy of continued terrorist activity. Until the end of the 1990s, these terrorist activities caused the death of approximately 800 people.

Francisco Franco died in 1975 and the King, Juan Carlos, nominated Suarez Gonzales, the Secretary General of the National Movement for the Prime Ministership. This was the beginning of major changes in Spain.

Autonomy

The Spanish constitution of 1978 re-established the framework for the development of autonomies. The Preamble states:

"The Spanish nation supports every Spaniard and every nationality in Spain in the exercise of their human rights and in the development of their culture, traditions language and institutions."

The second paragraph states:

"The constitution based on the joint and undissolvable unity of their homeland for the entire Spanish nation, recognizes and guarantees the right to self-government to the nationalities and regions constituting the country as well as their mutual solidarity."

The third paragraph states:

"Castilian is the official language of the country … the other languages of Spain are also official in the appropriate autonomous communities, in conformance with the Statutory provisions. The different languages of Spain are a part of our cultural treasures deserving of great interest and great protection."

The fourth paragraph states:

"The statutes may recognize the flags and coats of arms of the autonomous communities."

The 148th paragraph lists the affairs that properly belong to the administration of the autonomous communities. The most important of these are: The organization of the self-governing institutions, territorial arrangements, urban development, housing, agriculture and animal husbandry, regulation of commerce, management of mountains, forests, fresh water fishing, tourism, health care, social services, local water supplies, environmental protection, cultural matters, etc. The fiscal basis for all these is provided by funds received from the national budget, their own revenues and funds transferred from the territorial compensation foundation. There are legislative bodies in each of the autonomous territories and the administration is in the hands of governing council chaired by a president elected by the council but approved by the King. The administration of justice in the autonomous territory is supervised by a high court.

The central government is responsible for international relations, the armed forces, criminal justice, civil rights, social legislation, taxation and customs duties, fiscal matters, health insurance, social security and the national police. The 1979 Statute is the basis of the organization and structure of the autonomous Basque Country. In accordance with the constitution, it regulates the matters administrated jointly and individually and assures the use of both the Basque and Spanish language. In order for the Basque constitution not to conflict with the national constitution, the Statute omits the paragraph referring to the unity and integrity of Spain.

Belgium

Population (1995): 10,110,000
Ethnic groups: Flemish - 57.6%, Walloon - 32.5% and 60,000 Germans.
Official language: Flemish and French.

Belgium was formed from Low Country provinces in the 14th - 15th centuries. During the 15th century, it became one of Europe's richest countries under the rule of the Dukes of Burgundy. After the fall of Charles the Bold in 1477, the land was divided among its neighbors. The largest part, consisting of the 17 Low Country provinces was bestowed on Archduke Maximilian, the son of the German Emperor Frederic III, as the dowry of Maria, daughter of Charles the Bold. The smaller part became part of the French Crown. The Habsburg Empire thus acquired this area by marriage in 1488, while Burgundy was taken into the Empire in 1512, as a separate province. Since 1530, the Governor of the Low Countries was appointed by the Spanish branch of the Habsburgs. Philip II tried to withdraw the earlier autonomy of the region, initiated a merciless persecution of the Protestants and also exploited the area economically with high taxes, etc. During the fight against Spain, the animosity between the mostly Protestant northern provinces and the mostly Catholic southern areas was settled by the Union of Arras. The Catholic provinces also formed a union and eventually reached an agreement with Spain.

This meant the final division of the Low Countries. The northern areas formed the Union of Utrecht. Their independence was guaranteed by the Armistice of 1609 and was finally recognized by Spain in the Peace of Westphalia in 1648, making Holland an independent country. The liberated northern Protestant provinces now had an opportunity for unfettered capitalistic development. The southern Catholic provinces were handed back to the Austrian branch of the Habsburgs at the Peace of Rastatt, at the end of the Spanish War of Succession, in 1714. They were now known as the Austrian Low Countries. In 1795, France occupied all the Low Countries, but at the Congress of Vienna in 1815 reunited it with Holland under the name of the United Kingdom of the Low Countries. Functionally, Belgium was now under Holland's control and the religious, linguistic and cultural differences led to a revolt. Belgium declared its independence in 1830 and this was recognized by the Great Powers. In the 1870s and 1880s, the parliamentary struggles between the Liberals and the Christian Conservatives centered on the separation of church and state, on the replacement of the parochial schools with public schools and on the universal franchise. Around the turn of the 20th century, the Liberals and Labor joined forces to balance the Christian Conservative government Party.

In 1888 Flemish was made the official language to replace French. In 1898 Flemish and French were declared to be official languages of equal standing.

Language
Two large ethnic groups live side by side here and have for many centuries. They are the Dutch-speaking, Protestant and Catholic Flemish in the North and

the French-speaking Catholic Walloons in the South, along the French border. Since 1918 there has been a small German minority as well.

The economic differences between the two areas and the use of French as the official language were responsible for the Flemish struggle for equal rights. As Flanders developed and the Flemish-Walloon economic and political ties changed, a Walloon counter-movement started to develop. The first step in favour of the Flemish was the publication of all statutes in both languages, under the Equality Act of 1898. Equal rights in the legislature and franchise were obtained by the 1893 and 1921 amendments of the constitution. The linguistic-cultural and economic differences were aggravated by the political ones. Some of the Flemish sided with Germany in both World Wars and this led to a deterioration of the Flemish-Walloon relationship.

In the 1960s, the difficulties between the more advanced Walloon area and the economically struggling Flemish area were again accentuated by the unemployment in Flanders. It was declared at this time that no community was allowed to weaken the other. Resolution of the conflict was initiated by the constitutional revision of 1962 that divided Belgium into four linguistic regions, the Dutch, French, and German regions and the city of Brussels, which was bilingual. In this way, it was possible to draw boundary lines between Flanders and the Walloon area and between the latter and the German minority that inhabits 3% of Belgium's territory and represents 1% of the population. The boundaries of the communities and provinces were also adjusted. The implementation of the 1962 Language Law is supervised by a linguistic supervisory commission, but the conflict has so far not been satisfactorily resolved.

Autonomy

Starting in the 1970s, the linguistic areas were given autonomy to organize their cultural life. This process was completed in 1988 when they were given autonomy in all educational matters. About the same time, territorial autonomy was also established in Belgium. The Departments were given almost complete freedom in all administrative areas including foreign trade.

The central government retained only foreign policy, monetary policy, national defense and law enforcement matters. The 1993 constitutional amendment created the Belgian Federated Kingdom that consists of four autonomous regions. The Federal government and parliament, sitting in Brussels, makes decisions in and administrates foreign policy, defense, fiscal and law enforcement matters. The three regional legislative bodies, Walloon, Flemish and German, control all other matters in their jurisdictions.

Each region may even undertake international treaties, but these become law only if none of the other minorities veto them. The fiscal needs for the operation of the region are derived from local taxation (since 1980) and from the region's share of the national taxes (since 1988) and national subsidies.

Personal autonomy is granted to individual citizens living in a linguistic area not their own, but who wish to vote for a representative to the national parliament, representing the citizens' own linguistic area.

Switzerland

Population (1994): 7,019,000
Ethnic groups: Swiss German - 73.5%, French - 20% and Italian - 4.5%, Rhaeto-Roman
Official languages: German, French, Italian and Rhaeto-Roman

It is the country of linguistic communities, German, French, Italian and Rhaeto-Roman. The Swiss national consciousness of the ethnic and linguistic groups developed during their common history and defensive battles. They cannot be considered minorities.

During the great migration of peoples, the Germanic Burgundians settled the eastern part of the area and the Alemans settled the West. In the 12th century, the area was ruled by Princes of the House of Zahringen. They established the cities of Freiburg and Bern. After this family died out, the Habsburg Counts acquired large tracts of land along the middle-Rhine, Aar and Reuss rivers. The Princes of Savoy were moving in the direction of the northern shore of Lake Geneva and the course of the upper Rhone. The bishops of Basel, Geneva and Lausanne and the Abbot of Sankt Gallen controlled large tracts of land. Independent of them, free peasants lived along the shores of the Vierwaldstaetter Lake in village communities, under the protection of the German emperor. Since the Hohenstauffen emperors considered the security of the road to Italy across the St. Gotthard Pass vitally important to their interests, they were willing to grant freedom from villeiny to the armed peasantry in exchange for military service. When the Habsburgs were no longer willing to recognize the special privileges of the peasant communities in 1291, the three original cantons, Uri, Schwytz and Unterwalden formed a perpetual union and went to war. The war lasted from 1291 until 1386. In 1315, the Swiss defeated the imperial forces at Morgarten and this was followed by the cities of Luzerne, Zurich, Bern, Zug and Glarus joining the Union. This then was the foundation of the federation of the eight cantons (*Eidgenossenschaft*).

At the time of the Burgundian War in 1476-1477, the Federation repelled the attack by Charles the Bold, Prince of Burgundy. In 1499, the Federation separated from Austria, but its independence was formally acknowledged only after the Peace of Westphalia in 1648. In the beginning of the 16th century, the number of cantons grew to 13. The Reformation caused dislocations and religious wars in Switzerland, as well. The Reformation of the German territories originated in Zurich with Huldrych Zwingli, while the French territories were converted by John Calvin from Geneva. The original three cantons, as well as Zug, Luzern and Freiburg retained their Catholic religion.

In the 17th - 18th centuries, an aristocratic form of government developed in the larger towns and the occupied territories were oppressed and exploited by the ruling cantons. The dissatisfaction led to peasant uprisings. At the time of the French Revolution, the aristocratic governments were replaced by republican ones. Finally, in 1798, the French did away with the cantonal system, established a central government under the name of Helvetian Republic and annexed Geneva, Jura and Mulhausen to France. This led to an insurrection and to civil war until 1803, when Napoleon re-established the cantonal system, adding 6 more cantons to the federation. The Congress of Vienna, in 1815, added Neuenburg, Geneva and Wallis to Switzerland raising the total number of cantons in the Federation to 22. In the first half of the 19th century, political and religious differences again led to a civil war. Matters were resolved by the new constitution, enacted in 1848, according to which defense, foreign policy, customs and postal matters and coinage were the responsibility of the joint legislature of the Federation (*Bundesversammlung*). This body consisted of two chambers, the House of Representatives (*Nationalrat*) and another Chamber, representing the interest of the federated cantons (*Standerat*). The members of the standing Federal government are elected for seven years and the head of the government is simultaneously the Head of State.

Autonomy

In the constitution, first enacted in 1848 and amended in 1874, the Federal State granted large-scale autonomy to the cantons. In addition to the responsibilities mentioned above, the Federal government is responsible for the enactment of tax, commerce and bankruptcy legislation. A Federal judiciary has also been established. The self-government of the cantons, having their own constitution, is in the hands of their own legislative and executive bodies. Education, the Church, direction of the police and health services are cantonal responsibilities. Thus, minority problems surface at the local level in cantons with a mixed population and not at the federal level.

In 1815, the Congress of Vienna attached the Catholic and French-speaking Basel bishopric, later known as the canton of Jura, to Switzerland to compensate it for small areas of land lost along the borders. The City of Basel itself is German-speaking.

The Canton of Bern is German-speaking and legislation enacted by its parliament has frequently been found to be offensive to the interests and rights of the French minority.

The ratio between the two ethnic groups continued to shift toward the German side by virtue of the large-scale immigration of Germans who were granted very favorable loans and other advantages. The French population began to fight for the creation of an independent Canton Jura with a French majority. This was accomplished in 1978 and since 1979 there are 23 cantons in Switzerland.

There are tensions in Canton Fribourg, as well, where the French majority enacts discriminatory legislation against the German minority. The Germans are offended by the disproportionally small number of German representatives in the cantonal administration and in the inequality of language in naming communities and streets.

In Canton Graubünden, the Rhaeto-Romans complain about economic, educational and cultural discrimination, complicated by the fact that they have no literary language. Many cantons have one official language but there are cantons with two or three official languages. Instruction is everywhere delivered in the mother tongue of the students and at the University instruction is given in four languages.

Italy

Population (1994): 57,300,000
Ethnic groups: Italian - 95%, also Sardinian, Rhaeto-Roman (Ladin), South Tyrolean German, Slovenian, Albanian, Greek and Provençal.

Approximately 2.5 million non-Italians live in Italy. They include Sardinians,

Rhaeto-Romans (Ladins and Friulians), Germans, French, Albanians, Slovenians, Serbs, Croatians, Provençals and Catalans. Among the largest minority groups are the Germans in South Tyrol. They number more than ¼ million and live in a limited area.

SOUTH TYROL

Ethnic groups (1991): German - 288,000, Italian - 117,000, Rhaeto-Roman - 18,000.

The peace treaty of St. Germain, drawing the boundaries in Central Europe after World War I, attached the southern part of the Tyrol to Italy in 1919. This was the deal Italy made with the Allies in 1915 as the price of her entering World War I on their side. Italy, thus, received a territory of 74,000 km² and a population of 250,000, only 2.9% of whom listed themselves as Italians in 1910. This division destroyed the territorial integrity of Tyrol that, over the centuries, constituted a single economic, political and ethnic unit. The Tyroleans were refused even minimal autonomy by an Italy moving in the direction of Fascism.

After 1922, serious attempts were made to do away with the ethnic minorities. There was a strong campaign to promote Italianization, Germans were urged to move South and Italians to move North in order to loosen the German block and the use German was forbidden in the schools. The German-speaking teachers were transferred to Italian regions and they were replaced with Italian-speaking teachers. It was only in the so-called Catacomb-Schools that instruction continued in German. The same procedures were used against administrative and other officials. In 1925, Italian was declared to be the only official language and the names of all communities had to be listed and displayed in Italian only. The use of the term "Tyrol" was banned.

In 1939 the German and Italian governments reached an agreement under which the people in South Tyrol could choose either of two citizenships. Those who chose German citizenship had to leave their homeland. During the next few years 75,000 South Tyroleans were relocated, mostly to Eastern European German-speaking areas. Completion of this trend was hindered by the later stages of World War II.

At the end of the War, the Tyroleans requested a plebiscite, hoping to have the South Tyrol re-attached to Austria as its result. The Allies rejected the Austrian request for such a plebiscite and the peace treaty, signed on February 10, 1947 awarded the South Tyrol to Italy.

About the same time, the Austrian Foreign Secretary, Karl Gruber, and the Italian Prime Minister, Alcide de Gasperi, signed an agreement in Paris, the Gruber-de Gasperi Pact. According to this agreement, German was reintroduced into the schools, the town and village names could be displayed in both languages and the population could use the German form of their given and family names. Italy recognized the right of the South Tyroleans to autonomous legislative and executive activities within the given region. The matter of the "optants" was reviewed and two-thirds of those who chose to emigrate during the Hitler-Mussolini era were granted Italian citizenship and were allowed to return to the South Tyrol.

Yielding to both internal and external pressure, Italy approved the first directives for a South Tyrolean autonomous structure in 1948. Yet, contrary to the

Paris agreement, the German Bolzano (Bozen) region did not receive an independent administration but was attached to the predominantly Italian Trentino region. The Trentino-South Tyrol region was then given a parliament and self-administration covering the entire region having a two third Italian majority.

At the end of the 1940s, Rome supported a northward migration and with government help a 5,000-unit development was started in Bolzano by the local administration. The intent was quite obvious to the local German residents. It was the intent to have the ratio of the German population shifted in favor of the Italians in the very center of German culture in the South Tyrol. By the end of the 1950s, the tensions resulted in large demonstrations, bombings and other terrorist activities.

In 1956, Austria submitted a memorandum to Italy and made recommendations for the resolution of the problems. Since the discussions proved fruitless, *Austria submitted the matter of the South Tyrol to the 15th General Assembly of the United Nations. The UN General Assembly's resolutions urged Italy*, in both 1960 and 1961, to settle this conflict directly with Austria. In the mean time, the absence of progress had further embittered the Tyrolean extremists and the bombing attacks were resumed. During the night of June 11, 1961, 37 bombs were exploded in different locations. The situation was clearly untenable and Rome was forced to return to the bargaining table. In 1971, an amendment of the Italian constitution enacted the basic legal requirements regulating the autonomy of the region that took effect on January 20, 1972. According to these, the region would be headed by a Regional Council, a Regional Government and a President.

Thirty-five deputies would be elected to both the Bolzano and Trentino parliaments and thus the joint Trentino-South Tyrol parliament would have 70 members. The sessions would be chaired by an Italian during one half of the session and by a German during the other half. Administrative, budgetary, economic and cultural matters would be managed autonomously by the separate regional parliaments and governments sitting in Bolzano and in Trentino.

The publication of newspapers and magazines was started for the German minority in Italy, the local radio stations were broadcasting in German and the Italian Television network introduced a program in German.

In the academic year 1994-1995, there were 127 German, 64 Italian and 13 Rhaeto-Roman (Ladin) elementary and middle schools. Educational autonomy meant not only an independent network of schools but allowed for different curricula, in accordance with differing cultural and historical traditions.

German-speaking South Tyroleans were allowed to complete their education abroad and thus, in the mid-1990s, about 3,500 of them studied at the University of Innsbruck in Austria. The establishment of a University in the South Tyrol is being planned. Of the 116 communities in Bolzano Province, the Italians have a majority in five and the Ladins (Rhaeto-Romans) in eight. In recent years, the increasing numbers of the German minority clearly justified the autonomy. In accordance with the legal requirements, the ethnic ratios, established by the latest census, must be taken into consideration in governmental services and in employment in government offices. Since 1996, the Province may fly its own flag.

The smallest nationality group is the Ladin. They are considered to be the descendants of the Rhaeto-Roman tribes Italianized by the Romans. The oldest inscription indicating their presence in the region dates to 1,400 BC. Together with the Rhaeto-Romans living in Canton Graubünden and Canton Friuli in Switzerland and the Rhaeto-Romans (Friuli) living in another autonomous Italian province (Friuli-Venezia Giulia), they constitute the Rhaeto-Roman linguistic community. They never developed a higher social group that could have maintained and protected their language and traditions and thus many of them assimilated into the surrounding German language and culture.

The Ladins live in the regions of Trentino-South Tyrol and Val d'Aosta, in the Provinces of Bolzano, Belluno and Trieste. Their total number is between 30 and 40 thousand. The only sizable block lives in the South Tyrol, in five valleys in the Dolomite Mountains. For a long time, they were considered to be Italians and that their language was just an Italian dialect. In the 1920s-1930s, the Ladins were declared to be a foreign ethnic group and were forced to accept German citizenship that led to the re-settlement of about 2,000. After the Second World War, they demanded recognition by petitions and demonstrations.

In the 1950s, their presence in the Province of Bolzano was finally and officially recognized and some of the nationality laws were extended to them. They could display the names of the communities in Ladin and they could teach Ladin in school but many of the other privileges granted to the Germans were withheld from them. The 1972 amendment of the autonomy regulations markedly improved their situation. In 1977, in one of the centers of Ladins in the Laderthal (St. Martin in Thurn), a cultural institute was established for the preservation of Ladin language and culture. They have newspapers in their mother tongue and there are brief, daily radio and television broadcasts in Ladin. *The Ladins have no motherland to turn to for support* and their numbers are too small for an effective fight for their rights. According to a 1983 Regional Act, two representatives at the Regional Council are charged with the protection of their interests, in the South Tyrol Provincial Assembly.

The *French-speaking Valle d'Aosta Province*, similar to the Swiss cantons, enjoyed autonomy until the 18th century when it became subject to the Principality of Savoy. In 1960, it became part of the united Italy. The Italian government slowly abolished the use of French in schools, forbade the use of French in the legal system and in administration. After World War II, the province was given autonomy and this was made a part of the 1948 constitution. In practice, however, the autonomy was never fully implemented. Claiming financial difficulties, the Italian government in Rome, in 1965, vetoed the erection of the television relay stations necessary to broadcast Swiss and French programs in the area. At the same time, the Aosta regional Council was given the authority to establish 64 primary and secondary schools where instruction was provided in French. A number of cultural activities were also resurrected.

The situation of *the Slovenes, Serbs and Croats* were regularized by agreements between Italy and Yugoslavia, signed in 1954 and 1975, which assure the rights of the nationalities in the Trieste area. These rights have not been extended to the Slovenes in the area of Udine.

The *Albanians* living in Calabria have been considered a minority since 1860. They came, or were brought, to the south of Italy in the 15th century and later they played an important role in the renaissance of the Albanian nation. Even though their rights are somewhat curtailed, their standards of living are much higher than those in their mother country.

Sweden

Population (1994): 8,800,000
Ethnic groups: Swedish - 91%, Lapp - 4%, Finn - 4%.
Official language: Swedish.

Throughout history, a number of national groups settled in Sweden: Germans, Finns, Dutch, Scots and Walloons, but, with the exception of the Finns, they all rapidly became assimilated. The original inhabitants of the area were the Lapps. The later conquerors first colonized them and later tried by all means to assimilate them.

Today, the approximately 50-100,000 Lapps live in an area about 1,500 km. long and 3-400 km. wide, in the Kola Peninsula and in the northern regions of Sweden, Norway and Finland.

The Shamanist Lapp society was based on the symbiosis of large family groups. Some of them, the fishermen, lived in permanent settlements but the majority, engaged in hunting and reindeer breeding, led a nomadic existence. As soon as the Lapps began to trade with the neighboring people, these became aware of the natural riches of the area. The Lapp legends speak of thieves and robbers who came to steal their goods. The 17th - 18th century wars between the Scandinavian nations were partly over the ownership of the northern territories.

The Lapps were first subjected to taxation and then missionaries were sent to convert them. Since, however, Lapp culture differed widely from Christian culture these attempts were not successful. The missionaries were followed by settlers. The Swedish government encouraged the northward movement of the free peasants and those who settled on Lapp lands were exempt from taxation and military service. Colonization began.

Forceful intervention and major changes came at the end of the 19th century when increased industrialization made the natural wealth of Lapland, minerals, hydroelectric power and lumber, increasingly important.

Swedish minority policies were similar throughout the centuries to the Norwegian assimilation policies. Beginning in the 17th century, schools were set up for the Lapps, but, partly because of the nomadic lifestyle of the Lapps and partly because the language of instruction in these schools was Swedish, the experiment failed. In the first decades of the 20th century, mobile schools were set up for the purpose of assimilating the communities by giving them "small sips of civilization". These attempts were stopped in the 1950s and 1960.

An Act of 1971 codified the centuries-old Lapp systems of reindeer breeding, as practiced in the Lapp villages. This law limited the practices to these villages and thereby significantly increased their economic status. The strongest Lapp communities can today be found in these areas. Unfortunately, the regulations do not extend to the fishing villages and to the Lapps engaged in other occupations. The demand of the Lapps to preserve their language and culture raised little interest abroad until the 1960s and 1970s. At this time, a number of Lapp groups asked the Swedish government for permission to preserve their language and culture. Lapp-speaking schools were set up and the Lapp language was taught in other schools as well. While the Lapps may not have been satisfied with the conditions, they did make substantial progress. In 1974, at the University of Umea, a chair was established for Lapp language and culture and Lapp is taught at the Uppsala University as well. A commission established by the Swedish government recommended that a Lapp Representation be set up and function as a governmental agency for the protection of Lapp economic and cultural interests. This was done in 1989.

During the past ten years no progress has been made. The petitions concerning the extension of the protective laws governing reindeer breeding, to fishing and hunting - reiterated repeatedly - have to date been unsuccessful.

Norway

Population (1995): 4,348,000
Ethnic groups: Norwegian - 97%, Lapp and Finn.
Official language: Norwegian.

The Norwegian parliament enacted a law in 1851 establishing the Lapp Fund for the teaching of Norwegian to the Lapps. This was the first step in the Norwegianization process lasting a hundred years. During the first 30 years, the Church stood at the helm of the Norwegianization process and in the regions where a majority of the students understood Norwegian, this immediately became the language of instruction. Where the majority did not speak Norwegian, the language of instruction remained Lapp or Finnish. After 1880, the assimilation policies entered their firmest period. A new system of instruction was introduced, the bilingual textbooks were withdrawn, instruction in Finnish or Lapp was discontinued and it was even forbidden that the students converse with each other in their native tongue during break periods in school. The practice of favoring teachers who took a teaching position in the Finnmark and who could instruct successfully in the official language became universal. These teachers received a higher salary and an allowance for moving expenses. The situation was made even worse by the Education Ordinance of 1898 that remained in effect until 1959 and was designed clearly to accomplish the assimilation of the Lapps. *All this was accompanied by large-scale settlements with which the government endeavored to change the ethnic ratios.* Significant Norwegian blocks were established, primarily in the border regions. Between 1870 and 1930, 50 - 60,000 Norwegians settled in the two northern counties. The purpose of the settlements was stated by Benjamin Vogt, the Norwegian Minister of Commerce at the border negotiations between Norway and Sweden, "We wished to have a patriotic population and we knew that Norwegian agriculturists who, by virtue of their occupation, were tied to the soil and who are Norwegian patriots, would represent the strongest defense against the Eastern (i.e. Russian) threat."[84]

Naturally, the settlement was accompanied by a rapid spread of Norwegian culture. New schools, boarding schools and churches represented the new trend. The Norwegian presence was strengthened by the 1902 Land Act, which was not repealed until 1960, and according to which land could be purchased in Norway only by a one who spoke and wrote Norwegian and who had a Norwegian name. This discriminatory legislation deprived thousands of Lapps of the right to own land.

---

[84] Béla Jávorszky: Észak-Europa kisebbségei (The Minorities of Northern Europe). Magvető, Bp. 1991. p. 38.

Cultural autonomy

Taking advantage of the apparent changes, a number of national Lapp and All-Lapp organizations emerged after 1970. One of the first was the Scandinavian Lapp Council, in 1979, that is today the highest Lapp forum in Norway and is subject only to the Scandinavian Lapp Conference. Since 1953, the Lapps hold a national convention every 2-3 years.

Similarly to Sweden, Lapp is now taught at the Universities of Oslo and Tromso in Norway and Helsinki and Oulu in Finland. In 1989, Norway started to train Lapp teachers, and students were accepted from Sweden and Finland as well. The Lapp Institute, located in Norway, serves as a research establishment for educational methodology and also serves as a center for international Lapp cooperation. Today, even in Norwegian and Finn areas, instruction is provided in Lapp if there is a high enough concentration of Lapp inhabitants.

Finland

Population (1994): 5,098,754
Ethnic groups: Finnish - 93.6%, Swedish - 6% and 5,700 Lapps.
Official languages: Finnish and Swedish.

In order to understand the history of the Swedish minority's role in Finland, a review of Finnish history is required. In the area of present Finland, there has been a Swedish-speaking population ever since the 12th - 14th centuries when crusades were conducted in this area to convert the Finns from Paganism. During the Swedish rule, Finland had no autonomy. As a consequence of the 1808-1809 Swedish-Russian

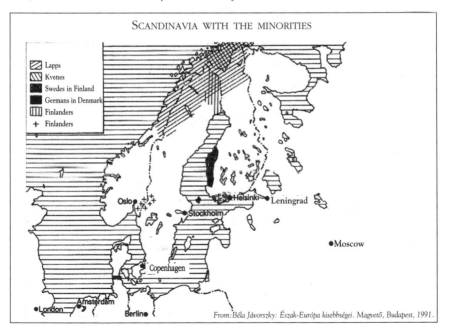

SCANDINAVIA WITH THE MINORITIES

Lapps
Kvenes
Swedes in Finland
Germans in Denmark
Finlanders
+ Finlanders

From:Béla Jávorszky: Észak-Európa kisebbségei. Magvető, Budapest, 1991.

97

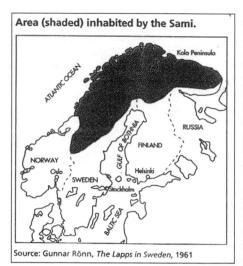

Area (shaded) inhabited by the Sami.

Kola Peninsula

ATLANTIC OCEAN

RUSSIA

GULF OF BOTHNIA

FINLAND

NORWAY

Oslo   Helsinki

SWEDEN

Stockholm

BALTIC SEA

Source: Gunnar Rönn, *The Lapps in Sweden*, 1961

war, Finland became a part of the Russian Empire. Alexander I treated Finland generously. As an autonomous Grand Duchy, it could preserve its separate parliament, its civil and criminal code dating back to the Swedish rule, its Swedish-type administration and the Swedish language. The situation is described well by the patriot and academician, A.I. Arvidsson, who stated in 1809 that, "We can no longer be Swedes, we cannot become Russians, we must become Finns".[85] The Finns became a nation and the Turku Academy and the University of Helsinki became bastions of Finnish linguistic and cultural development. When Nicholas I marched into Hungary in 1849, the Finns, sympathizing with Hungary, translated and published the story of William Tell, upon which the Tsar prohibited all publications in Finnish, except agricultural and religious texts.

The special position that Finland enjoyed in the Russian Empire made it easy for her to become independent in 1917, but independence was followed by a bloody civil war.

Autonomy

In the 1919 constitution of the independent Finland, the Swedes were not considered a minority. The constitution concludes that the national languages of Finland were Finnish and Swedish and that every citizen has the right to execute his own affairs in his own language. It was in this spirit that the 1922 Language Act was drafted. The Finnish settlements were categorized on a linguistic basis and *a settlement had to be bilingual if the non-Finnish-speaking segment represented at least 8% of the population or numbered more than 8,000. The county had to be bilingual if one of its communities was bilingual.* The linguistic ratio in the settlement was reviewed every ten years when the citizens had to indicate their language on the national census form. The Swedish-speakers could demand that they be drafted into a Swedish military outfit. The language used for training was Swedish in these outfits, but all commands were given in Finnish. In the Finnish Lutheran Church, the Swedish congregations were under a Swedish-speaking bishop. Even within the Church the linguistic ordinances pertained and *the congregation was considered bilingual if at least 50 members spoke the "minority" language.*

Since in Finland both the constitution and the educational statutes guarantee that learning may be done in both official languages, there is a completely parallel and equal Swedish system. The local government must operate a Swedish-language school if there are at least 13 children who demand it.

The currently Finnish, but Swedish-speaking Aland Islands were Swedish until the 1808-1809 war when, together with Finland, they came under Russian rule. In 1921, a ruling by the League of Nations assigned the islands to Finland, subse-

---

[85] Jávorszky: op.cit. p. 39.

quent to the signing of a Finn-Swedish agreement that the language and culture of the Islands would be preserved. Statutes about the control of the islands, first issued in 1951 and amended in 1970 and 1991, gave the islands territorial autonomy. The islands constitute a Department having 24,000 inhabitants. It is governed by a 30 member Departmental Parliament that appoints the Departmental government. Industrialization, public information, postal services, administration, police, social matters, environmental protection, public transportation, education and culture all fall under its jurisdiction. The independent budget is assured by local taxation, by central government subsidies, loans and grants (0.5% of the entire Finnish budget is devoted to the islands).

There are 5,700 Lapps (called by themselves "Sami" people) in Finland who are primarily involved in reindeer breeding, fishing and forestry. The Language Law guarantees official status to the Lapp language in their settlements. It is only in Finland that the Sami nation has been officially recognized and accepted. The implementation of the 1991 Lapp Language Act is complicated by the fact that there is no uniform Lapp language, that there are many dialects and that a significant percentage of the Lapps are illiterate. The Finnish government makes sure that there is instruction in the Lapp language and the two Universities guarantee admission for Lapp-speaking applicants. The Lapps are represented in a 20 member Lapp Parliament that is elected every four years and that must be heard by the Finnish Parliament in all matters pertaining to the Lapps.

The situation of the Finns in Sweden is a very sore point. There are no Finnish schools, universities or state-supported communications media even though there are as many Finns in Sweden as there are Swedes in Finland.

Finns have been living in Sweden since the early Middle Ages. It was the availability of employment that, from time to time, started a migration, or it was to escape from war. In the 1970s, a wave of repatriation began. Since the support of minorities in Sweden has practically vanished, the Finnish families are threatened by total assimilation and by the loss of their Finnish roots.

Russia

Population (1996): 148,100,000
Ethnic groups: Russian - 82.6%, Tartar - 3.6%, Ukrainian - 2.7%, Tsuvas - 1.2%
Dagestani - 1%, Mari, Baskir, Polish, German, Udmurt, Buryat, Osset and Yakut, etc.
Official language: Russian.
The 18th - 19th centuries
Russia's minority policies were quite different toward Poland or toward Finland, than when the Empire was moving toward the East and was "colonizing". Poland and Finland were formerly independent and Russia had to decide about the best way to make them a functional part of the Empire. Forceful assimilation was not an option since illiteracy was significantly higher in Russia than in the two countries that derived their culture and education from Western Christian civilization and had traded their independence for Russian suzerainty.

In Russia, education of the average person took place in the parochial village schools ever since the time of Peter I. By the 19th century, this type of education was no longer sufficient.

The priests, who did the teaching, had many other priestly functions and were frequently without adequate pedagogical training or sufficient education. Even the ecclesiastic papers spoke of the negligent and routine educational system. It is not surprising, therefore, that ever increasing numbers of students studied in the schools maintained by the village communities just as they did generally in the Europe. In the 1900s, the state made an attempt to improve the level of education in the parochial schools under its sway, mainly by increasing the subsidy granted to the Orthodox Church, but this endeavor was not successful. In 1897, in the Romanov Empire, the literacy rate of the various nationalities was as follows: German 60%, Latvians 52%, Jews 49%, Poles 35%, Russians 30% and the Asiatic populations 0.2%.

JEWS

Learning from the difficulties the Habsburgs had in trying to accommodate their nationalities, the Tsars tried to use forced Russification to try to preserve the integrity of their empire.

One of the targets of this Russification program were the Jews. Even though Catherine the Great and Alexander I can not be considered anti-Semites, they still considered it prudent to settle the Jews along the western borders of the empire. Because of their distinctive religious symbols, appearance and language, the Jews were frequently the targets of Russian nationalism. Their participation in the terrorist group, *Narodnaja Volja* (The Wish of the People), and its successful murderous attempt against Tsar Alexander II, triggered local pogroms against the Jewish communities in 1881. The Tsarist government enacted discriminatory legislation against the Jews in May 1882. The statement, "One third of the Jews will convert, one third will emigrate and one third will starve to death" was attributed to Pobyedonostzev, the Procurator of the Holy Synod. In fact, only about three of every 10,000 converted to the Orthodox Creed and about 22% emigrated. The Congress of Berlin gave all of Bessarabia to Russia in 1878 and all foreign Jews were expelled from there in 1880. During the winter of 1891, 30,000 Jews were expelled from Moscow alone. The area along the border assigned to them became overpopulated and their numbers were decimated by epidemics and hunger. Consequently, very large numbers of them sought a better life and an opportunity for advancement in Austria or Hungary and, even further, in Germany, England and the United States.

BALTIC NATIONS

The principle of "divide and conquer" proved to be particularly applicable to this area. During the mid-19th century, the Tsarist government supported the Estonians and Latvians against the economically and politically dominant Germans. Starting in 1890, however, they supported the local German minorities to balance the increasing strength of the Estonians and Latvians.

The same happened in Lithuania where the government first supported the Lithuanian endeavors against the Poles. Starting in the 1890s, Russia supported the more pliable Poles against the Lithuanians. Actually, at this time, the Baltic nations were not striving for independence but only for administrative autonomy within the Empire.

An attack was launched against the guardian of their national identity, the Church, as well. During the 1820s and 1830s, the leaders of the Unitus (Greek Catholic) Church were urged to convert to the Greek Orthodox religion. Consequently, the members of Unitus in the West-Ukraine converted to the Greek Orthodox religion in 1839. For the unsophisticated people, there could be no doubt about the advantages of belonging to the Orthodox Church and of learning the Russian language, if they wanted to better themselves. Tsar Nicholas I empowered the Orthodox Church to convert 100,000 Lithuanians, Estonians and Latvians Lutherans back to the Orthodox Church. In this endeavor, the Tsar could reasonably count on the animosity of the peasants against their German landlords, who made their life miserable with crushing taxation. The policies of Nicholas I were followed by the advocates of forceful Russification at the end of the 19th century.

BYELORUSSIANS AND UKRAINIANS

Because of the interest in Russification, an electoral census was introduced in 1897 and when it was found that the Russian population numbered only 44.3% of the total, an increased program of Russification began.

The Russian government believed that Russification of the Byelorussians (4.7%) and of the Ukrainians (17.8%), living within the borders of the Empire, offered the best chance of increasing the percentage of the "Russian" population. After 1839, the Byelorussian language, viewed as a Polish dialect, was forbidden and the guardian of the Byelorussian national consciousness, the Greek Catholic Church, was forced to return to the Greek Orthodox religion. Use of the Ukrainian language in the administration was also forbidden and this retarded the development of this language into a literary one. During the process of becoming a nation, the Ukrainians participated in the more developed Polish political and cultural movements. Ukrainians even took part in the 1830 Polish revolutionary organizations. Their paths branched off only after 1848.

SMALLER NATIONALITIES

The Eastern expansion gained strength during the 18th century. Its purpose was primarily economic. The conquering Russians took advantage of the animosities of the nomadic tribes fighting for grazing land and, after the 1730s, increasingly assumed an overlordship over the nomadic Central Asiatic Turkic and Iranian (Muslim) tribes living on the steppes beyond the Urals. The fate of the small nationalities depended, to a large extent, on the strategic importance of the land they inhabited. In the occupied areas, fortresses were erected and territorial organization began. Russian troops advanced to the eastern littoral of the Caspian Sea in 1869 and, by 1874, the Trans-Caspian military district was organized. In 1885, a Russian-British conflict was about to break out when, in 1887, the two Great Powers reached an agreement about the division of the Turkmen steppes and drew the boundary lines for Afghanistan, Persia and Russia in the debated territory. This agreement was expanded in 1895 to include the boundary line drawn in the Pamir, between the two colonizing Great Powers.

The fate of the nomadic and semi-nomadic, small, Shamanic tribes was assimilation because they lacked the intellectual upper classes which might have been able to preserve their national consciousness. The conquering Tsarist troops were followed by Pravoslav missionaries and, whenever they could, the tribes migrated into the depth of the impenetrable forests or along the banks of unnamed rivers. This is what the Voguls did. Even so, they were unable to meet the taxes to be paid in immensely valuable furs and many tribes lost their land when mineral deposits or oil were found on them. In the border areas, particularly where the Christian and Muslim cultures met, the colonizing endeavors were considerably more restrained than in the interior of the country where whole populations were transplanted without any hesitation and where Russian administration, language and culture ruled over the occupied areas. The strongly individualistic Muslims were in a different situation. The Edict of Toleration, issued by Catherine the Great, in reality pertained only to the Muslims.

It is of interest to study the Crimean Tartars from among the Muslim nations because the assimilative endeavors practiced on them were more or less typical of those practiced on other nationalities in that general area.

CRIMEAN TARTARS

The occupation of the Crimean Peninsula was inevitable in Russia's drive toward a warm sea. Hungary's liberation from under the Turkish yoke at the Peace of Karlóca, in 1699, and the occupation of Azov by Russia signified the decline of the Turkish Empire. At the end of the 17th century, this affected the Crimean Tartar Khanate and led to its gradual decline.

At the same time, the Russian expansion moved South and conquered parts of the Ukraine and Kiev from the Poles. It was only after this that the path for further southward expansion was open. Peter the Great was unable to proceed in this direction but Catherine II was successful. Listening to the advice of her councilors, she ordered the occupation of the Crimea in 1776. In this case, Russia again used the technique, used successfully by other colonizing nations, namely interfering in local disputes.

In 1776-1778, Russian intervention brought St. Petersburg's protégé, Sahin Giray, to power. In order to save the Khanate, he initiated inevitable reforms, but in doing so, he used the much more advanced Russian system as a model and demolished a number of traditional establishments. This made him many enemies. On Catherine's request, he settled refugees from Turkish rule, including Albanians. Opponents to this policy rebelled and this opened the doors to overt intervention. In 1778, the Russian army, assisted by local Albanian troops, occupied the town of the rebels. Turkey was not in a position to assist her Muslim brethren. The Russian-Turkish agreement of 1779 acknowledged that the Crimea belonged to the Russian sphere of interest. When another rebellion erupted in 1781, the Russian army under Archduke Potemkin had no difficulty in dealing with it. The Tartars were forced to agree that the Crimea was a part of the Russian Empire and thus, by 1783, the incorporation of the Crimea was an accomplished fact.

There actually were two phases in this process. The first phase, which coincided with Potemkin's governorship, had as its goal to gain the support of the local leadership, the Muslim clergy, in exchange for a certain degree of autonomy. The second phase was the period of ruthless imposition of Russian rule.

Potemkin, who was the Governor of the southern areas, urged the military authorities to treat the Tartars as friends. The administrator appointed to take charge of local affairs, Igelstrom, was responsible to Potemkin, and tried hard to maintain the illusion that the situation had changed very little since before 1783. He endeavored to adapt the structure of the old Khanate to the new administration and he made a particular effort to gain the support of the local Muslim Church leaders who, by virtue of their religious and cultural ties, were Turkophiles and anti-Russian. These men had a great influence with the devout Muslims since they were in charge of the local educational and administrative matters. The clerics were put on the government payroll in 1783 and their lands were guaranteed by the Russian state. They could also maintain their tax-exempt status.

In 1785, Ingelstrom was transferred to the Volga area and the forceful Russification of the Crimea, phase two, began. It caused serious dissatisfaction among the lower income nobility, increased their affection for Turkey and ultimately led to anti-Russian revolts. Many of them emigrated to Turkey.

The Russian administrators gave the land of the emigrants to Russian settlers or to local nobles who were willing to cooperate with the Russians. The higher nobility of the former Khanate Court became impoverished. The towns formerly engaged in commerce regressed since the Russians established new key trading centers, such as Sebastopol, Cherson and Odessa. The earlier merchant towns decayed and the merchants moved to other cities, such as Simferopol. Commerce was largely taken over by Slavs, Greeks and Armenians. The impoverishment of the urban population meant that the segment of society that played the dominant role in preserving the national consciousness and culture was becoming much weaker. In Simferopol, for instance, the representatives of the former Tartar urban population were excluded from the city administration. Yet, the Russian landowner class did not have the complete control over their villeins, as they had in Russia, because Catherine protected the free Tartar peasantry from subjugation. She did this because she needed the Tartar peasants to fight in her armies. In fact, Potemkin established a Tartar division in 1784. After the 1853-1856 Crimean War, the landowners tried to use a very high rate of taxation to prevent the Tartar peasants from returning to their land so that these lands could be settled with obedient Russian muzhiks.

The settlement policy introduced by Russia had, as its goal, settling the empty lands, not inhabited by the free Tartar peasantry, with Armenians fleeing from Turkey, with Orthodox Slavs, Greeks, and even Germans and Swiss. Between 1820 and 1860, the 150,000 Tartar population were diluted with 100,000 foreigners, of whom the Russians numbered approximately 70,000.

A result of the 1877-1878 Russian-Turkish War was additional Crimean emigration to Turkey. The changing Russian attitudes are illustrated by the slogan of Alexander II, "The Crimean Tartars will have to choose between loyalty or deportation."

The end of the 19th century was the period of national renaissance among the Muslim Turkish people. Pan-Islamic and pan-Turkic movements developed. The essence of the pan-Islamic movement was defined by the newspaper *Ang* published in Kazan. It stated, "We define the concept of a nation spiritually.

The nation is the sum total of Islamic Law and the Muslim Religion."[86]
According to them, Islam did not distinguish between Tartars and Arabs.

The Russians viewed Tartar culture as a barbarian heritage. The local governors demolished the traditional buildings, with the exception of the Bahtsiseray. This fact was noted with amazement by British travelers of the period.

The Church of the Crimean Tartars

While Catherine II did not touch the Muslim Church, and even salaried the clergy, this privileged situation came to an end with the Tsarina's death. An 1831 ordinance limited the previous autonomy of the Muslim Church by setting up the Crimean Muslim Religious Affairs Committee that was in charge of religious matters and could regulate ecclesiastic monetary and land problems. Yet, under this Committee, the local authorities could make decisions concerning education and could even rule in judicial matters, thus preserving some of their old autonomy, a situation unparalleled anywhere else in Russia. In contrast to the upper layers of society who were loyal to Russia and who were in favor of modernization, the Muslim clergy endeavored to preserve the traditions and the national heritage at the end of the 19th century.

Education of the Crimean Tartars

The schools operated under Muslim supervision. The first Russian schools were established in the1850s. In view of the fact that the Muslim schools were a function of the Muslim ecclesiastic organizations and the teaching was largely limited to religious matters, the graduates of these schools could not compete with the graduates of the Russian schools who had received a more modern education. Consequently, the number of Russian schools increased markedly after 1877 and there was a keen competition among them. Graduates of the Russian-language Simferopol school, established in 1828 for Tartar students, were eligible for enrollment at the Sebastopol Russian University. The attraction of Russian culture was enhanced by the fact that medical care was much better in the areas inhabited by Russians.

Evolution of national consciousness of the Crimean Tartars

Ismail Bey Gasprali (1851-1914) was the first modern Tartar intellectual who, under the influence of Pan-Islamism, fought for a united Turkestan. He also began his education in a Tartar religious school and then studied in a local Russian school. From there, he went to St. Petersburg and thence to Paris. Finally, he went to Turkey and there became acquainted with the aspirations of the "Young Turks" movement. Returning home, he announced his program in his newspaper, the *Tercuman*. He recognized the dangers of Russification based on the inadequacies of Tartar education and demanded high standards in Muslim elementary schools and a renewal of the Tartar literary language. When he saw that it would not be possible to achieve any significant results against the aggressive nationality policies of the Russian government, he sought paths of cooperation and joined forces with the Russian Liberals and the Constitutional Democratic party. The 1905 Russian bourgeois, democratic revolution resulted in the formation of the first Duma (National Parliament) in 1906. It was open to nationality representatives and to

---

[86] Ang. 1913 No.8., p. 138. It is cited by Magda Katona: A közép-ázsiai konfliktusok (The Central Asian conflicts), ELTE Ruszisztikai Központ, Bp., 1996. p. 10.

their demands. The Volga Tartars were in a more unsatisfactory situation and demanded territorial autonomy, while the Crimean Tartars would have been satisfied with a cultural autonomy. The second Duma excluded the nationality representatives, saying "the Duma must be Russian in spirit".

Realizing that cooperation with the Russians was hopeless, the new Crimean Tartar intellectuals abandoned Gasprali's policies and chose to follow a Turkophile line. Gasprali, incidentally, came into conflict with the Muslim leadership as well, mainly because of his radical tendencies. The new, nationalist generation labeled Gasprali as a compromiser and a reactionary. A third group was formed in Istanbul and started spreading its wings in 1907, at the time the Young Turk movement came into its own. In 1908, this group established the Crimean Student Association, which set as its goal the creation of an independent Crimean State.

Pan-Turkism spread among the small mid-Asiatic nations, as well, and their goal was to create a united Turanian country for all the Turkic people.

World War I led to an increased organizational activity among all the minority nationalities. In 1916, in Lausanne, the League of Non-Russian Nationalities was formed. In 1917, in St. Petersburg, after the abdication of the Tsar, the Muslim Congress of All the Russias met and demanded territorial autonomy. It set up the National Deliberative Council as its bargaining arm. During June and July of that year, the Crimean national party was established and began to make much more radical demands. In November, the Tartar *Kurultay* (National Assembly) was called together in Bahtsiseray. It made decisions in December concerning a new constitution and a new government but the Bolshevik revolution put an end to all Crimean independence.

Minorities under Sovjet Power
The victorious outcome of the 1917 Russian Revolution meant that the nascent Bolshevik state had to confront the many problems raised by the nationality areas having a varying degree of social and cultural development and a wide variety of demands for politically motivated territorial and cultural autonomy.

Soviet Power and Violence
In the newly formed Soviet government, Stalin was given the post of Commissar for the Nationalities. He was considered an expert in this field by virtue of his 1914 paper on "Marxism and the National Question" in which he took a position favorable to the right of the nationalities for self-government. Similarly to Lenin, he emphasized at the Third Soviet Congress in January 1918 that, "The principle of self-government must be a weapon in the fight for Socialism, but this principle must be subjugated to the principle of Socialism." This meant, in practice, that for both economic and strategic reasons the young Soviet state could not permit any secession. In all areas, it supported the local organization of the Bolshevik Party and put in place a Soviet government. The bourgeois organizations, whether for the preparation for autonomy or for organizing local elections, were declared to be capitalist machinations and were destroyed by military force or by the use of the Secret Police. The Soviet power structure was fully in charge. Clever agitators took advantage of social antagonisms and of the peasants' yearning for land. The period of civil wars lasted until 1921-1922, when all outside intervention ceased

that could have been of assistance to the local bourgeois forces. The telegram that Stalin sent to the Ukrainian Soviet government is characteristic of the way in which the situation was managed: "...you have played long enough at being a government and a republic. It is time to put an end to all this."[87]

According to Stalin, the individual republic had to become a member of the Russian Federation, as an autonomous republic. At the beginning of 1918, Stalin was active in the border regions, establishing Russophile governments and setting up the Communist power structures. The Tartar-Bashkir Soviet Republic that he organized became the model for subsequent autonomous republics. The nationalities, unhappy with the oppressive policies of the Tsarist government, now demanded total territorial autonomy or complete independence. In 1922, the Georgian Communists opposed entry into the Russian Federation and demanded greater independence (Georgian conflict). Lenin, on the other hand, was thinking in terms of a federation of Soviet republics, having equal rights. In one of his letters to Kamenev, he wrote, "We consider ourselves as having equal rights with the Ukrainian SSR and with all the others and, together with them, we enter into a new alliance, a new federation, the European and Asiatic Union of Soviet Republics." Lenin, Stalin and other Bolshevik leaders believed that the national differences and the antagonisms between the nationalities could be gradually resolved by the equalizing force of Socialism and they rejected federalism and territorial autonomy that could have been established on an Austro-Marxist basis.

In contrast, they were picturing a regional autonomy where the political units were not divided from each other on a nationality basis. According to them, the interests of the local self-government had to be subjugated to the interests of the Proletarian State and believed that only a limited cultural autonomy, subservient to the interests of the Proletarian Dictatorship, was permissible.

In the first phase of the Soviet nationality policies, lasting from 1918 to the 1930s, the smaller nations, which had no written language, were issued a Roman alphabet that in and of itself was a divisive force. At this time, nationality officials were appointed to serve with the Russian ones.

In the second phase, from the 1930s to the 1960s, a forceful economic transformation and socialist industrialization were imposed and all writing had to be with the Cyrillic alphabet.

New Administration and Ethnic Homogenization in Lieu of Autonomy
The Empire was divided into republics according to the model proposed by Stalin. Russia was also a Union of Republics that included, in addition to the Russians, a number of other nationalities, which formed autonomous republics, autonomous territories or national districts. It was joined in April of 1918 by the Turkestan Autonomous Republic, which gathered together the majority of the small Asiatic nationalities. The so-called autonomous republics, like the Tartar one, the Bashkir or the Komi, did not have the option of seceding - not even in theory. The small nations were gathered into autonomous territories or districts. In all the free and equal republics Russian was the official language.

Naturally, in the formation of the boundaries of the various administrative units, the centralizing and divisive endeavors of the Bolshevik state were real-

[87] László Béládi and Tamas Krausz: Életrajzok a bolsevizmus történetéből (Biographies from the history of Bolshevism), ELTE, ÁJK, Bp., 1988. pp. 89-92.

ized. Until 1936, when Tajikistan was the last of the republics to be established, the State attempted to divide the nationalities with repeated redistricting and by inciting territorial and ethnic animosities. Thus, for instance, Bokhara and Khorezm, having a predominantly Tajik population, were placed into Uzbekistan. The Soviet government, wishing to counterbalance the Pan-Turkestan ideas that arose from the Pan-Turkic ideas, supported the ethnic, linguistic and territorial separateness of the Uzbeks. For the same reason, they elevated the Kipchac dialect of the Uzbek language to be their literary language, at the time they switched from the Arabic alphabet to the Roman one.

Settlements
The gigantic building program of Socialism, its industrialization program and its environmental reconstruction program caused huge migrations of the highly privileged foreign workers, Russians, Ukrainians and Byelorussians, who represented a dominant social stratum above the small nationalities. The influx of this enormous number of workers radically changed the ethnic ratios within two decades.

Linguistic divisions, the "birth of new nations" and Russification
In the spirit of Pan-Turkism, a number of Turkic intellectuals took a stand against Stalin's small-nationality policies. He wished to divide them by making their individual dialects into literary languages. They, in contrast, wished to unite the various dialects and create a unified Turkic literary language. The Turkish, the Azerian and the Turkmen languages were considered, until 1928, to be dialects of the same language, slowly separated from each other after this time. Also in 1929, the conversion to a Roman alphabet divided the Kazakh and Kirghiz languages. This reform in writing, introduced during the 1920s, also led to the unfortunate outcome that presently the ancient records, written in archaic Turkic are available only to the most highly educated few. Roman characters, separated the Tadzhic, from the neighboring Iranian literary traditions, written in Arabic characters. In 1941, the Turkic nations changed from the Roman to the Cyrillic alphabet and thus severed, or tried to sever, the literary and cultural threads tying them to Turkey. A number of small nations became literate at this time, for the first time in their history.

Some nations were given new names and thus the Uzbeks became Uighurs. In 1900, it was common knowledge that Turkestan was inhabited by Turkic people and that the Uzbeks assumed a central position between the Kazakhs and the Sarts. The latter term referred to the people living in the river valleys and in the towns. The term Uzbek, derived from the name of the Khan Uzbeg who lived in the 14th century, was reintroduced in 1924. The Dzungars, another Turkic-speaking nation, were renamed Uigurs, after a people long since gone. In this fashion, the various literary languages were created and separated from each other, but in the process the well-to-do peasantry, the artisans and the intellectuals were destroyed and the entire Turkestan society was functionally decapacitated.

In reality, there was no chance for autonomy where everything was economically and politically controlled by the Party. Yet, it is true, that experts leading the eastward extension of the Russian Empire tried to improve the life of the small nationalities whose languages and customs they were studying. The

Russian Csernyekov, who devoted his entire life to the Vogouls, constructed the first Vogoul alphabet. The famous specialist of the Ostyak language, the German W. Steinitz, prepared the first Ostyak alphabet and textbooks in the 1930s.

The developments starting in the 1920s still needed an intellectual layer in these nationalities. The small nationalities, without a written language, were given first the Roman, and later the Cyrillic, alphabet and developed their own literature. The gifted youngsters were selected and sent to schools. After growing up, many of them became assimilated into the more developed and more promising Russian culture. From the end of the 1920s, the sons of the small Siberian tribes, (Ob-Ugrians, Samoyeds, etc.) could get an education at the Institute of Nordic Nations and it was here that teachers of the native languages were trained. In the 1930s, there was a significant improvement in the Soviet educational system in Western Siberia and, in addition to elementary schools, there were more advanced schools in the larger centers, such as Chanti-Mansijks, where teacher colleges were also established. The first flowers of Vogoul literature were published at the end of the 1920s by the Institute of Nordic Nations.

Second Phase, Economic Reorganization, and Urbanization

The greatest obstacle to the Socialist industrialization of the 1930s was the existence of the small landowner and military communities maintained by the Asiatic Turkic nations. The battles between 1917 and 1921, and the subsequent settlements, already cut the traditional routes of the nomadic herdsmen and made the sale of livestock difficult. The Soviet leadership used drastic measures, including the army and police, to force the nomads to settle down. During their seasonal journeys, the government forces swooped down on the tribes when they were most vulnerable, in the desert or steppes, far from water, and surrounded them with barbed wire.

The animals died quickly and the men were decimated by epidemics. This was the fate of the Kazakhs, the Turkmens and the Karakalpaks. During the first 5-year plan, designed to settle the nomads, the Kazakhs drove their herds to Afghanistan, to Siberia and to China to protect them from confiscation. Hundreds of thousands starved to death. Many killed their own animals as a sign of protest - 2.3 million cattle and 10 million sheep perished, representing approximately 80% of the animals. The new collective farms lacked equipment, building material and seed. There were a series of tribal uprisings. The tribal intelligentsia, evolving during the 1930s, raised its voice against the forced settlement policies, many of them having been appointed to administrative positions. Retribution came quickly and included the local Party secretaries if they belonged to the same ethnic group (Kazakh, Uzbek, Turkmen, Khirgiz). They were tried for bourgeois nationalism and tribal separatism, found guilty and executed. This process is categorized by Soviet historians as the "elimination of feudal remnants". It was during the 1940s that the collectivization was completed and the agriculture of Central Asia was converted to a one-crop system for growing cotton.

The 1920s were the years of collectivization and of the elimination of the kulak properties, followed by famine and dissatisfaction. During the 1930s came the "cleansing", the arrests for sabotage, the rapid change in local leaders and the forced industrialization. Nurturing the nationality culture was tantamount to a denial of internationalism and hence a sin. The sinners were

108

swallowed up by the labor camps. Education and the leadership became Russified.

After the Kirov murder in 1934, the era of the personality cult and of the Party-state dictatorship descended on the land. Forced labor camps were set up, there were preparations for the great show trials, entire tribes were transplanted and by 1937-1938 mass arrests and mass executions began.

Deportations and genocide

After the Molotov-Ribbentrop pact of 1939, the Sovietization of the Baltic provinces accelerated. The Estonian, Lithuanian and Latvian leading classes were transplanted, beginning in June 1941. The deportations, disappearances and other atrocities claimed 60,000 victims in Estonia, 35,000 in Latvia and 34,000 in Lithuania during 1940-1941. After the German invasion in 1941, the entire Jewish population of the area, fairly significant in Lithuania, was exterminated[88].

After the return of the Red Army and re-establishment of the Soviet system, renewed deportations affected approximately 20% of the entire Baltic population.

The Caucasian people, living in a strategically important area, could not escape their fate, either. Diligent NKVD officers "discovered conspiracies" and, in October 1943, the Karachevo-Cherkess autonomic republic was eliminated and 62,842 people were transplanted to Kirgizia and Kazakhstan. In March 1944, the deportation of 608,749 Chechens, Ingus and Balkars were reported in police memoranda - 23.7% of them died in labor camps. The Crimean Tartars were accused of trying to set up an independent Tartar state. Between May 18 and 20, 1944, 180,014 people were transported to Uzbekistan on 67 trains. 40,000 of the Tartars died in the process. On June 27-28, 1944, 15,040 Greeks, 12,422 Bulgarians and 9,521 Armenians were deported from the Crimea. From Georgia, 100,000 Turks, Kurds and other nationals were deported to Central Asiatic labor camps because they were "Turkish agents". The Germans living along the Volga were accused of having collaborated with the German troops during the war. Most of them were deported to Kazakhstan, together with approximately 2.5 million Poles from Eastern Poland.[89]

Birth of a national culture

Beginning in the 1950s, there developed even between the Volga and the Kama Rivers an increasingly prosperous group who could educate their children and among whom the idea of nationality arose. The group produced the first writers. The development of the nationality territories was a function of their industrial and commercial significance and development. In the 1970s, the Syryenians in the Komi Autonomous Republic, numbering about 322,000 people, had a well developed system of education with secondary schools and a university, radio, television and a publishing firm in their own language.

Artificial boundaries and resulting conflicts

In the 1920s, the newly formed Tadzhik and Uzbek nations competed for the land where previously they had lived in harmony. Conflicts erupted in 1989 between the original population of Central Asia and the expatriated Turks,

[88] Sz. Bíró Zoltán: Szovjet felügyelet alatt (Under Soviet control), História 1998/4. p. 17.
[89] Varga Lajos: Világháború és népek deportálása (World War and deportation) História, 1994/1. p. 17

Chechens and Kurds. Pogroms were started to force the resettlement of the nationalities that were settled here as punishment during the Soviet period.

Absence of autonomy in the mercy of future colonization
De-Stalinization in Central Asia was rapid and efficient. The local nationality leaders cooperated with Brezhnev and with the Moscow leadership that followed him. A two-tiered economy developed in Central Asia, as well, but there it was manifested by extending agriculture beyond cotton to opium poppies and marijuana and joining the international drug trade. Following the economic collapse of the Soviet Union and of the East-European Socialist countries, the fight for independence beginning in 1989, reached Central Asia in 1991. In a plebiscite about the future of the Soviet Union, they voted for the preservation of the Union but after the unsuccessful coup in Moscow during the second half of that year, Uzbekistan, Kirghistan, Turkmenistan and Kazakhstan all declared their intentions to become independent.

Among the small Siberian nations, the fate of the Hanti with 22,521 people, and of the Mansi, with 8474 people, was typical. Prior to the 1917 revolution, they lived primarily in villages and in the forests. The village-dwellers assimilated to the Russians while the forest-dwellers preserved their traditional life. The Soviet policy included the formation of nationality settlements, nationality boarding schools for the children, Russification, prohibition of the religious cults. The introduction of the Russian language in instruction rapidly resulted in the original inhabitants losing their cultural identity. The young people moving to the cities were ashamed of their "barbarian heritage" and the number of mixed marriages increased. The original settlers living in the forests or engaged in pastoral animal husbandry rapidly decreased in numbers. The explosive increase in crude oil production in the 1960s and 1970s made reindeer breeding, fishing and hunting increasingly difficult and led to the disappearance of the traditional industry. The poorly planned and badly used financial aid just accelerated the assimilation. Pollution of the rivers and of the land, the aggressiveness of the newly arriving industrial workers and their increasingly large numbers, the strange way of life and the forceful imposition of laws and regulations not only increased the assimilation but also led to psychic and physical defects in Hanti and Mansi children, far more frequent than in a comparable group of Russian children.

HUNGARIANS AND RUTHENIANS IN THE KÁRPÁTALJA

The Kárpátalja was briefly under Hungarian control (1939-1944) and then became a part first of the Soviet Empire and then of the Ukraine.

Collective guilt, retribution and ethnic cleansing
From September 1944 until late October, the Soviet army occupied the entire Kárpátalja, with the exception of Csap, and in the occupied territory, with the assistance of the Muscovite Hungarian Communists, reorganized the Hungarian Communist Party. The Czech hopes of having this area returned to them were not realized and the area was incorporated into the Soviet Union.

The second Order of the Day, issued by the commander of the Soviet troops on November 13, 1944, ordered that within three days all former soldiers who had served in either the Hungarian or German armies, who were members of either the gendarmes or the police or who were of military age (males between 18 and 50) had to report. All of these were taken away, allegedly for three days of work, but only a fraction of them ever returned. Hunger, typhoid fever and inhuman conditions in the death camps led to the death of 30% of the detainees, including whole families from certain villages. According to Stalin, the Carpatian-Ukraininan Hungarian question was one of rail transportation.

After this little episode, a Congress was called to Munkács for November 26, 1944 with "Popular representatives". The "invited representatives" did not represent the population since they did not include any Hungarians or Germans. The Congress issued a proclamation according to which it would fulfill the centuries-old demands of the "local Carpathian Ukrainians, the unification with the Ukraine." Czech administration came to an end in January 1945 and the Kárpátalja, for the first time in history, belonged to Russia, i.e., the Soviet Union. History was revised and it was claimed that the Kárpátalja had been a part of the Kiev Principality.

The Presidium of the Supreme Council of the Soviet Union, in its ordinance of January 22, 1946 incorporated the Kárpátalja into the Ukrainian SSR of the Soviet Union, under the name of Transcarpathian Territory.

In the Kárpátalja, the Soviets used the same techniques as elsewhere: first they gave some rights and then they took them back again. In fact, the inter-pretation of the laws was largely at the discretion of the local officials. In all arrangements, the policy tested in other nationality areas was used, namely, there was a definite pecking order, Russians, Ukrainians and Hungarians. Conditions improved only after Stalin's death.

The Hungarian books were removed from the public libraries and Hungarian could not be spoken in the offices and workshops. They were forbidden to trav-el to Hungary and Hungarian tourism was directed only toward the major Russian cultural centers. The Kárpátalja became a forgotten land and only Munkács and Ungvár could occasionally host small Hungarian tour groups.

The establishment of Hungarian cultural associations was highly suspect. István Soós, a teacher in Aknaszlatina, was sentenced to 10 years of hard labor, for having put the play János Vitéz on the stage. Hungarian writers, poets and intellectuals could meet only at each others' homes.

The publishing of Hungarian books improved after Stalin's death and even books published in Hungary appeared in the bookstores. During the *perestroika*, a number of Hungarian scientific and artistic circles and cultural establishments were organized. Finally, in 1989, the Hungarian Kárpátalja Cultural Association was established in order to protect the interests of the Hungarian population.

Education and use of the mother tongue

In addition to the six-year Hungarian schools, ten-year schools were established on the Russian model. Hungarian teacher education was started in Huszt but was transferred to Munkács in 1950. The teacher training school in Ungvár was closed in 1954 and the Hungarian students were reassigned to the Russian department of the University of Ungvár. The 1956 Hungarian Freedom Fight, gave an excuse for eliminating Hungarian intellectuals and clergy by means of ideological trials and executions. As a sign of concession on the part of the authorities, the teaching of Hungarian language and literature was introduced at the University. The Party leaders, however, emphasized the future of the internationalist Russian schools and, in the hope of a better life, many Hungarian parents enrolled their children in the Russian schools. The number of students attending Hungarian schools decreased, leading to their gradual decline. Even in 1993, of the 87 Kárpátalja Hungarian schools, 30 were "international" and the teaching was bilingual.

Destruction of the Churches

During the academic year 1945-46, the crucifixes were removed from the class-rooms, religious instruction was forbidden and priests were not allowed to enter the schools. Later, religious instruction outside the schools was also punished. The estates of the Church were confiscated, the priests' home was also national-ized and the priests were expelled. The congregation could lease the church - for a very high fee. The priests were taxed heavily and attending church was con-sidered a crime. Nineteen Roman Catholic priests, 20 Protestant ministers and the Chief Rabbi of Munkács were thrown into jail. One Protestant minister was exe-cuted, three died in prison and so did the Roman Catholic Archdeacon of Beregszász. It is not surprising that the Russian Orthodox Church considered the Greek Catholic Church its worst enemy. Bishop Teodor Romzsa was brutally murdered in 1947. The Greek Catholic churches and monasteries were expro-priated and handed over to the Pravoslav Church. Force and intimidation were used to coerce the Greek Church to secede from Rome and to recognize the Patriarch of Moscow as the Supreme Pontiff. Many of their priests were arrested and, in 1949, the Munkács Greek Catholic diocese was disbanded. At this time, there were 265 Greek Catholic parishes, 384 churches and 450,000 members. Some of the churches became warehouses, some became Museums of Atheism and 234 Greek Catholic churches were handed over to the Orthodox Church. In addition to bishop Romzsa, 5 other priests were murdered and 128 priests were imprisoned or sent to labor camps. Until the *perestroika*, the Church operated underground and it was only when Gorbachev took over the government that the priests dared to celebrate mass in the open, not infrequently in the cemetery. Approximately one fourth of the expropriated ecclesiastic property was returned but the buildings were totally pillaged and in lamentable condition.

Autonomy?

In a plebiscite conducted on December 1, 1991, the majority of the population of Beregszász district voted in favor of establishing an autonomous Hungarian district. In spite of this plebiscite, the autonomy has remained an empty promise. Yet, the plebiscite was important until the birth of the Ukrainian-Hungarian Basic Treaty (1993), that was ratified over the objection of the Hungarians and also of some of the Ruthenians.

As a consequence of the Russian settlement policies, a number of nationali-ties were moved and the ethnic balance has shifted in favor of the ruling major-ity. Between 1910 and 1989, the Hungarian population decreased by 28% and the German population by 10%, signaling the disappearance of the latter as an ethnic group.

Without a jointly operated territorial and personal autonomy, self-government by the original inhabitants, Hungarians and Ruthenians, has been impossible. The Ruthenians, and the Hungarians living among them in scattered settlements, are the strongest proponents of the autonomy for the entire Kárpátalja. The population of this area in 1990 was 1,252,000, of whom the Ruthenians represented 78%, the Hungarians 12.5%, the Romanians 2.4% and the Slovaks and Germans 0.3%. The Kárpátalja Hungarian Cultural Association is presently endeavoring to fight for a territorial autonomy that would include the Hungarians living in a block in Beregszász and in the neighboring districts.

The two greatest stumbling blocks for the autonomy of the Kárpátalja within the Ukraine is the frightening example of the Crimea and that the Ukrainian nationalists do not recognize the identity of the Ruthenians as being different from the Ukrainians. At the present time, there is a slow and gradual development of a separate economic belt along the boundaries. It does not grant territorial autonomy to the Hungarians having a majority in the Beregszász district, but it does improve the standards of living in that area.

Poland

Population (1995): 88,600,000
Ethnic groups: Polish - 99%, Ruthenians, Byelorussians, Germans, Gypsies, Ukrainians, Lithuanians, Slovakians, Greeks and Tartars.
Official language: Polish.

The Divided Poland under Russian, Prussian and Austrian Rule
In the 18th century, Poland was divided on three different occasions between Russia, the Habsburg Monarchy and Prussia. After the 1795 division, 54% of the Poles came under the rule of the King of Prussia. German was made the official language in administrative offices in the courts and in many schools. The expropriated Polish royal and ecclesiastic estates were given to German officials. In Galicia, under Austrian control, the Treasury expropriated the ecclesiastic estates, closed monasteries and introduced German into the schools. At this time, in the Russian controlled area, a Polish University was established in Vilnius and a network of Polish schools was set up in Volhinia. In Krzemieniec, an institute of higher education was in operation.

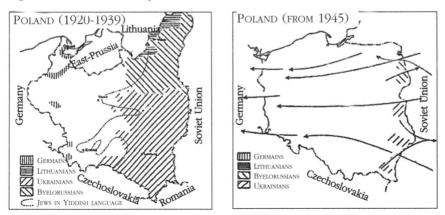

113

In the 19th century, there were a series of insurrections attempting to re-establish national unity and independence. During the Napoleonic era, Poland was unified but the Congress of Vienna, in 1815, again returned much of Poland to Russia with the stipulation that the Romanovs would grant the area autonomy similar to the one granted to Finland.

Under Russian rule

The Poles could not acquiesce in the Russian rule and, in 1830, the junior officers of the remaining Polish army attacked the palace of the Russian governor in Warsaw, leading to a general military insurrection against the Tsar. Unfortunately, the haughty behavior of the Polish nobility toward minorities living in their area and their refusal to listen to the legitimate complaints of the peasantry doomed the insurrection to failure. The nobility was isolated in its antagonism against the Tsar, thus national solidarity could not develop. In response Nicholas I, who had long since regretted his promise of autonomy, disbanded the Polish army in 1832 and enrolled its members into the Russian army. The highly developed Polish agricultural areas along the Southwestern border were incorporated into Russia and drastic methods were used to remove the Poles. The Vilnius University and the Krzemieniec school were closed and their place was assumed by the Orthodox Tsarist University in Kiev. Young teachers from Byelorussia and the Ukraine went to Poland and settled there. It was from this group that the new Ukrainian intellectual class evolved over the next 20 years. In 1836, instruction in Polish was discontinued in all public schools.

The emigration following the 1831 rebellion deprived Poland of its most important political personalities. The country declined into poverty and lost its ability for political initiatives. In 1846, there was an uprising in Krakow, the capital of Austrian controlled Galicia. The insurgents added the liberation of the villeins to their plans for a free Poland, but the Vienna Court had no difficulty in overcoming this rather lackluster uprising and incorporated the hitherto autonomous Krakow Republic into the Monarchy. These events were of great interest to the Hungarian politicians of the Reform Period. Kossuth learned from the Galician events that it was pointless to speak about the future of a country if there was no national unity and so long as, "the hate-generating walls of feudalism were standing". The 1848 Hungarian revolt had no parallel event in Poland but a Polish Legion, under General Bem, fought first in Vienna and then in Hungary against the oppressive Habsburg despotism.

At the beginning of 1860, Tsar Alexander II graciously consented to the Finnish request for their own constitution, for which the grateful Finns erected a statue in his honor. Under the effect of this event, the Polish governor, Wielopolski, petitioned the Tsar to reestablish the Polish autonomy, as proposed at the Congress of Vienna. This initiative was considered by the Polish nobility as a weakening of the Tsarist regime and in 1863 a revolt erupted in Warsaw. At this time, the nobility promised a distribution of land and the revolt was supported by the nascent Polish intellectual class. They relied much too heavily on French support, ignored the nationality drive of the Ruthenians and Byelorussians and so alienated these minorities from the freedom fight.

The victorious Tsarist regime did away with all the remnants of autonomy. A governor ruled in Warsaw and by the 1880s, Poland was entirely integrated into the Russian administration. A Russian director was put in charge of all Polish institutions. The most painful wound inflicted upon Poland was the elimination of the name of the country. From that time on, it was referred to only as the province along the Vistula. The Polish Universities were replaced by Russian ones, the development of cultural institutions was curtailed and in the public schools only religion was taught in Polish while all other use of the language was prohibited. The authorities tried, unsuccessfully, to subjugate the Catholic Church to the State. They built Greek Orthodox churches and tried to make the Greek Catholics convert to the Orthodox religion. In 1865, publication in Lithuanian and Byelorussian was prohibited and all publications had to be printed in the Cyrillic alphabet.

After 1874, Ukrainian publications were also prohibited, even using the Cyrillic alphabet, and in 1885, the Polish Bank was taken over. Economic separatism was brought to a halt. A period of silence ensued, followed by a period of economic and cultural growth until the turn of the century when the re-establishment of the autonomy, promised by the Congress of Vienna, again began to be very cautiously explored as a political goal.

Under Prussian rule

In the period following the unification of Germany (1871), Bismarck and his successors engaged in a vigorous Germanization of the occupied Polish territories. They were not satisfied with the language of the administration being German and, in addition, city names had to be in German. In 1887, the teaching of the Polish language in the elementary schools was abolished. After 1900, even religious instruction had to be in German. The priests and bishops arguing against this action had their personal effects confiscated and some were jailed. One of the important tools used by the Prussians was the establishment of settlements of German immigrants. German banks advanced credit to German farmers settling in Poland and also to German industrial entrepreneurs.

Since these steps did not fulfill the expectations, 30,000 Poles and Jews were expelled from the German-controlled area claiming that they were Russian or Austrian subjects. In 1886, the Prussian Parliament approved 100 million Marks to encourage the settlement of Germans along the Baltic coast between Poznan and Danzig and this sum was raised significantly in successive years. The lack of success of these endeavors was due primarily to the resistance of the Polish co-operatives and banks.

Under Austrian rule

As part of the Austro-Hungarian Compromise, a number of autonomous rights were granted in the administration of the territories belonging to Austria. The same was true in Galicia, the former part of Poland (before 1772). Not only was the language of administration Polish, but all instruction, from the elementary schools to university was conducted in Polish, replacing instruction in Ukrainian. In 1873, the Academy of Sciences was established and in 1886 the Lemberg (Lvov) Historical Association was founded.

Poland was divided among her powerful neighbors in 1772, 1793, 1795 and again in 1815. It did not gain back its independence until the end of World War I when the 1919 Peace Treaties re-established the reunited, independent Poland. Additional territorial demands were met when the Polish army defeated the young Soviet Union and areas were ceded to Poland in 1921 at the Peace Treaty of Riga. In this Poland, there were 3.9 million Ukrainians, 1 million Byelorussians, 2.1 million Jews and 1 million Germans, in addition to the 18.8 million Poles representing 69.2% of the population. Danzig (Gdansk), lying on the shores of the Baltic Sea and having a predominantly German population, was made a free city under the aegis of the League of Nations.

Legal situation
The new Polish constitution included the international recommendations for the protection of minorities, assuring these minorities their cultural autonomy. The Polish statutes for the protection of minorities also guaranteed their property. This did not mean that the rights so guaranteed were in fact respected and, during the subsequent 10 years, the minorities filed 247 petitions with the League of Nations requesting a remedy for their losses. They did not get any assistance because the League of Nations was as impotent in this as in other matters. The Parliament voted in favor of autonomy for Eastern Galicia in 1922, but this autonomy was never implemented.

Numerus clausus and education
After 1924, the number of German schools gradually declined and later the number of German applicants admitted to the Universities was limited. Anti-Semitism, increasing in the 1930s, led to the emigration of a large number of Jews. In 1938, a system of selective admissions was introduced and consequently the percentage of Jewish university students was reduced from 24.6% in 1921 to 8.2% in 1938-1939. In the university classrooms, the Jews had to sit in segregated seats. The 1924 Education Act restricted education to the bilingual schools and this led to a reduction of the Ukrainian schools in Poland from 2,496 before World War I to 460 in 1928.[90]

Occupation and genocide
In September 1939, following the defeat of Poland in World War II, Poland was again divided between Germany and the Soviet Union, in accordance with the Molotov-Ribbentrop Pact. Consequently, about 3 million Poles remained in the Soviet Union (prisoners of war and deportees between 1940-1941). During the war, one million Poles were expelled from occupied Poland by the Germans and another 1.5 million were taken to Germany as slave laborers.

Revengeful minority policy
After World War II, the Germans were deprived of their citizenship and, for a while, they even had to wear a distinguishing mark. A 1946 decree proclaimed the collective guilt of all Germans, but this was reversed in 1950.

On the basis of an agreement made with the Soviet Union in 1946, the Ukrainians living in Poland were exchanged for the Poles living in the Soviet Union. In 1944-50, a civil war broke out between the Poles and the Ukrainians and when it was over, 160,000 Ukrainians were forcefully resettled from the Eastern part of Poland to the Western part previously inhabited by Germans.

[90] F. Glatz: A kisebbségi kérdés közép-Európában tegnap és ma (The minority question in Central Europe) História, no.11/1992. Európa Institut Budapest, MTA TTI, p. 34.

After 1945, similarly to other Central European countries, the Polish government expelled the Germans. The transfers lasted from 1945 to 1951 and in the process about 1.3 million Germans perished. The number of Germans remaining in Poland was about one tenth of the original German population of 9-10 million. Polish statistical data are generally unreliable and the data given for the 1960s and 1970s do not agree with those reported for a later date. Part of the confusion may be due to the fact that the members of the German minority, justifiably frightened by historical events, probably lied when asked on the census sheet about their nationality. From 1955 on, the expulsion of the Germans was continuous and between 1955 and 1970, a total of 368,824 of them are moved to Germany.[91] For historical reasons, this minority was considered to be dangerous to the State. At the 1990 national elections, several German minority representatives were elected to Parliament.

Today, approximately 180-200,000 Ukrainians live in the eastern parts of Poland. In the communities having a Ukrainian majority, the language of instruction in the public schools is Ukrainian. The Unitus churches were reopened and there are also two Ukrainian Universities. Starting in 1958, the Ukrainians were given the opportunity to resettle in the Soviet Union, but very few availed themselves of this option.

According to the 1989 census, there were approximately 190,000 Byelorussians living in the Byalistok region and there are 34 Byelorussian schools able to accommodate 2,400 students.

The Ruthenians number about 30,000. During the Polish-Ukrainian civil war, they lost a number of their Greek Catholic churches and by 1961 the number of Ruthenian schools had diminished from 17 to seven.

The Lithuanians are considered to be ethnically related to the Poles. The boundary adjustments of 1945 removed a large number of them from Poland and their total number in Poland today is only about 10,000. They have full cultural autonomy.

The records indicate that there are about 2,000 Czechs and 20,000 Slovaks living in Poland. They had a difficult time, but conditions have improved and they again have their own elementary and middle schools.

The 3 million Jews living in Poland after 1919 represented almost 20% of the world's Jewry. 90% of them were destroyed in the Holocaust. Due to the emigration beginning in 1960, their current numbers are estimated at 10,000.

The Tartars, who had a favored position between the two World Wars, were moved from the East of Poland to the West after the War. Their mosques were destroyed and a forceful assimilation policy was instituted.

The legal position of the approximately 500,000 Gypsies is not clear[92].

In 1921, the Poles represented 69.2% of the population. By 1990 the percentage of Poles rose to 98.7%. Thus, there is clearly no serious threat of an ethnic conflict.

---

[91] F. Glatz, Ibid, pp. 34-35.
[92] F. Glatz, Ibid, p. 36.

Post-Trianon Hungary

Population (1996): 10,214,000
Ethnic groups: Hungarian - 97.7%, German- 0.3%, Slovak - 0.1%, Gypsy - 1.4%,
Romanian - 0.1%, Croat - 0.1%.
Official language: Hungarian.

The 1920, the Trianon Peace Treaty deprived Hungary of 72% of its territory and of 60% of its population. The territory diminished from 282,000 km^2 to 93,000 km^2 and of the 18 million original population only 8 million remained. In parts of the detached areas, Romanians, Slovaks, Serbs, Croats, Ruthenians or Germans were in the majority but mixed and purely Hungarian territories were also detached, even some where the Hungarians lived immediately adjacent to the new Hungary without any intervening nationality groups. Of the original 10 million Hungarian-speakers, one third, or about 3.3 million, came under foreign rule. About half of these were detached in complete disregard of the ethnic boundaries, without plebiscite and purely on the basis of strategic considerations, such as the direction of branch railway lines. Hungary lost 86.6% of its forests and the ability of exercising ecological control over the watersheds of its rivers. All of the salt mines, almost all of the mineral resources and most of the stone quarries were lost. It lost 52.2% of its industrial potential and the industries most seriously affected included iron and steel, milling, lumber and paper. Hungary became a country dependent on imported raw materials. Losses in land and population of such magnitude affected about one out of every four families. The Peace Treaty even mandated that 3,950 km^2 of Western Hungary, with a population of 350,000, be given to Austria.

In this area, the loyalty of the 70% German city of Sopron was impressive. In August 1921, the students of the Selmecbánya Forestry and Mining University fled to Sopron. There, they organized a militia and, in the second battle of Ágfalva on September 8, defeated the Austrian gendarme battalion that came to occupy Sopron. Sopron was thus not occupied and negotiations conducted on October 11-13 resulted in the Venice Agreement, according to which the territory to be detached was divided. A plebiscite was ordered for Sopron and for eight neighboring communities. The vote was strongly in favor of Hungary (65%) and thus this area remained Hungarian. When the Austrian-Hungarian Border Commission arrived in the mostly Croat village of Szentpéterfa, the population received them waving Hungarian flags and singing the Hungarian national anthem. On their request, this village was returned to Hungary in 1922.

There were political groups in Trianon Hungary who were strongly antagonistic to the minority populations remaining in the country, fearing that their autonomous position might lead to further territorial mutilations of the country. The government, however, used great moderation in their policies. The 10.4% ethnic group consisted mainly of Slovaks (142,000) and Germans (550,000) who were scattered over a considerable area of the country. It was felt by the government that any hostile activity would trigger a very similar response against the Hungarians living beyond the border, where forceful assimilation undoubtedly would have been introduced on a reciprocity basis. The government also did not wish to alienate the majority populations in the neighboring countries but wished to impress them with its nationality policy.

118

Nationality policy ideals and legal bulwarks

The ideals of a new nationality policy were developed under the Bethlen government in the 1920s. Prime Minister Ordinance No. 4,800 of 1923 regulated the nationalities' right to use their language and their right to establish cultural and economic organizations. In the Trianon Hungary, the remaining nationalities were bilingual and for this reason the Minister of Religion and Education, Kúnó Klebelsberg, established three types of schools for the minorities from which the parents or the local administration could choose. In type "A", the language of instruction was the mother tongue of the minority with Hungarian as a required subject. In type "B", half the subjects had to be taught in Hungarian and half in the language of the minority. In type "C", the language of instruction was Hungarian with the language of the minority a required subject. This ordinance (110.478/1923) required that there be at least 40 school-age children for a minority school to be set up. It was also at this time that, in the context of the Klebelsberg school building program, it was possible to limit the number of students in any one class to no more than 40. Only a minority of the nationality schools was public and 80% of them were parochial. In these, the ecclesiastic authorities determined the language of instruction. The government attempted several times to convert the type "C" schools to type "B" but the local authorities and the parents opposed this move and, in fact, wished to move the schools in the opposite direction. Thus, the implementation of the 1935 Minority School Ordinance along these lines was motivated by fear of German intervention or of the population transfer proposed by Hitler.[93]

In 1930, there were 50 Slovak minority schools. Among the Croats, Serbs and Romanians, representing less than one percent of the population, the minority schools were of the "C" type. In the academic year 1929-1930, there were 454 German nationality schools. The 1930 census indicated a 1.4% decrease in the German population that alarmed the leader of the cultural association so much that, in a speech in Parliament, he mentioned the possibility of turning to Germany for assistance. Because of the lack of German secondary schools and of teacher training schools, the promising young people in the German minority obtained scholarships and studied at German Universities.

After Bleyer's death in 1933, Ferenc Basch and his associates represented an extremely radical group in the leadership of the German Educational Association of Hungary. They were graduates of German Universities and their thoughts reflected their strong identification with the German Empire. Among the historians and writers interested in the conditions of the 6.9% German minority in Hungary, such as Elemér Mályusz and Gyula Illyés, the fear of German propaganda and of the possible detachment of Western Transdanubia became manifest.

Territorial Re-Annexation, Increasingly Radical Minorities and Plans for Autonomy

In the territory re-annexed by the First Vienna Ruling in 1938, most of the population was Hungarian with 10.9% Slovaks. The leaders of the German minority, aware of the support of their mother country, wished to transform the Volksbund, already authorized by the Imrédy government, into a nationality structure with

---

[93] Loránt Tilkovszky: Nemzetiségi politika Magyarországon a 20. században. (Hungarian policy towards the nationalities in the 20th century.) Történelmi Kézikönyvtár, Csokonai, Debrecen, 1998. p. 78.

quasi-autonomous powers. Naturally, the political orientation would have been totally along the Nazi lines, facilitating the encroachment of German-Nazi policies into Hungary and encouraging the German expansive movements in this direction. It is not surprising that Prime Minister Count Pál Teleki insisted that all items in their charter which did not conform to the legitimate activities of a cultural association be expunged. The Volksbund endeavored to have German teachers teach from Nazi textbooks and to have their schools, 17 elementary schools, 3 middle schools and 2 high schools, taught according to National Socialist precepts. The other German schools throughout the country continued to teach in the spirit of Hungarian patriotism.

Kárpátalja was re-annexed on March 14-18, 1939 with armed force, bringing 501,047 Ruthenians, 72% of the total population, under Hungarian rule. Prime Minister Teleki, long an advocate of autonomy, was prepared to move in this direction. On July 23, 1940 he submitted to Parliament a legislative proposal on "The Kárpátalja Voivode and its Self-Government". Debate and implementation was postponed until after the war.

For the interim, Teleki introduced a bilingual administration. The planned introduction of autonomy frightened the small number of Hungarians living in that area, who well remembered the discriminations they were subjected to during the Czech rule. It infuriated the Volksbund, since the government, while planning autonomy for the Ruthenians had denied it to the Germans. This was particularly galling, since in the Slovak puppet state created in 1939 under German sponsorship, the German organizations were given a free hand, with their direction coming from Germany. Since the Carpathians became a potential front-line, the military authorities also objected to a Ruthenian autonomy in this area, for strategic reasons.

The Second Vienna Ruling of 1941 re-annexed North Transylvania to Hungary. In a follow-up meeting, in Turnu-Severin, the Hungarian delegation rejected a Romanian proposal for an exchange of population. Hungary was not willing to consider a population exchange involving about one million people. Thus, the larger and more populous portion of Transylvania remained under Romanian rule as did the natural gas fields that were of considerable strategic importance to Germany. The division could follow linguistic lines because by this time there were only 2 million Hungarians but 3 million Romanians, more than 500,000 Germans, almost 500,000 Jews and others living in the disputed area. The largest block of Hungarians lived far from the border, in the Székelyföld, and the population mix of the cities was quite different from that of the surrounding rural areas. Around the mostly Hungarian Kolozsvár, the villages were mostly Romanian and around the almost completely Hungarian Brassó, the villages were predominantly Romanian and German. While the First Vienna Ruling followed ethnic lines and the re-annexed population was largely Hungarian, the Second Vienna Ruling brought almost one million Romanians under Hungarian rule.

In the re-annexed territories, economic developments were sponsored by the government and important domestic social activities were extended to these areas. Teleki endeavored to reach accommodation and, therefore, ordered that in mixed population areas the high schools had to teach both languages and also required that officials serving in the administration of these areas take and pass an exam in the minority languages. Several plans for autonomy were considered to assure that nationalities living side by side with the Hungarians in the Felvidék, Kárpátlaja and Transylvania could develop independently. When count Teleki saw that he could not prevent Hungary's participation in the invasion of Yugoslavia, he committed suicide.

Under his successor, Prime Minister Lászlo Bárdossy, Hungarian troops occupied the Bácska, the Baranya Triangle, the Muraköz and the Muravidék. (Bánát came under German protectorate). In these areas, the population was 61% Serb, German and Croat. The Volksbund became very strong with German assistance, but the other nationalities also caused the government considerable difficulties with their demands.

The fact that the nationalities living in the re-annexed areas were strongly influenced by the anti-Hungarian attitude of Slovakia, Romania, Yugoslavia and Croatia made it very difficult to continue the moderate nationality policies of the Hungarian government. The government endeavored to assist those nationality cultural organizations that were not committed to separatism. The tensions were increased by the fact that the officials sent by the government to these distant and recently re-annexed areas were not always well educated and were ignorant of the language and culture of the local minorities. The local nationalities wished to appoint suitable individuals from among themselves for these administrative positions.

Population transfers
In the Délvidék, the Serbs were transferred to Serbia, until Germany stopped this transfer, and in their place about 13,000 Székelys from Bukovina were imported. An attempt to eradicate Serb partisan action led to the Délvidék "cleansing" that cost some 3,300 victims and was stopped only after vigorous governmental intervention. It is gratifying, and unique in the history of World War II, that those responsible for the so-called "Újvidék Massacre" were immediately called to account by the government.

Educational policies
So far as the educational policies of the government were concerned, Hungarian sections were established in the minority schools. The Slovaks had 118 elementary schools, 7 middle schools, 1 commercial school, I trade school and 2 high schools. The Ruthenians had 17 middle schools, 3 high schools and also preserved their 2 teacher education schools. In North Transylvania, there were 1,345 Romanian elementary schools, where Hungarian was also taught, 4 Romanian parochial schools, 1 Romanian high school and four other high schools that had a Romanian section. In all North Transylvanian middle schools, the instruction of the Romanian language was introduced, but little attention was paid to it. In the Délvidék, instruction in 94 communities was in the Serb language, there was a Serb high school in Újvidék and a middle school was reopened. In order to balance the Ukrainian and Russian influence, the government endorsed the use of the Ruthenian language and the endeavors to develop this into a literary language.

Census
Statistical studies about the nationalities began in the 18th century under the leadership of Mátyás Bél and András Vályi. In the 19th century, Lajos Nagy and Elek Fényes recorded the languages spoken in the villages. The distribution of

the various languages spoken in the country was mapped for the first time in 1851, during the Bach era. The original questions asked referred to the mother tongue of the individual and to the language he or she actually used. The questions were refined for the 1890, 1900 and 1910 census. In many countries, including Albania, France, the Netherlands and Great Britain, there were no nationality statistics kept at this time. In Hungary in 1941, the individuals were asked to state their nationality. In 1949 and 1960, the people were again asked to identify their nationality but it was not required that this question be answered. It is an open question whether the population at large would have dared to indicate their nationality, in view of the transplantations that had taken place on a nationality basis. Thus, for instance, the expulsion of the Germans after the war was initiated by the International Control Commission, i.e., the Russians, on the basis of the 1941 census. In the 1970 census, the question about nationality was omitted on the request of the nationality associations. In 1980, it was again included in the questionnaire and in 1990 not only the mother tongue and the spoken language were asked for but the nationality of the respondent as well. Naturally, many more indicated their mother tongue than their nationality. The responses were motivated not only by fear but also by regional loyalties. Many an old Slovak woman was heard to say, "We are Hungarian Tóts (the word comes from the medieval ethnic name: Teuton.)".

In 1949, only 22,455 Germans in Hungary dared to admit that they were of German nationality. In 1960, their number rose to 50,756.

It is also an open question, whether the number of the minorities was decreasing by spontaneous assimilation, such as was clearly the case among the smaller minorities who were scattered among the Hungarian population. In 1990, the census accounted for 5,353 Romanians, 15,272 Southern-Slavs, 6,691 Slovaks and 21,893 Germans, for a total of 49,209.

Nationality Policies – Under Soviet Direction
The Hungarian minority policies after 1945 were basically a function of Hungary's belonging to the Soviet block. Deviation from the general guidelines were possible only under the shadow of Soviet supervision and if the domestic conditions were entirely favorable. In Hungary, the nationality matters were controlled by the Allied Control Committee (ACC) that viewed all issues from a strictly Soviet perspective.

According to the Soviet Army's December 22, 1944 Order of the Day, the NKVD troops surrounded the German villages and dragged off for forced labor all males between 17 and 45 and all females between 18 and 35. In most cases, the selection was made also on the basis of German-sounding surnames. Approximately 55-60,000 Hungarians and Germans were deported, of whom only about half ever came back. On the basis of the 1943 Benes-Stalin agreement, a substantial percentage of the Germans living in Hungary were deported by 1949. Until 1950, the Germans were not included in the beneficial nationality legislation and the minority educational ordinances did not apply to them. At the same time, it was very noticeable that the Soviets strongly favored the Slavic minorities. Hungary was still largely occupied by Germany and the Russian troops had barely crossed the border when the "Hungarian Slavic Anti-Fascist Front" was established in Battonya. This Front actively participated in the Slovak population exchange, being urged to do so by the Slovak commissioners. The 1945-1946 school year started under favorable auspices, with Slovak schools being opened in Pitvaros and Tótkomlós. In the latter community, a bilingual administration was introduced in 1945.

In 1945-1946 in the Szeged area, the 1918 Serb proposals for annexing this area to Yugoslavia again surfaced but the affected communities unanimously declared on October 30, 1944 that they wished to remain in Hungary. In Mohács, as late as 1946 - 1947, this subject was again raised by certain individuals.

In 1945 - 1946, Serb, Croat and Slovene schools were opened with the Hungarian Slavic Anti-Fascist Front becoming very active in this matter.

According to the Prime Minister's Ordinance No. 10030/1945, issued on October 24, 1945, the parents of ten students could request, by secret ballot, that the language of instruction be the language of the minority. If there were twenty minority students, a separate nationality school had to be set up. A member of the Yugoslav division of ACC criticized the nationality policies of the Hungarian government in 1946 because no nationality schools had been set up in the South only, those in which the nationality language, usually a local dialect, was taught. The amended 330/1946 Prime Minister's ordinance required that a school teaching in the minority language had to be set up if there were 15 students from that nationality. In areas where no community had even that many students, the ordinance mandated that regional nationality schools be set up. A substantial number of the Slovenes requested in 1946 that the language of instruction be Hungarian, because they wanted to stay within the borders of Hungary and were concerned about possible forced evacuation. The Hungarian Slavic Anti-Fascist Front and the officers of the Yugoslav Division of ACC insisted everywhere on the establishment of nationality schools, even if this brought them in conflict with the local nationality population. They also insisted on the continued education for the teachers in Serbian, Croatian and Slovenian. In 1946, a Serb and Croat teachers' college opened in Pécs.

The Southern Slav Association organized from within the Hungarian Slavic Anti-Fascist Front, requested the Ministry of Religion and Education at the end of 1947 to ask Yugoslavia for 20 instructors. The Ministry pointed out that in Hungary there was already one instructor for every 15 minority students, while in Yugoslavia, where there were 32,000 Hungarian students, there was only one instructor for every 57 students and therefore Hungary did not need Yugoslav instructors but Yugoslavia could well use additional Hungarian instructors. In fact, no Yugoslav instructors ever came to Hungary.

It also happened that the local administration did not wish to establish a Slovenian language school and was coerced to do so by the county school board on instructions from the Ministry. This happened in the County Vas community of Apátistvánfalva.

Among the Romanians and Slovaks, the Hungarian government organized the schools. The parents usually requested that the language of instruction be Hungarian with the local language being taught as a separate discipline.

The Slovak-Hungarian population exchange filled those who wished to remain in Hungary with great fear. The Slovak division of the Hungarian Slavic Anti-Fascist Front met in Békéscsaba on July 27-28, 1946 to draft a recommendation to the Paris Peace Conference according to which the exchange of the Slovak population in Hungary and of the Hungarian population in Slovakia should become mandatory. In response, there was another meeting in Békéscsaba on August 18, 1946 at which some 10,000 people, representing the neighboring Slovak villages chanted over and over again, "We will not go to Slovakia". Hungary had suffered tremendous destruction during the war and was consequently very poor. Czechoslovakia was considered a rich allied country. The Slovaks reporting for transfer went voluntarily, leaving their poverty and few poor acres behind. At the same time the Slovak authorities in the Felvidék picked the richest Hungarian peasants and forced them to move to Hungary.

In addition to the Serb, Croat, Slovene, Slovak and Romanian schools, an attempt was made to set up a German school in some areas. On request of the Soviet military authorities, the local county school authority stopped the establishment of these schools.

In September 1947, the Minister of the Interior, again claiming foreign policy and nationality policies as an excuse, issued a revised ordinance regulating the rights of the Serb, Croat and Slovene nationalities. In order to assure them of the free use of their mother tongue, the ordinance threatened an investigation against any official who would in any way interfere with this mandate. In all official locations, announcements had to be bilingual and the street names also had to appear in both languages.

The Paris Peace Treaty, signed on February 7, 1947, contributed to the deterioration of the Slovak-Hungarian relationship by attaching the Horvátjárfalu, Oroszvár and Dunacsún communities to Czechoslovakia, even though they were located on the south side of the Danube. The alleged reason was the protection of Pozsony but in reality it was done to enable Czechoslovakia to build a Danubian power station. At the same time, the Groza government's misleading propaganda with which it wished to influence the Peace Conference and recover northern Transylvania, actually contributed to the improvement of Romanian-Hungarian relations and also allayed the fears of the Romanian minority in Hungary. In 1947-1948, an increasing number of Romanian schools was established for which teachers were brought in from Romania. At Gyula, a Romanian high school was opened with 30 students.

In 1948, a Stalin pronouncement condemned the Yugoslav Communist Party and the Rajk show trial that ensued from this led to a number of arrests. In 1949-1950, in a wide belt along the southern borders of Hungary, all the Serb and Croat residents were placed on record.

The number of students in the Serb, Croat and Slovene schools continued to decline. The fear of translocations had grown.

Relocation of the Germans

The Potsdam Declaration of the Four Great Powers did not approve the complete relocation of the Hungarians from Czechoslovakia. According to the Czechoslovak-Hungarian population exchange agreement, signed in February 1946, only as many Hungarians could be relocated from Czechoslovakia as there were Slovakians in Hungary who wished to return to Czechoslovakia.

The Hungarian Interim National Government, put together with Soviet assistance, received its orders from ACC and General Sviridov on August 2, 1945. Accordingly approximately 400 to 500,000 Germans had to be moved from Hungary. The government was forced to issue its edict of expulsion on

December 29, 1945. The Germans were to be gathered into 22 camps, placed into freight cars and shipped back to Germany. The process began in January 1946 in very cold weather. Every person was allowed 20 kg. of food and 80 kg. of personal property. Life was very hard for the people after their arrival in Germany and their archaic dialect made them difficult to understand. They were often and derisively called Hungarians. By June 1, 1946 120,000 Germans had been moved by the Hungarian government but ACC wished to have another 130,000 Germans expelled. American authorities in Germany refused to accept any more Germans after July 1, 1946 but, after renewed negotiations, translocations continued into the American sector of Germany until April 1947. Germans were also transported into the Soviet sector of Germany until October 1948. The Hungarians expelled from the Felvidék were settled into the houses left empty by the expelled Germans and so were the Bukovina Székelys from the area around Bonyhád, fleeing from the Serbs in 1945. Inhuman conditions prevailed when the freight cars containing the Germans were returned to Hungary, being refused entry into Germany by the Americans. Many Hungarians took milk and food to the miserable freight car residents. The older people were particularly affected and many of them died. The number of Germans forced to leave Hungary is estimated at 173,000 but, if those who were evacuated by the retreating German army and those who fled before the advancing Soviet troops are included, the total number may be as much as 250,000.

Ecclesiastic autonomy
The Greek Orthodox Church of Gyula called on all Romanians in August of 1945 and urged them to unite in a common cause. Romanian Greek Orthodox priests, supported by the Romanian Ambassador Vincze, started an organization that was political but also served to protect the interests of the Romanian community. They wished to establish a consistory to unite the 17 Romanian dioceses, to manage the internal ecclesiastic affairs and to serve as a political and cultural focal point for the Romanians. They also thought that this organization should have state support. In other words, *they were striving for the same type of ecclesiastic autonomy that they enjoyed under the Hungarian Kingdom.* The Hungarian Communist Party, following its Socialist guidelines, recommended the establishment of Hungarian Romanian Cultural Association, a "social organization" that could be controlled by its own cadre. Evidently, in a Communist dictatorship, no autonomous ecclesiastic organization could be considered and even the existing independence was destroyed by the nationalizations, trials and imprisonments of the 1950s. The Greek Orthodox Serb schools could not escape the fate of all the Hungarian parochial schools and were in turn nationalized. For the majority nation, this meant a decline of its morality and patriotism while for the minorities it meant a loss of their language and culture.

The Catholic Church also contributed to the education of the nationalities. In Hercegszántó, there was no room for the Bunyevác school. József Grősz, the Archbishop of Kalocsa, provided two classrooms for them in the so-called convent school.

In the domestic political life, a major uproar was caused by the position taken by the Roman Catholic and Lutheran Churches concerning the translocation of the Germans. The Churches considered this move un-Christian, shortsighted and based on collective guilt and compared it to the deportation of the Jews by the Nazis. After the persecutions of the Socialist era, the position of the Churches was regularized by the 1990 Act IV. In 1991, the return of expropriated Church property was begun or alternatives were offered.

The Croat, Polish and Slovene minorities are almost 100% Roman Catholic and the Germans and Slovaks are mostly Roman Catholics, with a certain percentage belonging to the Lutheran Church. The Armenians had their very own Armenian Church. *The Bulgarian, Romanian and Serb Orthodox Churches had their own independent ecclesiastic organizations* but administratively still constituted a part of the Churches in their Mother Country. They received an annual stipend to assist with the operation of their organizations and the maintenance of their public collections.

Changes in the Status of Minority Education as a Function of Historic Events
These events, up to 1970, had a repressive effect on the minorities and the Germans and Slovaks were particularly concerned about possible translocations. Even though the government, as part of its pseudo-democratic endeavors, assisted in the establishment of minority cultural or mass organizations, ever since 1948, the German and Slovak minorities refused to send their children to the nationality schools where instruction was in the nationality language. Thus, in 1949, Slovak-teaching schools could be opened only where this coincided with the desires of the community, usually in the South of Hungary. In the linguistically closed Slovak communities, in Pilis or in Nógrád, the villagers refused to have such schools established.

It was partly because of these failures that Slovak regional schools were established, first in Budapest and then in Sátoraljaujhely. It was hoped that a boarding-school approach would ensure that instruction was given in the Slovak language. Slovak secondary schools were established in other locations, including Nagybánhegyes, but in such day schools the attendance diminished over time because of commuting. In 1949, courses in Slovak were introduced in 40 Hungarian schools located in Slovak communities and, at the Budapest Teachers' College a Slovak chair was established.

As late as 1948, the rumor of attaching the region inhabited by Slovenes to Yugoslavia made the rounds of the Slovene villages. It was for this reason that in Alsószölnök the parents refused to allow the children to go to school and the schools closed, at least temporarily. It was also in 1949 that, at the Pécs Teachers College, a chair of the Serbo-Croat Language and of the Yugoslavian Literature was created. After the death of Stalin, the atmosphere lightened and in the period between 1953 and 1956, the number of requests by Yugoslav parents for instruction in their mother tongue increased.

A German cultural association was formed and in the 1952-1953 academic year German was taught in 66 schools. The following year the number increased to 76.

At this time, about 200-220,000 Germans lived in 158 communities in 11 counties. At the end of 1955, the Ministry of Education mandated the introduction of instruction in German, at least for the first four grades.

The thaw, following the 1956 Hungarian uprising, brought a noticeable improvement in the nationality issue. The decision of the Political Committee of the Hungarian Socialist Workers' Party of October 7, 1958 prescribed a

126

greater representation for the nationalities in the National Parliament and in the local administrative structures. Announcements were to be posted in two languages, the nationality programs of the radio were to be expanded, the level of the nationality press was to improve and the requests for instruction in the pupils' mother tongue were to be met.

In reality, however, the local Party functionaries confused integration with assimilation and very little was done to improve the situation. Starting with the 1960-1961 academic year, the schools where instruction was provided in the pupils' mother tongue were closed to promote "continuing education and social adaptation". This meant the implementation of the theory of "automatism" in real life. According to the theoreticians, in the process of building Socialism, nationality differences vanished and an integrated majority nation would emerge.

After 1961, nationality education diminished more and more. The schools where instruction was given in the minority language were replaced by bilingual schools or Hungarian schools were the minority language was taught as a separate course. In the beginning of the 1960s, 2,517 children participated in nationality-based education. By the end of 1968, this number rose to 21,615, which included the children in bilingual schools and schools where the minority language was taught.

During the 1970s, the era of increasing independence from Soviet Russia, the so-called gulyás-communism period, the fear of external interference abated. In 1972, the names of schools, cultural organizations and public institutions were displayed in two or more languages in 9 counties. In more than 100 communities, the teaching of the nationality language was reintroduced, kindergarten and other teachers were being trained and the number of nationality kindergartens was growing. A Nationality Chair was established in the National Teachers College. Folk art groups, clubs, study circles and dance groups were formed and the publishing of nationality books was increased. In County Tolna alone, the number of schools teaching the nationality language increased by 37% in three years. In 1974, new nationality curricula were established and institutes were established for the study of nationality history, culture and traditions. In Universities and other schools of higher education, nationality language and culture chairs were established to promote the preparation of nationality teachers. The last one of these was the Slovene chair established at the Szombathely Teachers' College.

All this proved to be too little. A number of studies, censuses and research programs, conducted in the 1980s, demonstrated that in the bilingual educational systems, where only the language, history, literature and geography were taught in the minority language, assimilation could not be arrested among the small, scattered minority populations. A contributing factor to assimilation was the regular occurrence of mixed marriages. In the middle of the 1980s, the Romanians had 6 schools with instruction in the Romanian language, and 8 where Romanian was also taught. The corresponding numbers for the Slovaks were: 5 and 82, and for the Southern Slavs: 6 and 49. The Germans had 183 schools where German was also taught.

Pursuant to Party resolutions, the renewal and refurbishing of the nationality schools began. The paradox, however, was recognized, that while the constitution guaranteed instruction in the student's mother tongue and not in a bilingual system, even the bilingual schools did not have enough minority students to fill the classrooms.

Assimilation was also increased by the fact that the beginning students were not instructed in the local dialects, such as Bunyevác, Sokác, Gragyistye Croat, etc., but in a literary language not spoken in the homes. These literary languages, Slovak, Serbo-Croat and Romanian, were ideal for "good neighbor policy" but were in fact foreign languages that the children had to learn. These languages were not the languages of the community or of the family and were not suitable for the preservation of local traditions. This was a radical departure from the practice existing in Hungary until 1945, that made every effort to teach the beginning students in the dialect spoken in the region.

Safeguarding the interests of the minorities
According to the 1949 Constitution, and under the supervision of the Hungarian Workers' Party, the Nationality Associations were controlled by the Nationality Division of the General Education Section of the Ministry for Religion and Public Education. By 1950-1951, the local chapters of the Nationality Associations were closed and only the central offices remained open. Their primary functions were the class struggle, the removal of ecclesiastic reactionism, destruction of the kulaks, etc. Beginning in 1958, the Secretaries of the Associations became members of the National Council of the Patriotic National Front. This meant that they had become officials of the State, in accordance with the centralizing and controlling system of the Communist Party State. In essence, the administration of nationality matters remained unchanged until the change in system in 1989. The Nationality Associations were effective only in the cultural arena. About the only factors preserving national identity and traditions were the nationality press and the few cultural organizations and folk dance ensembles.

The use of language
It is inherent in the nature of Socialism that there could be no legal protection of autonomy, even on the level of the communities. Assurance of any degree of autonomy was inconsistent with the governmental structure of Socialism where social organizations, mass organizations and trade unions were all under the direct supervision of the powerful Party State. It was only accidental when the local officials were conversant with the mother tongue of the community. In practice, use of the local dialect was restricted to the family circle and to the church, where preaching was allowed in the mother tongue.

Stopping discrimination against the Germans
After the ratification of the constitution of the German Democratic Republic in 1949, the existing restrictions of the civil rights and nationality rights of the German nationality minority were gradually lifted. The process was completed in 1956. The Council of Ministers resolved, in October 1949, that so far as selecting a place to live or a job were concerned, the Germans living in Hungary had the same standing as the Hungarian citizens. In fact, the legal recognition of the right to freely select a home or employment did not grant any advantage or preference and meant only that the previously existing restrictions were lifted, at least in principle. The March 1950 ordinance of the Council of Ministers, however, was no longer restricted to domicile and employment, but granted full citizenship rights to the members of the German

minority in Hungary. It was only now that any thought could be given to the reorganization of the educational system of the German nationality.

The active and passive franchise of the German nationals over the age of 18, lost to them after World War II, was first approved again by the electoral law of 1953. In February 1955, the Council of Ministers rescinded a standing resolution of the Ministry of the Interior that made the change of names very difficult for the Germans in Hungary.

The Minority Populations in the Various Nationalities and Minorities

The few scattered nationalities, left without an intellectual class by the Trianon Peace Treaty, were reduced by 300,000 people by the trials following 1945, the mass deportations, the translocations and the forced labor service. During the years of the Communist dictatorship, deprived of all opportunities for nationality organization, the total number was reduced to 49,209, at least according to official figures. It is, therefore, surprising that many more people voted in 1994 for the establishment of minority autonomies than the number of minority members believed to be living in the country. It was at this time that the Armenians appeared for the first time along with the "accepted" minorities as a group that was considering establishing a self-government, assuring to themselves a cultural autonomy.

In 1990, 98.5% of the population claimed Hungarian as their mother tongue and 97.8% claimed to be of Hungarian nationality. Of the 10,374,823 inhabitants of Hungary, 232,751 claimed a nationality, ethnic minority status and 137,724 claimed a language other than Hungarian as their mother tongue.[94] The huge increase in the German population between 1980 and 1990, 14.8% according to the criterion of mother tongue and 231.7% according to nationality, was largely due to the fact that the new political environment made people forget their fears and encouraged them in the preservation of their nationality.

The Gypsy nation showed a significant increase in numbers. During the Communist era, attempts were made to improve its condition with social regulations and by supporting its cultural associations, periodicals and folk ensembles, notably gypsy bands. Attempts were also made to raise the Gypsy language to a literary level. The adaptation of the various groups, which did not even speak the same language, into society was made very difficult by their traditional way of life, peculiar set of values and their ensuing low level of education. The traditional social and educational methods of advancement did not prove successful in integrating the Gypsies into society.

Local autonomy

The XXXI / 1989 Act of Constitution had the following to say about the nationalities: "The Hungarian Republic protects the national and linguistic minorities. Assures their collective participation in public life, the nurturing of their own culture, the use of their mother tongue and the right to receive education in their own language." Following the enactment of Act No. LXXVII of 1993, new demands were made and the activity of the minorities showed a marked increase, since this Act about the rights of the minorities offered not only cultural autonomy but also the

---

[94] Ibolya Dávid: J 1397. Sz. Beszámoló a Magyar Köztársaság területén élő nemzeti és etnikai kisebbségek helyzetéről (Report by the Minister of Justice on the situation of national and ethnic minorities living in Hungary), no. J 1397.

possibility of territorial autonomy. As a result of the 1988 elections, 1,360 local autonomies were established (Bulgarian, Gypsy, Greek, Croat, Polish, German, Romanian, Armenian, Ruthenian and Serb). In the capital alone, 9 minority autonomies were established. This represented a 65.5% increase over the previous election four years earlier. 658 local autonomies were created in communities that previously had no autonomous structure. The votes cast included the sympathy vote of the majority and reflected the societal support gained by the minorities.

Nationality representation in Parliament, outside of the established political parties, would be possible only in the context of a two-chamber Parliament.

The Czech Republic and Slovakia

Czech Republic: Population (1995): 10,330,000
Ethnic groups: Czech - 81%, Moravian - 13%, Slovak - 3%, German and Gypsy- 0.6%,
Hungarian - 0.1%.
Official language: Czech.

Slovakia: Population (1995): 5,367,800
Ethnic groups: Slovak - 86.6%, Hungarian - 10.8%, Gypsy - 1.44%, Czech - 1.2%,
Ruthenian - 0.33%, Ukrainian - 0.25%, Moravian - 0.11%, German - 0.1%, Polish -
0.05%.
Official language: Slovak.

The Minorities Between the Two World Wars (1919-1945)

The peace treaties at the end of World War I made 30 million people into minorities. Their protection should have been the responsibility of the minority protective organizations under the auspices of the League of Nations. It was the complete failure of these organizations that led to the growth of internal tensions in the new nations. This ultimately led to their ruin and consequently to World War II.

The Peace Treaty, signed on June 4, 1920 in the Little Trianon Palace, consigned a total of over one million Hungarians to an existence North of the new Hungarian-Czechoslovak border. Of these, according to the 1910 census, 893,586 lived in the former Felvidék (now Slovakia) representing 30.55% of the total population. In the Kárpátalja, also assigned to Czechoslovakia, there were 176,294 Hungarians, representing 29.6% of the population. Slovaks made up 58% of the population of the Felvidék, with the remainder being distributed between Ruthenians, Germans and Poles. At the Treaty of St. Germain in 1919, Czechoslovakia made a commitment to respect the individual and collective rights of the Hungarians living in that country.

Accordingly, the Kárpátalja should have been given autonomy and the Germans, representing about 25% of the population, should have been given special standing. Kárpátalja, in fact, never received autonomy, with the excuse that the political sophistication of the population was too low. The Czechoslovak constitution, enacted in 1920, declared that, "Its citizens were equal in law and enjoyed the same civil and political rights regardless of race, language or religion." Belonging to a minority could not be a detriment in filling official or other positions. The constitution guaranteed the free use of the minority language in com-

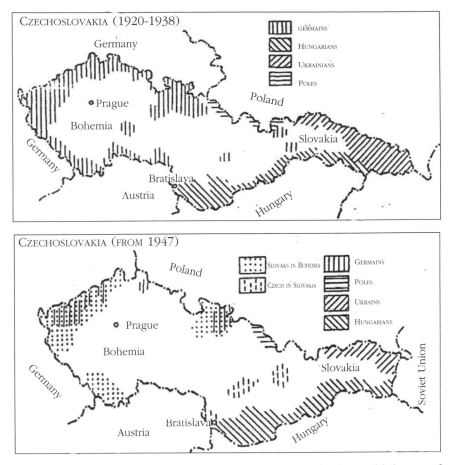

CZECHOSLOVAKIA (1920-1938)

Germany

| | | | GERMAINS
| | | | HUNGARIANS
| | | | UKRAINIANS
| | | | POLES

Prague
Bohemia
Germany
Poland
Slovakia
Bratislava
Austria
Hungary

CZECHOSLOVAKIA (FROM 1947)

Poland

| | | | SLOVAKS IN BOHEMIA
| | | | CZECH IN SLOVAKIA
| | | | GERMAINS
| | | | POLES
| | | | UKRAINS
| | | | HUNGARIANS

Prague
Bohemia
Germany
Slovakia
Soviet Union
Bratislava
Austria
Hungary

merce and in the press. The State assumed responsibility for the establishment of a school system in the minority language and even agreed that the minorities had a right to participate in national, regional and local budgetary matters on a proportional basis. It condemned discrimination between the minorities. "No system or effort leading to a loss of nationality was permitted. Any infraction of this principle was punishable by law." [95]

Denial of citizenship and replacement of public servants

From 1918 until 1924, a total of 106,841 voluntary emigrants moved to the Trianon Hungary from Czechoslovakia. They were mostly public servants refusing to take the oath of loyalty, railway employees and intellectuals and their family. Instead of the automatic right to citizenship, guaranteed even in the Peace Treaty, the Prague government tied the issuance of citizenship to a variety of conditions.

---

[95] Gyula Popély: Népfogyatkozás, (The Decrease of Population) Regio, Bp., 1991. pp. 41-42.

The language law, curtailment and taxation of the use of the language

The use of the official language was prescribed by Act 122 of 1920, the so-called "Language Law". It guaranteed the use of the mother tongue for all the minorities who represented at least 20% of the population in a given district. It also ordered that in all districts having at least 20% minority population, the official announcements of state offices, courts and authorities had to be made in the language of the minority as well and that all offices had to have identifying name plates in both languages. The Language Law set the 20% quota for the district and not for the cities, which meant that in Slovak districts the urban Hungarians could not muster the necessary numbers to reach 20% of the overall population. Thus, while the international agreements obliged Czechoslovakia to facilitate things for the non-Czech-speaking minorities in their contacts with governmental agencies and offices by allowing the use of their mother tongue, Czechoslovakia tied this privilege to the requirement of meeting a fairly high percentage of the total population. This, in fact, curtailed the use of the native language in many areas.

There were some individuals in Czechoslovakia who were critical of this law and of the political goals hiding behind it. Thus Emanuel Radl, a professor at the University of Prague, wrote in an essay examining this issue, "The Language Law is not an attempt to resolve the nationality problem equitably, but it is a tool in the fight against the Germans and the Hungarians".[96]

The Language Law was sabotaged by local authorities. Jozef Bellay, the Lord Lieutenant of County Trencsén, issued a circular on August 26, 1921, addressed to all judges, mayors, police chief, gendarmes and fiscal officer stations, in which he instructed the recipients to proceed in the most forceful fashion against those who dared to speak Hungarian in public places and thus "protect the prestige of our country against the provocative indecency of some people". Bellay justified his instructions by stating that, "After all, we are living in Slovakia and the language is the life of the country." In County Gömör, Sousedik, the judge of the Nagyrőce district, was one of the flag bearers in the fight against the Hungarian language. In one of his ordinances of 1922, he forbade the singing of Hungarian songs. He stated: "According to this ordinance, the singing of Hungarian songs in any tavern, public place, in the street or at an outing is strictly forbidden under the most severe penalties of law." Igor Thurzo, the Túrócszentmárton judge issued a proclamation on July 31, 1922 in which he stated: "It is incomprehensible and against nature that a part of our population still prattles in Hungarian and thereby provokes our peace-loving citizens."[97] It happened even in the 1970s, on a train, on a bus or in the street that somebody admonished the Hungarians that, "since they are eating Slovakian bread, they must speak Slovakian."

---

[96] Gyula Popély: A csehszlovákiai magyarság a népszámlálasok tükrében 1918-1945. (The Hungarians in Czechoslovakia in light of the census figures 1918-1945.) Regio Könyvek, Bp. 1991, p. 44. Some of the details are taken from a speech by Popély at the Kassa Zoltán Fábry Memorial, Oct.25.1992;
László Szarka: Adatok a csehszlovákiai magyar kisebbségről (Data about the Hungarian minority in Czechoslovakia): História: p. 32.

[97] Miklós Duray: Kettős elnyomásban, (In Dual Oppression) Madách, Polonium, Pozsony (Bratislava), 1993, p. 114.

Reorganization of the administration

In all of the successor states, the purpose of redrawing the district and county lines was to make sure that in the newly designed administrative units the Hungarians never reached the percentage of the population prescribed by the Language Law and thus, they could have the use of their mother tongue withheld from them.

The districts were reorganized in such a fashion that the number of them, where the minorities reached the required percentage, be kept to a minimum. Since the Hungarians lived along the new boundary line in a solid block, in a belt approximately 50 km. wide, the re-districting was done by the creation of long, narrow strips in a North-South direction. In the 1920s, the Hungarians were at a serious disadvantage in the districts of Pozsony, Kassa, Rimaszombat, Nyitra and Gálszécs. Since they did not represent 20% of the population in these districts, the Ministry of Justice prohibited the use of the Hungarian language. The highest administrative court ruled in the case of Rimaszombat that the ordinance was illegal, but even this could not implement a change since the 1930 census alleged an even smaller percentage for the Hungarians. In 1922, 35 five towns in Slovakia and the Kárpátalja were demoted to the status of villages, decreasing the influence of the Hungarians in the given territories, weakening the urban population, which was the guardian of the national identity and of the national culture and eliminating all autonomous organizations.

Elections and the gerrymandering of electoral districts

Even though the franchise was universal, direct and secret, the electoral districts could be arranged so that, in addition to Czechoslovak citizenship, there were clear distinctions between districts. In a Slovak area in 1920, 19,753 votes were required to elect a representative, while in a Hungarian district 27,697 votes (40% more) were needed to achieve the same purpose. In senatorial elections, the situation was the same. To elect a senator in Prague took 73,949 votes, in Érsekujvár it took 105,504 and in the Kárpátalja it took 143,007. Additional discrimination was shown by the fact that it took 100 signatures to nominate a candidate in the Czech provinces and 1,000 in Slovakia.[98]

Unreliable census figures

The last internationally recognized census in the Carpathian Basin was conducted in 1910. Because of intimidation and manipulation of the census data after World War I, there are no reliable figures on the number of Hungarians living beyond the borders of Hungary.

While the Language Law spoke only of linguistic minorities and linked the official use of the mother tongue to a population ratio of 20%, the governmental ordinance regulating the census required that the respondents identify their nationality. The 1921 census left it to the individual respondents to identify their own nationality, but reserved the right to modify the data by the census-takers, supervisors and political authorities. Needless to say, this opened the door to systematic abuses. In some locations, the Hungarians registered their complaints before a Notary Public. Jews were listed separately from Hungarians and everybody with

---

[98] Endre Arató: Tanulmányok a szlovákiai magyarok történetéből 1919-1945. (Essays on the History of Hungarians in Slovakia) Bp., Magvető Kiadó, 1977. pp. 54-59.

an "unregulated citizenship" was listed as a foreigner. The 1921 census showed 245,000 fewer Hungarians living in the area than at the time of the 1910 Hungarian census. At the 1930 census, the census-takers showed great ingenuity in recording "nationality".[99] Numerous abuses were committed and the result was that, according to this census, the number of Hungarians had decreased by 76,000.

Curtailment of the industrial development of the area
Between the two Wars, it was mainly the Czech industry that showed major developments. The Prague leadership penalized Slovakia with unfavorable tax and tariff restrictions. A large number of Slovakian factories were closed. Between 1919 and 1926, mining and smelting decreased by 25.7%, metal industry by 29.2% and the building industry by 2%.[100]

After World War II, major industrial investments were made, particularly in the northern, principally Slovak, areas. The southern areas, inhabited primarily by Hungarians, became economically the most neglected regions of the Slovakia. Of the investment portion of the national budget, between 1970 and 1975, 71-75% less was assigned per person in the Hungarian areas that in the other parts of Slovakia. When new industrial centers were established, as for instance in Kassa, Slovak skilled workers were brought in and this further diluted the ethnic ratios in the city.

Taxation policies
Income tax was 10% in Slovakia and in the Kárpátalja, while it was only 4% in the Czech provinces. While Slovak taxes contributed 15% of the national revenues, its share of the budget was only 6%.

Discriminatory credit policy
Almost two thirds (61.1%) of the former Hungarian financial institutions were now in the neighboring countries. In 1921, the assets of the Slovak banks exceeded that of the Hungarian ones. As a consequence of the subsequent Czech banking regulations, the number of Hungarian Banks and financial institutions was reduced from 30 to 7.

Land reform, resettlement and emigration
In the areas inhabited by Hungarians, about 35% of the estates were expropriated. The Hungarian agricultural workers and poor peasants received only about one quarter of the land to which they were entitled. Slovak settlers were brought to the Hungarian areas. Of the 94 new Slovak settlements, 64 were established in Hungarian areas. Of all the Slovak and Czech Legion settlements, 77% were located in Hungarian areas in order to dilute the Hungarian ethnic group. It is not an accident that the largest Czech and Slovak settlements were established in the purely Hungarian Csallóköz and Tiszahát regions. Those Hungarians who were left without land sought employment in the Czech provinces or emigrated.

---

[99] M. Duray, ibid, p. 101and Gy. Popély, ibid, pp. 68, 69, 77.
[100] Miklós Duray: Kettős elnyomásban (In Dual Oppression) Madách-Posonium, Pozsony, 1993, p. 101.

Reduction of schools, displacement of teachers, curtailment of the numbers of minority intellectuals and numerus clausus

On the Czech side of the Czech-German border, the so-called Sudetenland, the German schools and cultural institutions were preserved in the German majority districts. There was a German university in Prague and in Brno.

In the districts with Slovak majorities, all Hungarian schools were closed. Due to dismissals and expatriation of Hungarian teachers, their number decreased from 2,182 to 1,521 between 1921 and 1930.

In the districts with a Hungarian majority, the schools where Hungarian was the language of instruction continued to decrease in numbers. In the 1920-1921 academic year, approximately 90,000, of a total of 120,000, children attended in 720 Hungarian schools. By 1926-1927, their number was reduced to 66,260. In 1936-1937, there were 446 Hungarian communities where, regardless of the percentage of Hungarians, Slovak schools were established. During the same year, there were also 126 Hungarian communities, where there were more than the legally prescribed 40 students and yet no school was set up for them.

The Hungarian schools received less financial support that the Slovak ones and the Hungarian parents were given all sorts of enticements to send their children to Slovak schools. There were only about 900-1,000 Hungarian university students in Czechoslovakia in 1938, at a time when there were a total of 30,564 students. The number of Hungarian students did not approach the 5.5% set as the nationality quota.[101]

The Position of the Churches in the Absence of Autonomy

Church organizations were the principal transmitters of the language and of the cultural traditions of the nationalities and minorities. One of the criteria for this transmittal was that the services be conducted in the minority language and that the priests come from the minority group. The Church could also become the refuge for the intellectuals, anxious to maintain their national identity, who had been forced to leave their offices, schools and scholarly activities.

In the bourgeois, democratic Czechoslovakia only the Reformed Church had its autonomy. Only one Hungarian higher educational institute was established, the Losonc Reformed Seminary which, starting in 1925, produced the Hungarian Reformed clergy.

Promises of Autonomy

According to a Czechoslovak agreement reached with emigrant groups in Pittsburgh, Pa., May 1918, and also according to the Peace Treaty, Slovakia and the Kárpátalja were supposed to have a far-reaching autonomy. This never came about and the entire centralized country was governed from Prague with Czech officials replacing the German and Hungarian ones.

The appeasement policy vis-à-vis Germany, practiced by the British Prime Minister Chamberlain between 1937 and 1939, brought about a change in the direction of British policies. When Arthur Toynbee, the Director of the Royal Foreign Affairs Institute, visited Budapest in 1937, he spoke of the need to peacefully revise the boundaries of Hungary. By the end of 1937, A.C.

---

[101] Károly Vígh: A szlovákiai magyarság sorsa (Fate of the Hungarians in Slovakia) Népek Hazája sorozat, p. 83.

Macartney, an expert in Hungarian affairs, prepared a detailed recommendation for the revision of the boundaries for the above Institute.

Urged by Great Britain, the Little Entente countries brought their two-year old discussions to a successful conclusion on August 23, 1938. The Little Entente recognized that Hungary had equal rights to re-arm and agreed to improve the situation of the minorities in exchange for Hungary's agreement not to use force in its drive for boundary revisions. Under the pressure of events, a legislative proposal was prepared in 1938, according to which a certain measure of autonomy was to be granted to the minorities. This did not satisfy Hungary, which wanted nationality self-government with legislative and executive powers.

THE KÁRPÁTALJA HUNGARIANS AND RUTHENIANS IN CZECHOSLOVAKIA

In McKeesport, Pa., on June 26, 1918, The American Ruthenian National Council was established under the leadership of the attorney Gregorij Žatkovič in order to present a united front in Paris when the map of Europe was re-drawn. According to the 1910 census, the population of the Kárpátalja consisted of Hungarians (29.2%), Ruthenians (56.15%), Germans (10.66%) and Slovaks (1.3%). Following the McKeesport meeting, Žatkovič met with the future President of Czechoslovakia, Thomas Masaryk in Philadelphia, Pa. They signed a declaration, according to which "the Ruthenians in Hungary will join the Czechoslovak Democratic Republic as a sovereign nation with complete autonomy".[102] This was approved by the National Council in November. At the same time, the Ruthenians in Hungary, unaware of the American Ruthenian-Czech agreement, formed several organizations on the request of the Károlyi government, and agreed that the Hungarian Ruthenian National Council, established in Ungvár in 1918, would be the sole legal representative of the Hungarian Ruthenians. This National Council declared that it adhered firmly to Hungary and to Hungary's territorial integrity.

On November 24, 1918, the National Council and the Hungarian Government addressed a joint proclamation to the Ruthenian people, which announced the granting of full autonomy. During implementation, they could enjoy full nationality privileges, might use the Julian calendar, use the Ruthenian language in schools, offices and courts and even hinted at the possibility of a land reform. As part of the agreement with the National Council, the government appointed Ruthenian Lord Lieutenants to head the four counties that had a Ruthenian majority and also started to formulate a Ruthenian autonomy. The autonomy envisioned that foreign affairs, military affairs, railways, social services, citizenship issues and civil and criminal law would be jointly administered. At a meeting in Budapest on December 10, 1918 the representatives of the Ruthenian communities accepted the proposal and protested against being attached to Czechoslovakia. Act X of 1918, published on December 24, 1918 proclaimed the establishment of autonomous organizations and scheduled elections. On instruction of President Wilson, Lieutenant Goodwin visited Kárpátalja on March 2-12. In spite of the fact that Goodwin reported that the Ruthenians, having achieved autonomy wished to remain in Hungary, Clemenceau had already committed himself to the Czech point of view. On March 19, 1919 Colonel Vyx transmitted

---

[102] István Pirigyi: Kárpátalja In: Keresztény Magyar Vetés újság (Christian Hungarian Sowing paper), 1994, VII.31.

the Entente note to the Government in which the evacuation of a large part of the Tiszántúl was demanded under the pretext of establishing a demilitarized zone. This demand was unacceptable to the Government that had already met many of the Entente demands. At the same time, encircled by hostile and advancing Entente armies, the government considered resistance hopeless and resigned. The hopeless situation was a suitable environment for the Communist dictatorship that was the only group still willing to show some resistance. This, in turn, gave further excuse to the Entente to interfere and also gave justification for further territorial gains. Czech troops marched into the Kárpátalja.

Promises of autonomy with League of Nations guarantee
The Saint Germain Laye treaty assured autonomy for the Kárpátalja on September 10, 1919. This was guaranteed by the League of Nations on November 20, 1920. In practice, none of this ever happened. The Kárpátalja became a province of the Czechoslovak Republic under the name of Podkarpatska Rus.

Denial of citizenship and dismissal of public officials
Heeding the command of the Károlyi government, many officials and state employees refused to take the oath of loyalty to the occupying forces prior to the signing of the Peace Treaty. Many of them refused, even after the signing, and they all lost their jobs. Those who were not native in the Kárpátalja were expelled. Antal Papp, the Greek Catholic bishop of Munkács was forcibly put across the border in 1925. The officials were replaced with Czech citizens. The Hungarians, to survive, frequently claimed to be Ruthenians or Slovaks.

The only Hungarian high school was in Beregszász, but even this one was led by Czech principals. There could be a public or parochial elementary school in every Hungarian village.

Land reform and settlement of the border regions
Land reform was based on political considerations. The native Hungarians could not get any land along the Trianon border and Ruthenians from the mountain areas were settled there. The purpose was clearly to change the ethnic ratios to the detriment of the Hungarians who had lived in a block along the border.

The situation of the Churches
It was due to the cooperation of the clergy of all the denominations that Jenő Ortutay, the Greek Catholic Archdeacon, was elected mayor of Beregszász. The Pan Slavic movement gained strength in Russia around the turn of the century. This led to an orientation toward the Ukraine and toward Russia, which in turn inspired large numbers to convert from the Greek Catholic religion to the Greek Orthodox one. The Czech authorities supported this schismatic movement, since right from its onset, it had a strong anti-Hungarian coloration. The Ruthenian Greek Catholic Church, Unitas, was essentially destroyed. Churches were demolished and atrocities were committed against the congregation. The "Greater Russian" trend was promoted by the Orthodox clergy fleeing to this area from the Communist regime in Russia. This trend was opposed by the Galician Greek Catholic Ukrainians, known as "Little Russians". The language and religious struggles were only a façade for the Ruthenian search for identity. In actuality the majority wished to return to Hungary.

Territorial re-annexation and its consequences

The 1938 München agreement not only mandated the transfer of the Sudetenland to Germany but also ordered bilateral discussions concerning the Polish and Hungarian minority areas of Czechoslovakia. In case these discussions were unsuccessful, an arbitration panel was to render a judgment. The Polish and Hungarian demands were mentioned only in the appendix of the München agreement. Great Britain notified the Prague government that, "under the present circumstances, it has become necessary to make territorial concessions to Hungary and that the Czech government had to accept this immediately and honestly."[103]

It was after these preliminaries that the autonomous Ruthenian government was established on October 9, 1938 under the leadership of András Bródy. Since at the Joint Ministerial Council meeting on October 25, he recommended that a plebiscite be called to determine whether the area should belong to Hungary or to Czechoslovakia, he was jailed and Augustin Volosin was appointed in his place.

Because the Hungarian-Czechoslovak negotiations in Komárom did not produce any results, the issue was referred to an international arbitration panel for a decision, which had been the original intent of the Czechoslovak delegation, consisting almost exclusively of Slovaks. According to the First Vienna Decision, handed down on November 2, 1938, Ungvár, Munkács, Beregszász and the surrounding territories, a total of 12,000 km² were returned to Hungary. The population of this area was 85% Hungarian. Thus Kárpátalja was divided into two parts. The Czechoslovak portion, under the leadership of Volosin, moved its capital to Huszt. On November 22, the Czechoslovak Parliament recognized the constitution of the autonomous Kárpát-Ukraine.

When Czechoslovakia disintegrated in March of 1939, an independent Slovakia was proclaimed on March 14 by Volosin, who was elected President on the next day. Germany notified Hungary about the collapse of Czechoslovakia and urged it to take advantage of the power vacuum.

Between March 14 and 18, 1939, Hungarian troops marched into the Kárpátalja and a territory of 12,171 km² and 496,000 inhabitants were re-annexed to Hungary. Because of World War II, the promised autonomy for the Kárpátalja could not be implemented, but the Ministerial Council ruled on May 23, 1939 that in the Kárpátalja, the Hungarian and Kárpát-Ukrainian (Ruthenian) languages were both official languages of equal standing. This ruling was announced by the Prime Minister, Count Pál Teleki.

In 1941, the Allies recognized the Czechoslovak émigré government in London, under the former President of the country, Eduard Beneš, and accepted restoration of the former boundaries, at least in principle.

At the Moscow negotiations between Beneš and Stalin, in 1943, Stalin promised that after the victory, the Hungarian minority would be expelled from Slovakia.

---

[103] Ignác Romsich: Helyünk és sorsunk a Duna-medencében (Our place and fate in the Danube Basin), Osiris, Bp., 1996, p. 102; Romsich, ibid. p. 107; Csicsery-Vigh: Teleki Pál és kora (Pál Teleki and his Era), p. 40; C.A. Macartney: Teleki Pál miniszterelnöksége (The Prime Ministership of Pál Teleki), p. 137.

The Years when the Minorities in Czechoslovakia were Deprived of their Rights (1945-1948)

The Soviet army reached the eastern area of Slovakia in the fall of 1944 and, as soon as the front moved on, the Slovak National Council was organized. The manifesto of the Council was published on February 4, 1945. It began, "The new Czechoslovak Republic will be a Slavic People's Republic." In March 1945, the program of the returning Czechoslovak government was worked out jointly by the London and Moscow refugee groups. This program was approved by the leader of the London Czech émigré government, Eduard Beneš.

Denial of citizenship and dismissal of public officials

Chapter VIII of the government program announced in Kassa on April 5, 1945 declared that the Germans and the Hungarians were collective criminals and demanded that all citizen rights be withdrawn from them. Only those could expect a return of their citizenship who actively fought against Fascism, the others were declared to be expatriates who were expelled from the Republic "forever". According to Chapter IX, their property with all buildings standing on it became the property of the State.

Ordinance 44/1945 of the Slovak National Council, issued on May 25, 1945 echoed the spirit of the governmental program of Kassa and stated that all public officials of Hungarian extraction had to be dismissed immediately and that, after May 31, payment of pensions to former public officials of Hungarian extraction would be halted. The justification was simply, "Hungarian nationality".[104]

Presidential Decree 33/1945, promulgated on August 2, 1945 made the Hungarian and German population in Czechoslovakia homeless. This had happened to the Slovak Jews in 1942 with constitutional ordinance No. 68, but they were also ordered to be deported. Loss of the citizenship meant that the Hungarians and Germans could not join any of the regular political parties, could not participate in elections, lost their pension and were ineligible for any public employment.

Ethnic cleansing, imprisonment, retributions and intimidations[105]

During the spring and summer of 1945, large numbers of Hungarians in Slovakia were interned or removed to labor camps. During the fall and winter of 1944, approximately 10,000 Hungarians were deported from the eastern parts of Slovakia to the Soviet Union from where the survivors could return only after 3 1/2 years. At the People's Court sessions, Hungarians were often found guilty by former Slovak fascists, Hlinka Guardists or members of the Hlinka Party. Thousands of the Hungarian defendants were declared to be war criminals. The politically unreliables could be held in jail for years without any judicial action.

As a result of the imposed 1946 Hungarian-Czechoslovak people exchange, 76,616 Hungarians were forcibly relocated to Hungary. During the "re-Slovakization campaign" of 1946, 326,679 Hungarians were sufficiently intimidated to claim to be Slovaks and about 10,000 fled to Hungary. Presidential decree 71/1945, issued on September 19, 1945 ordered that all men who had lost their

---

[104] Katalin Vadkerty: A reszlovákizáció (Reslovakization) Kalligram, Pozsony, 1993, p. 11.
[105] K. Vadkerty: Magyar sors Csehszlovákiában (Life of Hungarians in Czechoslovakia) História, 1997/2, pp. 3-7.

citizenship, and who were unemployed, had to report for labor. The edict of October 1, 1945, No. 88/1945, addressed the forced labor issue. Accordingly all men between 16 and 55 and all women between 18 and 45 could be condemned to forced labor for periods up to three years. This process was contemporaneous with the settling of Slovakians into the Hungarian areas of southern Slovakia and affected 9,247 Hungarian men and women.

In November 1946, the deportation of the Hungarians from southern Slovakia to Bohemia and Moravia began. The authorities had the Hungarian villages surrounded by troops, made the residents pack a few essentials and then herded them into cattle cars for transport to Bohemia. There were a total of approximately 60,000 Hungarians in this area, of whom approximately 44,000 were deported from 393 locations. Because of the frost and the rough handling, many died on the trip. The authorities then settled Slovaks into the houses and estates of the displaced Hungarians. According to estimates, the Hungarians abandoned property worth approximately 235,550 Czech K. The terrified Hungarians started to flee. The escapees heard frequent rifle fire and the precise number of the victims is not known.

State Secretary Vladimir Clementis calmed concerned parties by saying: "We can treat the Hungarians living within our borders any which way we want to."[106]

Loss of property
Ordinance No.4 of the Slovak National Council was approved on February 27, 1945 and was titled, "On the confiscation of the agricultural property of the Germans, Hungarians and traitors and enemies of the Slovak Nation." Confiscation of all property was decreed by the Presidential decree No.108/1945. The confiscation of Hungarian agricultural real estate began. Katalin Vadkerty estimates that the total area confiscated amounted to 614,462 hectares. Hungarian small and medium-sized enterprises were taken into state custody. In the towns, the Hungarian apartments and houses were expropriated. All real and other assets confiscated were distributed among Slovak claimants.

As a consequence of the population exchange that was not completed until the end of 1948, the Hungarians moved to Hungary left behind much greater assets in land and houses, than the Czechoslovaks did in Hungary. In the agreement of Lake Csorba, in 1949, the Hungarian Communist regime relinquished all claims for this property. The so-called Beneš decrees have never been rescinded and the compensation of the Hungarians in Slovakia had not been enacted to date.

Changes in community and personal names
The attempts to change the names of Hungarian communities go back to the first half of the last century, when the Slovak language became a literary one. It was at this time that the name Bratislava was first coined for the city of Pozsony. In 1948, the changing of the Hungarian name of the communities began again. At the same time, the Slovak officials insisted that Hungarian family names be spelled according to Slovak pronunciation and spelling. A special permit was required for the bestowing of a Hungarian first name.

---

[106] Vadkerty, Ibid.

140

Reduction of the number of schools, dismissal of teachers and curtailment of the number of minority intellectuals

According to decree No. 1944/6, all Hungarian and German schools opened after the re-annexation in the Felvidék had to be closed.

When the Slovak National Councils took over administrative control from the Soviet military authorities in May 1945, all Hungarian schools were closed, all Hungarian teachers were dismissed and all Hungarian printed material was banned. All Hungarian cultural and protective organizations were disbanded and their assets were seized.

The so-called Local National Councils mandated that the use of the Hungarian language in public places be forbidden. When the Communists came to power in 1948, conditions improved and elementary and secondary education in Hungarian was restarted. Yet, even in the 1970s, there were so few Hungarian middle schools that only 30-35% of the 15 year-old Hungarian students could receive instruction in their mother tongue. At the same time, a ministerial edict required that only those could apply to a foreign university, including in Hungary, who had graduated from a high school where the Slovak was the language of instruction. Parents frequently entered their children in Slovak schools because they were afraid of, or intimidated by, the local, urban, National Councils.

When the first classes in Hungarian began in 1949, only 110 Hungarian teachers were available, about 5% of the former number. For many years, untrained teachers taught the Hungarian children. At the beginning of the 1950s, the Hungarian schools were in deplorable shape and many of them were in temporary buildings. In many schools, there was no running water, the walls were damp, etc. The repairs were made by the older students, the parents and the teachers.

No new buildings were erected for Hungarian education until the late 1960s. Only Slovak children were taught in good buildings. In 1921, there were about 720 Hungarian schools in Slovakia, their number decreased to 376 by 1977. Between 1950 and 1978, 233 Hungarian schools were discontinued. Only 30% of the Hungarians graduated as compared to 43% of the Slovaks. Even today, training for the skilled trades is largely limited to Slovaks.

The greatest deficiencies were in higher education. In 1977, for example, only 5.9% of the 19 year-old Hungarians were admitted to a University or other establishment of higher education.

The Period Between 1948 and 1990

The year 1947-1948 was a turning point in the post-World War II Soviet sphere of interest. By this time, in every country, the alleged multi-party democracy was put aside and power was everywhere concentrated in the hands of the Communist Party. By nationalization and expropriation, the Soviet-style economic and social system was implemented. The minorities no longer represented a threat to the centralized economic and political powers and therefore, on the model of the Soviet nationality policy system, and in accordance with "shop-window policy", certain cultural organizations were permitted, albeit only under Party supervision.

In October 1948, citizenship was returned to the Hungarians, although this did not grant minority rights. The November 4, 1948 edict exempted land holdings of less than 50 hectares from confiscation, if the owner had his citizenship restored. The edict did not apply to land that had been distributed to Slovak settlers and repatriates.

In the life of the Eastern European countries, the death of Stalin in 1953 and the relaxation following the XXth Party Congress, brought significant improvements. The faulty economic policies of the 1950s led to political insecurity and to the appearance of more moderate, "revisionist" elements within the Communist Party. The Polish and Hungarian events of 1956 also left their mark on the minority policies of the neighboring countries. According to the Czechoslovak July 1956 Constitution, "Favorable conditions must be assured for the economic and cultural life of the Hungarians and Ruthenians." According to the 1960 Constitution, "The State guarantees every opportunity and all necessary tools for the Hungarian, Ukrainian and Polish citizens to receive instruction in their mother tongue". This law still excluded the Germans and the Gypsies. The 1968 Constitutional Act, in section 143, converted the Republic into a Federation and thus the Hungarian nationality issues became a matter of domestic policies for the Slovak Federal State. The cultural and educational improvements promised by the 1968 Act, section 144, remained largely unfulfilled since no implementation legislation was ever enacted.

Establishment of Border Protective Belts and Administrative Changes
Czech and Slovak settlers moved into the areas from which Hungarians had either emigrated or were expelled. The Government organized it carefully and after 1945, about 30 new settlements were created. Between 1945 and 1948, at least 150 villages, previously 100% Hungarian, acquired a mixed population and this process continued for a long time. The new settlements and the villages becoming increasingly Slovak were placed at a great advantage when the administration was reorganized in 1960. In 1960, the administrative districts were reorganized. The small districts were fused into larger ones and these larger districts were organized into provinces. The boundaries of the districts were drawn so that the Hungarian population became a minority. Only two districts remained largely Hungarian, Dunaszerdahely and Komárom.

Discriminatory economic policies
By the end of the years when the Hungarians were deprived of their civil rights, the Hungarian intellectual and official class had all but disappeared while the farmer class was decimated by deportations. The rural population escaping into industry could find only menial jobs as unskilled labor. The investment and employment statistics reveal that industrialization was promoted almost exclusively in the Slovak settlements, on the Slovak side of the linguistic border and in the increasingly Slovak cities, like Kassa, Vágsellye and Rimaszombat. The skilled workforce required by the newly developing industries in Kassa was recruited exclusively from among the younger Slovak generation. The southern Slovak districts, populated largely by Hungarians, had significantly smaller budgetary allocations than the Slovak districts. Thus, these areas had to remain primarily agricultural. Even in this, they were placed at a disadvantage. In several districts, the Hungarian cooperatives were more economically successful, but in these areas the governmental allocation of equipment strongly favored the weaker Slovak cooperatives.

In the 1970s, the Slovak agricultural cooperatives were fused with the Hungarian ones, but the leadership was almost always Slovak and any adjustment necessary was always made in favor of the Slovaks. The results of the discriminatory economic policies became evident in the 1970s statistical data. The number of Hungarians employed in industry increased slightly, but mostly as auxiliary work force and as warehouse workers. The bulk of the Hungarian workforce was still employed in agriculture. The average income in the Hungarian districts in southern Slovakia was far below the national average, even as late as the end of the 1980s.[107]

For all these reasons, the capitalist entrepreneur group, emerging after the change in the system, came almost entirely from the majority Slovak population even in the areas with large Hungarian minorities.

Industrialization and the Change in Population Ratios
The employment opportunities created by rapid industrialization and all the new jobs made available by new industries and improved and expanded services were largely and intentionally reserved for Slovaks.

Because of this scarcity of employment opportunities, Hungarian youth had to seek employment far from home. Almost half of the Hungarian population was thus forced into such a commuting existence even today, since industrial expansion was very slow from the northern industrial regions in the direction of the primarily agricultural southern districts.

Because of their inadequate training, most of the Hungarian workforce finds employment in the building trades.

Lack of autonomy for the churches
In every country under a socialist regime, the clergy was tightly controlled, religious education was restricted to the church buildings, the clergy was harassed by the Ecclesiastic Affairs administration and individual clergymen were frequently under police observation.

The Slovakian Hungarians had fewer and fewer clergymen of Hungarian extraction and they were subject to Slovak bishops. Teaching and preaching in Hungarian became increasingly rare and the number of Hungarian parishes decreased very rapidly. Catholic priests were trained only in Pozsony and, until the end of the 1980s, the authorities regulated the number of seminarians. Of about 130 to 150 seminary students in the middle of the 1970s, only ten spoke Hungarian. Instruction was in Slovakian and it was not permitted that Hungarians be trained in their mother country.

The only Church with any autonomy was the Reformed (Protestant) one and hence it was diocese-based and uniformly Hungarian in character.

The smallest denomination was Lutheran, numbering only a few thousand. The Hungarians no longer have any individual congregations and there is no independent training for Hungarian Lutheran clergy.

In Slovakia, the Hungarian population decreased by 20% between 1910 and 1991, while the Slovak population increased by 30%. The German population has, for all practical purposes, disappeared.

Nowadays, in Slovakia, the Hungarians wish to exchange their minority status for a federal nation status and wish to have a complete local, regional and national autonomy.

[107] Miklós Duray: Kettős elnyomásban (In Dual Oppression) Madách-Posonium, Pozsony, 1993, pp. 99-102.

The Hungarian regions with the junction of local governments in the south, inhabited by Hungarians, would emerge.

Romania

Population (1994): 22,730,622
Ethnic groups: Romanian - 78.3%, Hungarian - 10.8%, Gypsy - 0.9%, German - 0.9%
Ukrainian, Ruthenian, Croat, Jew, Turkish, Tartar and Slovak - 0.9%.

Ethnic groups in Transylvania (1992): Romanian - 73.6%, Hungarian - 20.7%, Gypsy - 2.5%, German - 1.7%, Serb - 0.4%, Slovak - 0.3% and Ruthenian - 0.7%.
Official language: Romanian.

The Minority Situation at the End of the 19th century

The small Balkan states emerged from several hundred years of Turkish rule during the second half of the 19th century. This delayed achievement of national status led them to develop impatient minority policies, which implied fear of their minorities, based partly on the self consciousness of their newly acquired independence and unity. The countries created after the dismemberment of Hungary in 1919 were not homogenous states but multi-nationality structures with a real identity problem, composed of regions that had been historically independent.

They also lacked the democratic governmental traditions that went back several centuries in the Catholic and Protestant countries. The Byzantine spirit of the hierarchical Orthodox Church was quite different in its relationship to the governing structures of the State than its Western counterparts. This relationship, and the powerful but variable Turkish-type governance, can be traced in the domestic policies of the national states born at the end of the 19th century to this day. The laws did not necessarily have to conform to the constitution and the local ordinances did not necessarily conform to either. Since their concept of a constitutional state was quite different from the one held in the West, the minorities, accustomed to the western type of constitutional government, had no means for effective self-protection in the absence of autonomy within which protection of the community would have been possible. This situation also led to the economic decline of the minorities, their loss of status and ultimately to their decrease in numbers.

Census taking without the nationalities

In Romania, there were only two census counts during the 19th century, in 1859 and in 1899. Neither of these asked about nationality. According to some calculations, the number of non-Romanians constituted approximately 20% of the entire population. The most ethnically mixed area of Romania was the Dobruja, annexed to Romania in 1878 and in 1913. Turks, Tartars, Bulgarians, Russians, Germans, Jews and Armenians lived together in the province. They did not have the franchise and could not be elected to office. The officials were all Romanians, and the people had fewer rights than under Turkish rule. After 1880, Romanians were settled in Dobruja and this group was granted political privileges.

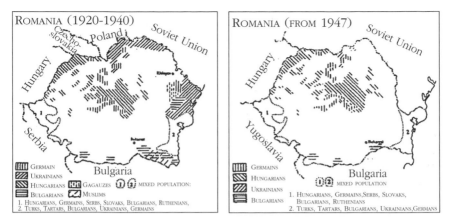

ROMANIA (1920-1940)

GERMAIN
UKRAINIANS
HUNGARIANS GAGAUZES MIXED POPULATION:
BULGARIANS MUSLIMS
1. HUNGARIANS, GERMAINS, SERBS, SLOVAKS, BULGARIANS, RUTHENIANS,
2. TURKS, TARTARS, BULGARIANS, UKRAINIANS, GERMAINS

ROMANIA (FROM 1947)

GERMAINS
HUNGARIANS
UKRAINIANS
BULGARIANS
MIXED POPULATION
1. HUNGARIANS, GERMAINS, SERBS, SLOVAKS,
   BULGARIANS, RUTHENIANS
2. TURKS, TARTARS, BULGARIANS, UKRAINIANS, GERMAINS

Beginning at the end of the 18th century, a large number of Jews settled there - but were given permission to live in the cities only. At the end of the 19th century, 256,500 of a total number of 270,000 were considered homeless and enjoyed no political rights whatever.

An attempt to create a state religion

The census reports are characteristic of the Romanian ecclesiastic policy. The census does not distinguish between the Greek Catholics and the Greek Orthodox, since the former religion was considered to be anti-Romanian. The Lutherans were counted with the Reformed Church members. In the Kingdom of Romania, before 1920, there were approximately 70,000 Hungarians and most of these were Csángós. Until 1848, most of the priests living among the Moldova Csángós were of Hungarian ethnicity, but after this date most of the new priest were not Hungarian-speaking. In 1884, a bishopric was organized in Iasi (Jászvásárhely) and in 1886, a seminary was established, where the language of instruction was strictly Romanian even though the congregations were Hungarian. In Szabófalva, a parochial school was organized, but the language of instruction was Romanian there, as well. The hymnbooks and other religious texts had to be written in Romanian.

Exclusively Romanian education

The Education Act of 1864 did not permit education in any language except Romanian. Hence, the Csángó Hungarian schools had to close. The Education Act of 1886 directed that the entire educational system be under the complete control and supervision of the State. Further amendments stated that only those schools would be licensed that followed the state-prescribed curriculum and where instruction was only in Romanian, even in those areas where the population was not Romanian. In the approved public schools, only licensed Romanian-born teachers were allowed to teach.

In Romania, the Hungarian-speaking Csángós, separated from their mother country for centuries, were without priests who could preach in Hungarian and without schools where the instruction was in Hungarian. From the 1660s on, the Vatican sent Italian and Polish Franciscans who could not speak Hungarian, to the Moldova Csángó-Hungarian settlements. Their situation deteriorated further during the second half of the 19th century. When the Public Education Act of 1893 was implemented, even religion had to be taught in Romanian. In all churches, the official language, Romanian, became the language of liturgy. One of the reasons why Hungarians became Romanians was the absence of their own priests. They did not have a single school where the children could have studied in Hungarian.

In Dobruja, 5 Turkish elementary schools were authorized, for a total population of 35,000. In the diocese of Bucharest, there were first 2, and later 3, schools where the language of instruction was Hungarian.

The 1906 report of the director of the Constanta high school was characteristic, "In addition to teaching and education, this school, just as all other schools in the country, has the goal to make the children into Romanians even though at home with their parents they are speaking in Greek, Bulgarian or Armenian."[108]

The Minority Situation 1919-1945
In 1919, the century-old dream became reality and by increasing its territory to twice its original size, Greater Romania was born from five regions having very different traditions.

The Western territories, annexed to Romania by the Trianon Peace Treaty, Bukovina, Transylvania, Partium and a portion of the Temes Bánság, represented 34.8% of the territory and 30.7% of the population of the new country. From Hungary alone, 103,000 km² were annexed to Romania, more than the entire area of the new Hungary. In this area, in 1930, of the active population, 75.8% worked in agriculture, 9.5% in industry, 3.0% in commerce and 11.7% in other occupations. In Transylvania, 82.7% of the population lived in villages and only 17.3% in towns. Officially, there were 49 towns but only 6 of them had more than 50,000 inhabitants.

In the Gyulafehérvár Decrees of 1918, mandating the union of the nationalities, the Romanian leaders in Transylvania held out the possibility of autonomy, "Total nationality freedom for people living together. Every nationality has the right to its own education and self-government and to courts conducted in their own language. They will have their own administration led by their own people. In the Legislative Assembly and in the Administration all nationalities will be represented according to the proportion of their population to the total population."

Contradiction between the international agreements and the constitutional practice
On December 9, 1919 Romania and the Allied Powers signed a minority protective agreement in Paris. Paragraph 8 of this agreement, signed by the Romanians stated, "Differences in religion, denomination or belief may not be a detriment to any Romanian citizen in the enjoyment of their political or civil rights, namely, eligibility for public positions, occupations and honors and

---

[108] Ernő Raffay: A vajdaságoktól a birodalomig, az újkori Románia története (From voivodeship to empire, the history of modern Romania) JATE, Szeged, 1989, p. 97.;
Pál Péter Domokos: A moldvai magyarság (The Moldavian Hungarians) Magvető Kiadó, Bp., 1987. p. 132.

engagement in any trade or industry. No Romanian citizen may be barred from using any language freely in business or trade or in church..."

Paragraph 11 promised a limited autonomy to the Székelys and to the Saxons, "Romania agrees to grant local autonomy, under governmental supervision, to the Transylvania Székely and Saxon communities in religious and educational matters." Romania agreed to recognize some of the requirements of the agreement as the fundamental law of the land and that no law, ordinance or official action would be in opposition to these requirements. Further, that any law, ordinance or official action in opposition to these requirements would not be implemented.

In spite of these international obligations, the 1923 Constitution included practically nothing of the above international agreement. The Constitution declared the country to be a Romanian National State and revoked the important promises of the Gyulafehérvár Decrees.

Paragraph 1 stated, "The Kingdom of Romania is a homogeneous national state." Paragraph 5 revealed that the concept of a nationality minority was not accepted, "...The Romanians enjoy freedom of conscience, freedom of education and freedom of the press regardless of racial, linguistic or religious differences..." Senator C.G Dissescu, a professor at the University and the drafter of the constitutional statutes wrote, "The term homogeneous, mentioned in Paragraph 1, excludes any possibility of discussing and planning local autonomy. Regionalism is contrary to the letter and spirit of the new constitution and is condemned by the new constitution. Such activity can be construed into a crime against the State."[109]

Ethnic Cleansing

The Romanian army invaded Transylvania, with French assistance, at the end of the Great War, in December 1918, committed more and more violence, plunder, rape, flogging to death, torture, and murder during 1919. With the terrorization of Hungarians, they tried to ensure the success of their delegation's demand for new Romanian boundary.

Some examples: On April 19, 1919, in Kőröstárkány, 87 men and women between 20 and 83 years old were massacred. Erzsébet Oláh, a 49 year-old woman was buried alive. Mihály Izsák had his hands and feet broken before he also was buried alive. The massacre of Kisnyegerfalva, also on Easter Saturday, April 19, 1919 claimed 17 victims between 22 and 76 years of age.[110]

The language act, curtailment and taxation of the use of language

The Peace Treaty and the minority agreement prescribed the free use of language and the Gyulafehérvár Decree (1918) made the same promise. Bans on using the language before officials were instituted in 1921 and 1922. In 1921, an ordinance of the Ministry of the Interior instructed all courts to use only Romanian in all verbal or written communications. The 1925 administrative law proposal charged the leg-

---

[109] Lajos Nagy: A kisebbségek alkotmányjogi helyzete Nagyromániában (The constitutional rights of the minorities in Greater Romania) Minerva-nyomda Rt. Kolozsvár, 1944, p. 64.

[110] Dr. Kálmán Magyar: Magyar Holocaust 1917-67 (Hungarian Holocaust 1917-67, documents), Kaposvár, 1999. pp. 44-49; Ernő Raffay: Trianon titkai (The secrets of the Trianon treaty). Bp., 1990. pp. 62-67; M. Árpád Sárkány: Fekete-Kőrös völgyi magyar mártírok (Hungarian martyrs in the Fekete-Kőrös river valley) Erdélyi Magyarság, 1994/17. pp. 43-44.

islative council to permit the use of the local minority language, which in practice meant that the use of the minority language was going to be forbidden. Even in the villages, an announcement was posted in the administrative offices, "Only Romanian spoken". The new administrative law of 1936 threatened serious punishment if the minority language was used by the local council. The use of language in the courts, also mandated by the minority protective agreements, was not regulated and interpreting was done by the lawyers and the clients. After 1929, the books of all the cooperatives had to be in Romanian. After 1935, the tradesmen and merchants who did not keep their books in Romanian were charged an additional tax. People entering stores had to be addressed in Romanian, under severe penalty of law. After 1936, motion pictures were not allowed to have a Hungarian soundtrack.

Reorganization of the administration
In all the successor states, the administrative units, districts and counties, were re-drawn in order that in the new administrative units the number of Hungarians remain below the percentage defined by the Language Act and thus the permission to use the minority language in the schools might be withheld.

Discriminatory land reform, emigration and loss of property
The Romanian Land Ownership Act unmistakably favored the Romanians to the detriment of the Hungarians. As Senator Hossu Longhin stated, "…if we wish these areas to acquire a truly Romanian character, if we want to make them truly Romanian, then we must give the land to the Romanians."[111] Of all those who were given land, 14.8% were Hungarians and 78.1% were Romanians. This was particularly hard on the peasants who were settled on Hungarian Crown lands after 1885 and consequently 1,802 families emigrated. Jointly owned lands in the Székelyföld (Székelyland) and privately owned land in Csík were also confiscated. With the excuse of land reform, more than 10,000 Székely peasants were deprived of their modest livelihood. The Romanian Minister of the Interior wished to expropriate the land belonging to the Tusnád spa facility and, when this met resistance, the Minister dismissed the village council and appointed a new council from among the newly settled Romanians who agreed to his demands. It was thus that Tusnád's commonly held lands became the property of the Romanian National Tourist Agency.

While the Romanian churches gained landed property, the Hungarian churches lost more than 314,000 cadastral yokes, even though the income from these lands was traditionally used for cultural and educational purposes. The existence and estates of the so-called Catholic Status came into question. Under the heading of land reform, 84.54% of the ecclesiastic, educational institutional and foundation estates were expropriated.

Settlement of the border regions and formation of a cultural zone
After the distribution of land, almost entirely from land confiscated from Hungarian ecclesiastic and private owners, huge tracts still remained in the hands of the State. The largest of these tracts were in Counties Bihar, Csík, Háromszék and Szatmár.

---

[111] Sándor Biró: Kisebbségben és többségben (Románok és magyarok 1867-1940) (In Majority and Minority (Romanians and Hungarians 1867-1940) Európai Protestáns Magyar Szabadegyetem, Bern, 1989. p. 309.

The Romanian Minister of Agriculture, Constantinescu, stated on November 10, 1923, in the Romanian Senate that, "The lands confiscated in the Temes-Torontál-Arad-Szatmár region were retained by the government in order to settle Romanians from beyond our borders and from the mountains on those lands. It is my opinion that these expropriated land properly belong to those who represent the cradle of Romanian nationalism."[112]

At the same time, Deputy Minister Victor Jinga, one of the greatest experts of Romanian settlement policies, defined the goals of land ownership policy in 1928 as follows, "We must make the foreigners brought to this land understand, regardless of their language and religion, that this land is preserved for the total and eternal use of the Romanians and therefore the Romanian State has engaged in a decisive and wide-ranging activity as a duty toward the preservation of our people. The first and foremost purpose of this activity is to cleanse the Romanian sphere of all elements that do not belong there."[113] According to Jinga's data, a total of 111 Romanian settlements were established along the Trianon borders. Forty five were in County Temes-Torontál, 19 in Szatmár, 19 in Szilágy, 15 in Arad, and 9 in Bihar. A total of 4,973 Romanian families were settled on 69,223 hectares. In order to accomplish the above-stated goals, no Hungarian could have any land in these areas. It is not surprising, therefore, that in this border region the number of Romanian villages multiplied and the Hungarian presence correspondingly diminished. Starting in 1924, the Romanian State wished to accelerate the Romanization of the almost purely Hungarian-speaking Székelyföld and of the mixed population along the border. To accomplish this, a so-called cultural zone was established in 10 of the counties in this area and, allegedly to intensify Romanian education, teachers were imported from the Regat who were paid 50% more than the local teachers and who were also given a free gift of 10 hectares of land. The State viewed education as the most powerful tool of assimilation.

In 1938, a military border zone was established. The Act stated that in this zone any property could be confiscated for military purpose. A 1939 amendment of the Act stated that land acquired by the State in the mixed-population border zone could be sold for settlement purposes exclusively to Romanians.

Migration and assimilation
The Székelyföld counties were not designed by nature for agriculture. There was practically no industry, credit was not readily available and thus the major portion of the young men were forced to migrate to the former Kingdom of Romania area. Their number was estimated at 100,000. A significant part of the intellectuals and of the aristocracy fled to Hungary, the owners of mid-sized estates became impoverished and their children moved to the cities in search of jobs or they emigrated. Until 1935, approximately 350,000 Hungarians fled from Transylvania, their native land.

Discriminatory taxation
"We follow a policy that you will be forced to follow…if you have a Romanian soul. It will be a policy that will place economic and fiscal matters on a national basis" said Vintila Bratianu, in presenting his economic policies.[114]

---

[112] Sándor Biró, op.cit. p. 323.
[113] Sándor Biró, op.cit. p. 324.
[114] Sándor Biró, op.cit. p. 306.

The discriminatory tax law, enacted in 1934, was trying to assist the debtors who were in difficulties because of the worldwide depression, but did not apply to the Székelys with medium-size estates. Yet, the Romanian landowners with medium sized estates, who formerly belonged to the 2nd Naszód and 13th Karánsebes border guard regiments, were included and were granted tax relief. These Romanian families had received their land for fighting against Hungary in the 1848-1849 war.

The differences between the Romanian and non-Romanian populations was evident not only in taxation but also in the way the taxes were collected. Thus, between 1934 and 1936, many more taxes were collected in the Székely counties than in the Romanian ones. According to official estimates, in the Romanian counties only 38.2% of the assessed taxes were collected, while the figure in the Székely counties stood at 96.5%. By 1926, the taxes in the old Romanian Kingdom were lowered by 11% for tradesmen and merchants, while at the same time the taxes in Transylvania were raised by 24.6%. If the merchants wished to display the stores name in Hungarian, the ordinary taxes they had to pay were increased several fold. According to the figures of the Romanian Ministry of Finance for the period between 1924 and 1926, the people in Transylvania paid 205 million more in direct taxes that the entire old Romanian Kingdom.[115]

Discriminatory credit policy
Even though, after 1920, 61.1% of the Hungarian financial institutions wound up in the neighboring states, the fiscal policies everywhere served the majority interests.

The Romanian National Bank, under Liberal leadership, was reluctant to grant Hungarian banks any credit and thus these banks were limited in the amount of credit they could grant, while at the same time the Romanian banks were granted the same preferential credit as before. Consequently the Hungarian economic life in Transylvania had to struggle against very heavy odds.

Expulsion of teachers, name analysis and reduction in the number of schools and of the minority intellectuals
After 1924, Hungarian teachers could obtain a teacher's certificate only if they could pass a Romanian language test. The teachers in parochial schools were not eligible for State salary support and the Churches could not guarantee the teachers' salary, since the foundations created to support education lost their funding and their estates had been confiscated during the land reform. Yet, at the same time, the Saxon and Romanian teachers continued to enjoy the benefits they had during the Hungarian regime. They received State subsistence, traveled on the trains for half fare and kept their pensions. After 1933, Hungarian teachers could serve in the army only as enlisted men because they all failed the officer candidate exam. Many of the teachers emigrated to Hungary.

Instruction in Hungarian, after 1919, was limited to the parochial schools and as a consequence more than 1,000 Hungarian public schools were closed. In the academic year 1930-1931, 483 Reformed schools were operated, 297 Catholic ones, 36 Unitarians and 6 Lutheran ones. 57.6% of the Hungarian children of school age

---

[115] Sándor Biró, op.cit. pp. 326-327.

attended these schools. The others were supposed to attend the Hungarian language public schools or the Hungarian division of the Romanian language schools. The number of these decreased year after year. Thus, a significant percentage of the Hungarian children had to attend Romanian language schools and, in the Székelyföld, children having a Hungarian family name were forced to do so. During the era of Dualism, both Hungarian and Romanian schools were maintained by the state but now, when state support was no longer available, the Romanian parochial schools went public and the Hungarian ones were closed.

According to Paragraph 19 of the 1924 Public School Act, parents who wished to send their children to private schools had to report such intent. If the principals of the public schools found that the Hungarian child's name was offensive to the Romanian ear, the parents were not granted the certificate they needed to send the child to a private school. This process of exclusion was referred to as Name Analysis.

In the Hungarian parochial schools four subjects, geography, history, constitutional history and the Romanian language, had to be taught in Romanian, which made the school, for all practical purposes, bilingual.

After 1924, the Hungarian language public schools and the Hungarian division of the Romanian language schools were gradually changed to regular Romanian public schools, with all instruction being delivered in Romanian. The Hungarian divisions were usually converted by an order from the school superintendent. In the high schools, the situation was even worse:

In the 1930-1931 academic year there were only 23 Hungarian language schools and these were parochial schools of a lower order that had lost their foundation-based support. There were 17 secondary schools for girls, 7 teacher colleges, 4 higher trade schools and 4 schools of commerce. These numbers indicate that more than half of the schools functioning in 1918 had disappeared.

About 75% of the Hungarian students were unable to take the baccalaureate exam, made mandatory in the Romanian language, after 1925. In 1927, 91.5% of the Hungarian students failed this exam. During the 1930s, the law was made even more stringent, thereby further reducing the number of Hungarian students who could attend institutes of higher learning. After 1934, most Hungarian applicants did not pass the entrance exam. By 1938, lawyers had to take a language test to practice.

In 1919, the Hungarian University in Kolozsvár was taken over by the state and the following year it opened its door as a Romanian State University. Approximately 2,500 students were admitted annually, of whom about 300 were Hungarians. Only a few of them actually completed their studies. During the first ten years, only 31 students received a degree, representing about 6-7% of all the degrees awarded.

In 1919, the Hungarians, relying on the Minority Protective Agreement and on the Gyulafehérvár Decree, and with the cooperation of all the Hungarian churches, planned to open a Hungarian university. The government stopped this endeavor and forbade it for all time to come. This meant, in practice, that the replacement of Hungarian intellectuals disappeared, because even those who went to study in Hungary only rarely returned to Romania where job opportunities were extremely limited.

The divinity school continued to receive state support but the maintenance of the buildings became the responsibility of the diocese.

Numerus clausus

During the 1930s, even private companies introduced the so-called "*numerus valachius*", i.e., the requirement that the majority of the employees, and the language used in the business, be Romanian.

The ratio set for nationality students at the Universities was 5.5%, but only 3.1% of the places were ever filled by Hungarians.

After 1933, the *numerus valachius* movement, organized by A. Vaida, resulted in yet another language exam for the public officials leading to further dismissals.

The 1938 Constitution made it a fundamental principle that in governmental employment, the Romanian element, being the majority power in the country, had to be given preference.

Loss of place names

Decree No. 1 of the Governing Council stated, in 1919, that, "every nationality may use the place names in their own language." After 1921, it was required that in the Hungarian press the Romanian place names be used. Even in Hungarian poetry, all place names had to be in Romanian.

The position of the Churches in the absence of autonomy

When the Romanian troops occupied Budapest in 1919, they decreed that there had to be church services in honor of the occasion and that the bells had to be rung everywhere in the country. Clergymen who refused to do so were thrown into jail and severely beaten.

The ecclesiastic organizations were severely damaged by the Trianon Peace Treaty and their strength and survival was largely dependent on whether they could function under an independent Hungarian hierarchy or whether they had to become integrated into a majority national ecclesiastic organization. The latter would have led to the loss of their autonomy and eventual atrophy. The Reformed Church scrupulously followed the law and took all the necessary steps to create a new Reformed diocese. They organized a meeting of all of the dioceses, announced the formation of the new Királyhágómellék Reformed Diocese and elected a new bishop and new officers of this diocese. The Romanian approval did not come for 20 years and during this time the new diocese applied in vain for the State support, which was provided to all the other dioceses and to their leadership.

Romania reached an agreement with the Holy See in 1927. The Vatican authorized the establishment of the fifth Greek Catholic bishopric and thus the Romanian bishops had a majority in the joint council of the Romanian Greek Catholic and Hungarian Roman Catholic bishops. This also meant that the Patrimonium Sacrum, established with Hungarian funds, was henceforth managed by ecclesiastic leaders whose majority was Romanian. There was also a 20 year-long struggle to keep the Romanian State from disbanding the Roman Catholic *Status* and confiscating its funds. The Status was a characteristically independent Transylvanian organization. It was an elective body, established centuries ago under Protestant Princes, and survived until the end of World War II. Early on, it was responsible for ecclesiastic administrative duties. Its lands and forests were almost totally expropriated by the 1921 Romanian land reform.

The fight against the Transylvanian Hungarian Catholic Church was led by Ghibu Onisifor, a professor at the University of Kolozsvár, whose writings were published at Government expense.

The Hungarian parochial schools were under the authority of the Central Education Directorate, having lost the independence they enjoyed under the Dualism. The regulations concerning the equipment and maintenance of the buildings and the requirements of excluding all students of different religion led to the closing of hundreds of parochial school during the early 1920s. At the end of 1920, there were 1,184 Hungarian parochial schools. By 1928 their number decreased to 818 and more schools were closed in the Székelyföld than anywhere else in the country. The Romanian churches were favored in all ordinances, such legal discrimination being incorporated into the 1928 Education Act and into the 1939 Constitution. British and American Protestant missions kept records of the mistreatment, incarceration, torture and robbing of the Hungarian churchmen. In the Székelyföld (Székelyland), designated as a cultural zone, forceful conversions were started.

In the 1930s, the Székelyföld peasants were forced to build churches for the Romanian officials and for those who were forcefully converted. The peasants also had to build the Romanian public schools.

The League of Nations minority agreements did not specify precisely to what extent the territorial or ecclesiastic autonomy of a minority had to be respected. Consequently, the state could institute discriminatory credit policies, other economic discriminations, deprive minorities of their civil rights and intimidate them at will. In any and all of these cases, the injured parties could appeal to the League of Nations, but this was a totally useless exercise. International intervention was clearly not a reasonable possibility.

Territorial Re-Annexation (1940)

After the March 1939 dismemberment of Czechoslovakia, the foreign policy of Great Britain took a turn. It signed a treaty of mutual assistance with Poland and, together with France, it guaranteed the independent statehood of Greece and Romania. Another modification of British foreign policy took place in June 1940, when the Soviet Union demanded the cessation of Bessarabia and North Bukovina from Romania.

Romania had to yield and on August 2, Bessarabia became a part of the Soviet Union. Apprehensive of Hungarian territorial claims, Romania renounced the British and French guarantees on July 1 and turned to Germany for support. Great Britain was prepared to accept any territorial readjustment that was arrived at by mutual consent but the Turnu-Severin negotiations were unsuccessful. Romania then asked for arbitration through its ambassador in Berlin. The arbitration decision and the protocol were signed on August 30, 1940 in the Belvedere Palace in Vienna. In exchange for the territorial gains, Hungary was required to make large-scale shipments of agricultural products and raw materials to Germany and to make a number of domestic political changes requested by Germany. In November, Hungary joined the German-Italian-Japanese Tripartite Pact. The Vienna decision assigned an area of 43,000 km² to Hungary with a population of 51.4% Hungarian.

The Minority Policies of years 1945-1990

All socialist countries within the Soviet sphere of interest approached the minority question in a similar fashion. The dictatorial system of the socialist republics made the implementation of forced assimilation much easier. The centralized planning for all economic, cultural and organizational endeavors automatically excluded any possibility for autonomy and self-government. The principal goals of the dictatorship were the elimination of individually organized social structures, political parties and social associations. Trade unions were reorganized and subjected to the Communist Party. The Churches were economically constrained, intimidated and eventually destined for elimination. Individuals had to find their place in the administrative system that was controlled totally from above. At the same time, all the foreign and domestic policy trends that produced changes in the policies of the Soviet leadership, such as those of 1944-1945, 1947-1948, 1953, 1956, 1968, etc., weakened or strengthened the hard-line politicians vis-à-vis their foes the reformists. These fluctuations in policy affected the situation of the Hungarian minorities. The efforts promoting assimilation developed novel techniques to supplement the old ones:

Ethnic cleansing and the death camps

The September 12, 1944 Soviet-Romanian armistice agreement did away with the Second Vienna Decision and declared that Transylvania, or at least its major portion would be returned to Romania. In September 1944, the Hungarian government ordered the evacuation of Northern Transylvania and the advancing Soviet troops expelled the Hungarian administration. The approximately 10,000 strong semi-military organization, the so-called Maniu Guards, originally designed as a peacekeeping organization, kept all of North Transylvania in a state of terror for about six weeks. Several hundred men and women were brutally murdered, many others were interned and Hungarian books were burned. In Szárazajta, for example, two men were beheaded.

An entry in the Register of Death of the Gyanta Reformed Congregation for December 23, 1944 reads: "So far, in 1944, 32 men and 26 women have died, of whom 41 were the victims of the September 24, 1944 massacre by the 6th and 11th Alpine Chasseur companies". On the same day, in Magyarremete, 23 men were executed, 4 were taken to Kishalmagy and shot, and one died of his injuries at home. Men in Egeres were tortured by the returning former gendarme sergeant and there were some who had their extremities cut off. The Catholic priest of Bánffyhunyad, Károly Keresztes, was also tortured, but his life was spared when Emil Petru, the Greek Catholic priest in the same village, interceded on his behalf. Similar events took place in Váralmás, Kispetri and Magyarbikal. In the forest of Körtvely, mutilated corpses were found. At last, the Soviet military authorities became incensed by these atrocities and, for a time, the Soviet Army took over the administration of the area.[116]

Immediately after the switch in sides, on August 23, 1944, Romania declared war on Hungary and considered the South Transylvanian Hungarians as enemies. Teachers, priests, physicians, engineers and manufacturers were

[116] M. Gál, B. A. Gajdos, F. Imreh: Fehér könyv az 1944. Őszi magyarellenes atrocitásokról. (The White Paper on the atrocities against Hungarians at the autumn of 1944.) Kolozsvár (Cluj), 1995. p. 32; Z. Szász: Erdély története, III.kötet, (History of Transylvania) vol. III Akadémia, Bp., 1986. p. 1761.

154

deported to labor camps, like the one Tirgu Jiu, in Oltenia. The Transylvanian Saxons and the Bánság German intellectuals were interned in the same camp. From there, about 1,500 Germans were taken to the Soviet Union as slave laborers in the mines. In Földvár, in County Brassó, the camp originally designed as a Russian prisoner of war camp, was now used for Hungarians and a few Germans. They were brought there from North Transylvania, mostly from the Székelyföld but as well as from the Szilágyság or County Szatmár. The returning Romanian officials identified all the men of military age and those who had served in the Székely border guards and all of them were taken to the camps. In Kolozsvár, during large-scale screening in the streets, all men with a Hungarian sounding name were arrested and taken to the camps. The Csángó historian, László Mikecs, died in a prisoner camp in Taganrog in 1944. There was only one avenue for escape, as revealed by a report of the Notary Public of Kökös village, (1220/1945): conversion to the Greek Orthodox religion. The people of Kökös chose not to convert. The number of inmates in the camps was decimated by typhoid fever and starvation. After repeated requests, a small number of the inmates were released in March 1945.

Using concessions to divide and circumvent

One of the important techniques of the Romanian minority policy was to offer a compromise to the moderate political leaders in order to eliminate the more radical aims. The next step would wait until the foreign political situation had sufficiently improved, at which time the compromise would be withdrawn.

Prior to the Paris Peace Treaties, in 1945, concerned about a possible transfer of land to Hungary, Romania issued the Nationality Act (86/1945) which guaranteed the use of the mother tongue in the courts and in the administration, provided that at least 30% of the population belonged to the nationality group. So far as the University of Kolozsvár was concerned, the aim was to develop a bilingual university. By this time, it was no longer possible for the minorities to take their political grievances to the League of Nations. In 1946, an ordinance issued by the Council of Ministers specified how the above act would be implemented. This ordinance actually took a step backward and was less generous than the Nationality Act.

Yet, in 1945-1946, Hungarian, German and Yiddish theaters were established with government funding and schools in their mother tongue were opened for the Turks and Tartars. On request from the Hungarian People's Association and from other organizations, the Groza government, in power since March 1945, made a promise to extend administrative autonomy to all of Transylvania. Yet, during the same month, the freely elected councils in the 11 north Transylvanian counties were disbanded. The left-wing Hungarian People's Association, which opposed the return of any land to Hungary at the Paris Peace Negotiations, proved to be a very useful tool for the Romanian government in splitting up the Hungarians in both the domestic and foreign policy arena.

While the peace negotiations were still in progress, this organization was entrusted with the drafting of a nationality act and a promise was made to create an independent administrative nationality area, wherever the minority represented 65% of the population. Signing the Peace Treaty and the victory of the Romanian Communist Party at the elections obviated all of these promises.

Reorganization of the administration

The 1952 Constitution opened the possibility of the establishment of a *Hungarian Autonomous Province for the Székelys living as a block.* When the plan was submitted, the General Secretary of the Party, Gheorgiu-Dej, indicated that the goal was to follow the nationality policy practice initiated by Stalin. The autonomous territory did not include Aranyosszék, the Barcaság and the Hungarian areas of Moldavia. It was the "Socialist Territorial Autonomy" section of Stalin's 1936 Constitution that served as a model. Nobody suspected that this also meant that the currently accepted policy, namely the unhampered use of the native tongue in all of Transylvania, by the Romanians, Hungarians and Saxons, would henceforth be limited to the area of the Hungarian Autonomous Territory.

In 1960, N. Ceauşescu submitted a new administrative reform. The name of the Hungarian Autonomous Territory was *changed to the Maros-Hungarian Autonomous Territory and the percentage of Hungarians was reduced by the addition of Romanian areas and the separation of Hungarian areas.*

According to a 1960 resolution of the Romanian Communist Party, there was a further reorganization of the administration and the Maros-Hungarian Autonomous Territory ceased to exist. The new organization did not fully correspond to the pre-1918 one; the number of villages was reduced and the number of towns was increased to dissolve the cementing force of local communities.

Socialist industrialization, with settlements and with changes in the ethnic rates

Urbanization, tied by the State to industrialization, intentionally diluted the compact ethnic blocks. The ethnic composition of a given town or development was changed by the transfer of skilled workers from elsewhere. The Transylvanian towns were declared closed to Hungarians but opened their door widely for Romanians from old Romania. The newly imported Romanian intellectuals, officials and police were granted a number of benefits, such as increased salary and financial assistance for the move.

During the 1970s, the skilled workers who moved to Transylvania were trained in the trade schools beyond the Carpathians from where they were moved in large numbers to the previously Hungarian Transylvanian towns. They were domiciled in special blocks of apartments built to accommodate the workers of the newly established industries. The concept of the "closed city" was introduced according to the Soviet model and most of the towns in Transylvania and the Partium, including Kolozsvár, were declared "closed". In these towns only Romanians were granted permission to settle and a *numerus clausus* was developed in higher education and in employment.

The atrophy of theHungarian language educational network

After 1945, in addition to grade schools and secondary schools, higher education got under way as well. The Kolozsvár University had been established in 1872. It became Romanian in 1918. In 1940 it again became Hungarian. It was then succeeded by a new Hungarian university named after the great mathematician János Bólyai. It had a Medical School and a Pharmacology School that were later moved to Marosvásárhely. In Kolozsvár, there was also an Agricultural College and a Music Conservatory. In Marosvásárhely, a school of the performing arts and a teacher's college were established. Another teacher's college opened in

Bakó to provide teachers for the Csángó schools opened after 1948. All of these were short lived. The government first combined the minority schools with Romanian institutions, and then admitted fewer and fewer Hungarian applicants. Using the small number of Hungarian students as an excuse, the Hungarian sections were closed.

Soviet troops were withdrawn from Romania in 1958 as compensation for allowing Soviet troops to use Romanian soil in their preparation to invade Hungary and because the Romanians kept the leaders of the 1956 Hungarian revolt in custody in Snagov for a year. The political cleansing after the 1956 revolution gave a renewed opportunity to do away with the Transylvanian Hungarian intellectuals and politicians on the pretext that they had been in contact with the Hungarian "counter-revolutionaries". A number of Hungarian university students were expelled or tried before military tribunals. Trials began in 1957. In 1958, the last school of the Moldavian Csángós was closed. In 1959, the independent Hungarian Kolozsvár University was fused with the Romanian Babes University. The leader in this campaign to meld the two Universities was no other than N. Ceauşescu. Because of repeated tortures and continuous harassment by the Securitate (secret police), Professor László Szabedi and Prorector Zoltán Csendes committed suicide. Independent Hungarian secondary schools became the next target. The number of such schools was reduced by 50% and instruction in Hungarian became minimal.

In the 1970s, a number of the secondary schools were demoted to become trade schools and instruction in the minority language was authorized only in the trades with the lowest prestige.

In the 1980s, the minority schools became sections of the multinational schools, requiring a minimum number of minority students to maintain instruction in their language. The required numbers were 25 in the elementary schools and 36 in the secondary schools. Intimidation led to the closure of the Hungarian sections. At the same time the government insisted that Romanian classes be started if there were just 1 or 2 Romanian students.

The Marosvásárhely Hungarian Medical and Pharmacology Schools, originally part of the János Bólyai University, became independent during the 1948 Educational Reform movement. In 1962, in order to "strengthen Romanian-Hungarian brotherhood", the schools became bilingual. The Romanian section was steadily increased and the Hungarian section was forcibly diminished. In 1965-1966, Hungarians represented 99% of the student body but by 1988-1989, they represented only 29.67% of the entire student body. The Hungarian section of the Kolozsvár Agricultural College was closed in 1959. Teaching theory in Hungarian was forbidden at the Kolozsvár College of the Performing Arts and at the Music Conservatory after the academic year 1985-1986. Teaching techniques had been purely Romanian for some years.

Exclusion of the Hungarian intellectuals, closure of the cultural institutions and prohibition of all contacts with the mother country

The Educational Reform Act of August 3, 1948 started a new trend in the life of the Hungarian institutes of higher education. The professors, who were not Romanian citizens, had to resign from the Bólyai University and the new instructors were appointed from among high school teachers, research institutes and from various segments of cultural life. In the spring of 1950, "Marxist" evaluations were applied to the Hungarian cultural and scientific life in Romania. These included the Bólyai University, the Kolozsvár Hungarian National Theater, the Hungarian artistic associations, the writers' association and many others. These evaluations suggested that the independence of these organizations be brought to an end. Consequently, the Hungarian institutions were yoked with similar Romanian institutions. The previously independent Hungarian Music Academy and Art School became sections of the corresponding Romanian academies and the Performing Arts Academy was moved to Marosvásárhely. The integration of the Hungarian institutions was accompanied by a move to remove the Hungarian intellectuals from Kolozsvár, the former capital of Transylvania. *After 1953, additional Hungarian institutions of higher learning were closed and with the exception of the autonomous territory, bilingual city signs disappeared from Transylvania.* Hungarian newspapers, periodicals and books also disappeared and in the offices the use of the Hungarian language was curtailed.

When Czechoslovakia was occupied by Soviet troops in 1968, Hungarian soldiers had to march in, as well, to provide "international assistance", while Romania stayed away. This produced some temporary improvement in the situation of the Hungarians in Romania. The *Kriterion* was established and new Hungarian newspapers and periodicals appeared. Bilingual signs could again be seen.

The 226/1974 legal ordinance assigned severe punishment to those who had foreign visitors stay with them.

According to a 1977 agreement, a Hungarian Consulate was opened in Kolozsvár in 1980 but, eight years later, it was again closed.

Cleansing within the party, cadre policies

By 1952, the power struggle within the Romanian Communist Party was over. The position of Gheorghiu-Dej was consolidated and thus it was possible to expel the minority politicians who participated meritoriously in the early days of the party. The so-called "Moscow leadership" was expelled from the Party, among them Vasile Luca, who was of Hungarian extraction, and Anna Pauker, who was Jewish. Several famous professors were also removed from the University, including Attila T. Szabó and Zsigmond Jakó. Many officials were removed from their positions and many university students were expelled or arrested. In connection with the 1956 Hungarian events, a number of instructors and many students were charged and sentenced to 10 and 20 years of incarceration or forced labor.

In the 1980s, the change of cadres accelerated rapidly and Hungarian urban and county officials, county party secretaries, leading officials of the People's Councils, directors of industry, and Hungarian military, police and State Security officers were replaced by Romanian nationals. Changes implemented in the Hungarian schools followed and between 1984 and 1987, half of the Hungarian school principals were replaced by Romanians. Similarly, Hungarian cultural institutions had Romanian leaders appointed to them who did not speak Hungarian.

Breaking the Churches

In 1947, the Romanian government canceled the agreement made with the Holy See in 1927 and in 1948, the Greek Catholics were coerced to join the Greek Orthodox Church. The Romanian Greek Catholic Church, with 1.5 million members, was fused by edict with the Greek Orthodox Church in 1948. The former leaders of the Greek Catholic Church were replaced with a hierarchy totally subservient to the State. On the basis of the 1950 Religious Affairs Act, the government recognized only one Hungarian Roman Catholic Bishop, namely the Bishop of Gyulafehárvár. The other three bishoprics were demoted to deaneries. The Romanian Legislature wished to enact a statute that would have granted the government far-reaching authority in making ecclesiastic appointments. Bishop Áron Márton, who strongly objected to the nationalization of church schools, was arrested in 1949, together with Catholic and Greek Catholic bishops, and this was followed by a number of church dignitaries being imprisoned.

The leadership of the Protestant Churches reached an agreement with the State in 1949, according to which the State selected the highest church dignitaries and laymen from a panel submitted by the Church. This, naturally, resulted in many of the important positions being held by people obligated to the State.

The religious orders, so important in Catholic education, were disbanded. *Status*, the centuries-old independently wealthy organization that had been in charge of the economic and cultural affairs of the Roman Catholic Church, was disbanded.

One characteristic example: In 1972, after several years of negotiations, the World Reformed Alliance donated 20 thousand bibles to the Romanian Reformed Church. These were kept in Romanian warehouses until 1984 when they were moved to the paper factory in Braille and converted into toilet paper. No Hungarian book or periodical could be imported into Romania and even travel guides were confiscated at the border. Bibles were smuggled in by young people in their backpacks. There was no religious press.

Starting in the 1980s, the State attempted to impose a *numerus clausus* on the training of both Reformed and Catholic clergy, wishing to reduce their number in this way. During the last few decades, about 1,500 Orthodox churches were built, many of them in purely Hungarian areas. These churches were built with State support, while the subsidies for the Catholic and Protestant churches were delayed and economic assistance for church construction or maintenance can be expected only from Hungarian population.

Assimilation

From 1910 to 1992, the percentage of Romanians in Transylvania grew by 20% while the percentage of Hungarians declined by 11% and the Saxon's percentage declined by almost 90%. In the 1980s, during the Ceausescu-period, Saxons (Germans) were ransomed to Germany for 5,000 DM a child and 9-10 000 DM an adult. Between 1980-1988, about 13,000 people resettled yearly.[117] In total, 414,226 person resettled to Germany from 1950 to 1993.

The Romanian Hungarian Democratic Association (RMDSZ), the political representatives of the Hungarians in Romania, proposed at its 1993 annual congress, that the term *"Territorial Autonomy" be replaced with the more acceptable term, "Regional self-government"*. Unfortunately, in the absence of decentralization and the maintenance of a centralized distribution of funds and governmental control, as manifested by a prefect being appointed to supervise the Self-Government, there could be no real division of authority or effective democratization.

---

[117] Prof. Friedrich Blahusch: Aussiedler / Spataussiesdler. Fachhoschule Fulda, Fachbereih Sozialwesen. p. 3. http://www.unics.uni-hannover.de/bollm/wandel/blahusch.htm

Yugoslavia and Serbia

Population (1993): 10,811,000
Ethnic groups: Serb - 63%, Albanian - 3.5%, Macedonians - 5.5%, Hungarian - 4%, Croat - 1.6%, also Bosnian, German, Slovak and Romanian, "Yugoslavians".

In the Vajdaság (Voivodina), belonging to Serbia (1992): Serb - 54.4%, Hungarian - 18.9%, "Yugoslav" - 8.2%, Croat - 5.4%, Slovak - 3.4%, Romanian - 2.3%, Macedonians - 2.1%, Ruthenian - 1.1%, Gypsy - 1%, other - 2.4%.
Official language: Serb.

The first Serb nation was established in the 12th century. It had its most glorious period under Tsar Dusan at the beginning of the 14th century. After the defeat of Rigómező (Kosovo Polje)in 1389, it became a vassal of the Turkish Empire and was incorporated into it in 1459, where it remained there for the next four centuries. Under Turkish rule, the Balkan populations were repeatedly exchanged and continuously in motion, producing a very complex ethnic and religious picture. The two anti-Turkish uprisings at the beginning of the 19th century, in 1804 and 1815, resulted in the Serb Principality receiving autonomy from the Sultan in 1830. The autonomous area consisted of approximately 100 km radius around Belgrade. In a few towns, there were still some Turkish guards but generally Prince Miloš, of the House of Obrenović, was in complete control of his principality. In 1842, Alexander Karadjordjević became the ruler. His very talented Minister, Ilja Garašanin, worked out a proposal (Načertanije) in 1844 for the creation of a Yugoslav State under Serb leadership. He assumed that the Ottoman Empire was about to collapse and thus it would be possible to incorporate its former Yugoslav territories. This could be accomplished either with Russian assistance peacefully or by force of arms. The Serbian State, strengthened by these acquisitions, could then hope to obtain the Yugoslav parts of the Habsburg Empire if the international situation would prove favorable.[118] The 1878 Berlin Congress, bringing to a conclusion the 1877-1878 Russo-Turkish War, recognized the independent Serbia. The peace treaties after the two Balkan Wars and after World War I increased Serbia's territory fourfold. Much of this was due to its powerful patron, Russia.

Using the Pan-Slav movement, Russia was actively participating in the events leading up to World War I. According to Henri Pozzi, during the years preceding the War, Baron Hartwig, the Russian ambassador in Belgrade, gave the Ujedinjenje ili Smrt (Unification or Death), a secret Pan-Slavic organization, 45,000 Francs. Hartwig also gave 15,000 Francs to Commander Voja Tanković, on July 19, 1914, for the two week long training that Tanković had given to Princip Gavrilo, the murderer of Crown Prince Francis Ferdinand. Tanković allegedly taught Gavrilo how handle a revolver and how to shoot. While in 1908, at the time Bosnia and Herzegovina were annexed to the Habsburg Monarchy, Nicholas II refused Russia's active participation in a war against the Monarchy because Russia was not yet prepared for war. In 1914, however, Russia immediately stood with Serbia. Hartwig assigned two of his military aides, Colonel Atamov and Captain Werchowsky to Colonel Dimitrijevic-Apis, the Grand master of the Black Hand, a secret organization.

---

[118] Emil Niederhauser: Illirizmus és Nagyszerb tervek. (Illyrism and the Greater Serbia plans) In Historia 1992/4, pp. 11-13.

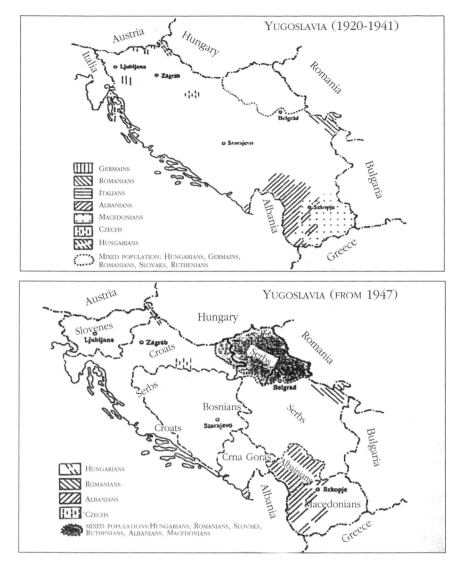

The telegram from the Serb Minister in St. Petersburg, Spalaiković, to Pasić on July 22, 1914, sheds light on the secret Russian-Serb relationships: "…Sasonov urges our military preparedness. Public demonstrations are to be avoided until the Russian preparations are complete…" Following the July 24 Russian Council of Ministers meeting, Splaiković cabled about the mobilization of two thirds of the Russian military forces and also said, "Sasonov requests that our answer to the ultimatum be peaceful in form but negative in content… It is the Tsar's request that we mobilize immediately, but if Austria initiates the conflict, we should withdraw our army without resisting in order to maintain our armed

161

forces intact…" The secret anti-Monarchy agreement of March 1912 between Bulgaria and Serbia was followed by a similar agreement between Russia and Romania in 1914. A vigorous and successful propaganda campaign helped to bring the interests of Romania and Serbia to the attention of the Western press. Take Jonescu met twice in 1912 with Grand Duke Nicholas who tried to use Russian money to convince Jonescu to organize a propaganda campaign against Austria. Starting in 1909, Isvolski, the Russian Ambassador in Paris, used Russian money to bribe the French press to publish articles unfavorable to the Monarchy. One of the recipients was Andre Tardieu, later Prime Minister, who at that time wrote the Foreign Policy column in Le Temps. The horrendous news items published in Paris during the War were generally written in the Serb Legation or in the editorial offices of Le Temps or the Agence des Balkans.[119]

Only 55% of the Serbs lived under Serbian or Montenegrin rule, while 45% settled, during the Turkish rule, on the northern side of the Danube and the Sava, in Croatia, Slavonia and Bosnia-Herzegovina. The Serb-Croat-Slovene Kingdom, known after 1929 as the Yugoslav Kingdom, was ethnically and religiously highly complex. The percentage of non-Serbs rose to 62.2% and included Croats, Slovenes, Hungarians, Germans Macedonians, Albanians, Romanians, Turks, Italians, Jews and others.

The Minority Situation, 1920-1945. Contradictions Between the International Agreements and Domestic Statutes

The representatives of the new Yugoslav state signed the Minority Defense Agreement of the St. Germain Peace Treaty only after lengthy debate and enacted it in 1920 only as a temporary measure. The Act guaranteed equality before the law and the right to hold office to all citizens including the minorities. The latter were allowed to establish and maintain benevolent, religious and elemosynary organizations and schools and other educational institutions, at their own expense. The Statute guaranteed the freedom of using the minority's mother tongue in instruction.

The 1921 Constitution disbanded the Croat Parliament, the Slovene Territorial Assembly, and the Újvidék National Council without mention of the nationalities. The following regulations were implemented:

Dishonest census

The last legitimate, and internationally recognized, census in the Carpathian Basin was the Hungarian one of 1910. In the successor states, intimidation was used and the census data were manipulated to such an extent that we have no reliable figures on the ethnic groups in these countries. The estimated figures differed widely from the official ones. Even in the statistical calculations the endeavors to favor the Serb position were manifest during the 1921 census. The population was not identified on a nationality basis and the only pertinent question asked was about the mother tongue. This made it possible to include in the Serb-Croat language family such diverse nationalities as the Serbs, Croats, Crnagorians, Muslims, and, for political reasons, the Macedonians.

---

[119] Pozzi, Henri: Századunk bűnösei… (The sinners of our century…) HOGYF EDITIO, Bp. 1996, pp. 16, 23, 31, 56, 58, 134, 136, 139-40, 145.

Settlements, populating the border zones, land reform and expropriation, altering the ethnic rates

Next to the officials, the landowners were considered to be the most important guardians of the Hungarian spirit. Consequently, arrests were made and a variety of atrocities were committed in an endeavor to make them leave their land voluntarily. The larger estates were immediately confiscated and the resettlement of Dobrovoljac on Hungarian land began already in 1919. The Dobrovoljac were Yugoslavs who served in the Austro-Hungarian army and deserted during the World War, fighting against their former comrades in the Serb or Russian army. These Dobrovoljac were settled on the estates and were given the breeding stock, the equipment and even the furniture of the former owners. It was in vain that the Bácska Agricultural Association protested, claiming that the Dobrovoljac slaughtered the breeding stock thereby causing great harm to Yugoslav agriculture. The Serb officials claimed that the steps taken were essential.[120] In the framework of the land reforms implemented during the 1920s, *Serbs were settled in a 40 km deep zone along the border and these settlements were designed to serve as a protective belt.* Minority nationals could settle within 50 km of the border only with the prior approval by the Minister of Internal Affairs or the Minister of Defense. Serb officials were moved to all the debated areas such as Kosovo, Macedonia, Baranya, Bácska and the Bánát. In all of these areas Serb settlements were established.

The expropriation and distribution of the large estates of the former "ruling nationalities", Germans, Hungarians, Italians, Turks and the Churches benefited, for all practical purposes, only the Slavs. Prior to 1940, more than 200 villages were settled in the Vajdaság and in Slavonia, and more than 100 in the Bánát. The new owners quite regularly leased the newly acquired land to Hungarians and Germans, who were not allowed to participate in the land reform because, according to a 1919 Council of Minister ordinance, non-Slavs "of uncertain citizenship" could not be given land. One third of those who emigrated from Yugoslavia to the United States, about 60,000, were German mid-sized landowners and Hungarian and Romanian cotters.

Replacement of public servants, loyalty oaths, language tests and settlements

The Hungarians in the Délvidék were already exposed to grave injustices as early as 1918, when the area was still technically part of Hungary, but was under the control of occupation forces. Accused of conspiring against the State, highly respected public figures were sentenced to long prison terms. The expropriation of land and other property began and a very unfavorable, 4:1, money exchange rate was imposed.

The large majority of the Hungarian officials and intellectuals refused to take the loyalty oath or sit for a language test. Losing their jobs, they moved to Hungary. Many others, mostly clergymen, were expelled later and approximately 50,000 of them moved to Hungary. The German and Hungarian officials were dismissed from the urban and village administrative offices, without pension or compensation. The reason given was that they had insufficient command of the official language. Their positions were filled with Slavs although some of them were transferred further South, to areas populated mainly by Slavs.

[120] János Csuka: A délvidéki magyarság története 1918-1941 (History of the Délvidék Hungarians) Püski, Bp. 1996, pp.34-35.

163

Use of the language

During the 1920s, signs appeared in the coffee houses, restaurants, offices and shops of the Délvidék towns with the inscription, "those who do not speak the official language are enemies of the State". It is indicative of the degree of intimidation, that these signs were posted even in shops where the owners' knowledge of Serb was limited to a few words. Hungarian signs were not displayed except in a few purely Hungarian villages. In Horgos, Topolya, Csantavér and Szabadka, the nameplates of Hungarian physicians and lawyers were painted over or defaced during the night, forcing the owner to take them down and replace them. The same happened in Zenta, Zombor and in the villages along the Tisza. In 1925, the only evidence that there were minorities living in Yugoslavia was the presence of five representatives of the German Party in the National Parliament.

Samuel Schumacher spoke during the debate on public education and said, "The population of my village was always purely German and the language of instruction was always 100 % in German. At present, only four of the 11 teachers know any German and, as may be imagined, the results of education are nil. In Estonia, the nationalities have educational autonomy. Before the War, the same was true in Hungary where the Serb National Church had educational autonomy. The history of this goes back 200 years. There were not only Serb nationality schools in Hungary, but there were even Serb teachers colleges in Zombor, Pakrac and Karlovci. There were also two Serb high schools and several high schools for girls. The Serbs in Hungary had substantial funds for the maintenance of their schools. In Hungary, the Germans also had their schools. The national minorities demand the same complete educational autonomy that the Serbs enjoyed in Hungary for 200 years..."[121] In 1929, Selimir Ostoic, a retired general, became the Mayor of Szabadka. He fired one his officials when he heard the man speaking Hungarian with a friend in the hall. The fired official was given a document indicating that he had been dismissed because he dared to speak Hungarian. The matter was taken to the League of Nations, but that organization did nothing to remedy the complaint.[122]

Reorganization of the administration

The non-Serb or non-Yugoslav ethnic blocs were fragmented by the administrative rearrangements introduced in 1922. The Albanian bloc was divided among 6 districts with Serb-Macedonian majorities and the Hungarian Tiszavidék was attached to Belgrade in order to produce a majority of the Yugoslav ethnic group. Later on, the same principle was applied when the Bánságs were established. Compromises were made only in response to threats from abroad, which is the explanation for the establishment of an autonomous Croat Bánság in 1939.

Curtailment of the territory's industrial development and the introduction of Serb workers

In 1921, the Vajdaság was the most industrialized province among the former Austrian provinces, second only to Slovenia. The intrusion of the Slavic element began at this time and it was at the same time, in the early 1920s, that the Hungarian element was forced out of their economic positions. The nationaliza-

---

[121] Csuka, op.cit.. p. 232.
[122] Csuka, op.cit. p. 365.

164

tion of the publicly held companies began and the Hungarians were excluded from the new managerial group. Serbo-Croat, Slovene, Bosnian and Dalmatian officials were brought in who increasingly diminished the opportunities of Hungarians to earn a living. Even more distress was caused by the activity of the Serb fiscal agencies that excluded Hungarians from the licensed trades and businesses. There were battles for every liquor license and the so-called *licno bravo* created such a desperate situation that men denied their Hungarian ethnicity in order to earn their livelihood. The licensed tobacco outlets were also taken away from the Hungarians. People realized the meaning of the saying attributed to Cardinal Kollonich, "The Hungarians must be first made poor and then be made into servants."[123] The development of industry and transportation gradually declined, since the Serbian territories, judged to be more reliable, were favored, and because the higher tax rate in the Hungarian areas scared investors away. Some capitalists were urged to move their companies to Old Serbia. The German and Jewish establishments were forced to employ Serb workers.

Taxation and tax collection
The tax rate varied from area to area and in every aspect of productivity, it was four times higher in the Vajdaság than anywhere else. The unpaid taxes of the Serbs were usually forgiven but, in the case of the minorities, immediate foreclosure was the rule.

Nationalization of the credit institutions
The majority of the banks had their Hungarian or German officials replaced or were closed. Many were forced to merge with Serb banks.

The elimination of schools, the displacement of teachers and the curtailment of minority intellectuals
The confiscation of the assets of the Hungarian educational and cultural institutions, without any compensation, began. The parochial schools were nationalized and Hungarian teachers were dismissed or transferred. The teachers were usually dismissed because "they did not speak the official language" and later a number of Hungarian schools were closed "for a shortage of teachers".[124]

Under the Name Analysis Act, those with a German or Slavic name could not claim to be Hungarian and go to a Hungarian school even though they spoke only Hungarian and their families had considered themselves to be Hungarians for several generations

The ratio of Hungarian-speaking students at the University was one fourth of the ratio of Hungarians living in Yugoslavia. Of the 500,000 Hungarians living in the country, only one one-thousandth (0.001%) gained a degree between the two World Wars. There was a shortage of Hungarian teachers, clergymen, physicians, veterinarians and industrial and agricultural experts. The new graduates frequently could find employment only in the Yugoslav districts. It is characteristic that the first Hungarian Teachers College was established in 1934, far from the Hungarian districts, in Belgrade.

---

[123] Csuka, op.cit. p. 97.
[124] Csuka, op.cit. p.pp 84-87

The position of the Churches in the absence of autonomy

The Hungarians generally submitted quietly to the arbitrary official rulings and it was only the Catholic clergy, which stood up against abuses of power. The younger clergy, ignoring the dangers, informed the press in Hungary about these issues. The active Catholic and Protestant clergy were harassed, imprisoned and expelled. Lacking an independent Hungarian bishopric, Croatian-speaking priests were assigned to the Hungarian churches after 1927.

The Minority Situation in Yugoslavia Between 1945 and 1990

In 1945, in a country controlled by the army under Tito's leadership, the Communist Party won the elections. The 1946 Constitution initiated the development of the Proletarian Dictatorship. According to 1945 data, one fourth of the homes were damaged or destroyed during the war. Two fifths of all industry was destroyed, roads, railroads and bridges became unusable and 1.8 million people perished. Of these, 1 million died during the civil war. During the War, 530,000 people were expatriated, 320,000 were interned, 270,000 were sent to forced labor and 40,000 Vajdaság Hungarians were murdered. In the strongly centralized, dictatorial Socialist system, exploitation of the minorities could be curtailed only by the supreme political leader, as we have seen already in the case of Romania.

The same thing was true in Yugoslavia. The foundation of the Second, or Tito's, Yugoslavia was laid in 1943, at the meeting of the AVNOJ (The Anti-Fascist Organization Established for the Liberation of Yugoslavia). Based on the experiences of the previous 25 years, it was decided to set up a federal system in Yugoslavia, giving equal rights to Serbs, Croats, Slovenes, Macedonians and Montenegrins, including the minorities. The number of planned federal units was identical with the number of nationalities. Bosnia-Herzegovina was not included.

The country was composed of 6 republics and two autonomous provinces. The basic principles of the Federation included the right of the Yugoslav people for self-determination, including the right to secede or to unite with other countries. The relationship with the Hungarian minority was affected by the position of Hungary within the Soviet Bloc, particularly after the Yugoslav-Soviet estrangement and the ousting of the Yugoslav Communist Party from the International, in 1948. Under the auspices of the so-called "show window politics", extensive rights were promised in both the constitution and in the statutes, but few, if any, were ever implemented in practice. It was at this time that, and in accordance with political guidelines, the class of "professional or Yugoslav Hungarians" was identified. This class had only statistical meaning and, if they really tried to protect the Hungarian interests, they were dismissed or transferred.

Ethnic cleansing and flight

On October 17, 1944, Commander-in-Chief Tito signed the Military Administration order that meant, in effect, that in the Bácska-Baranya-Bánát area all rights of the people had been suspended.

After the withdrawal of the German and Hungarian troops, the partisans entering the Hungarian villages, wishing to avenge the 1942 so-called Bácska massacre, committed dreadful atrocities and mass executions. These were done primarily to intimidate the people and also to eliminate the potential leadership

166

of the Hungarian minority. In many villages, such as Bezdán[125], the partisans arrived with death lists containing the names of those who, during the period of re-annexation to Hungary, accepted any economic, cultural or clerical position or who were in a leadership position. Large numbers of both Croats and Hungarians were arrested. Precise figures are not available about the numbers of victims of this retribution era but the estimates range from 20,000 to 40,000. There is documentary evidence for 20,000 deaths. About 30,000 Hungarians escaped to Hungary, including the Csángós and Székelys who were settled there in 1941. About 330,000 Germans escaped to Germany, 250,000 were killed at the front and in concentration camps. The number of uprooted and murdered Italians was approximately the same. The victims of the 1944-1945 Communist Serb retribution included about 100,000 Croats, 30,000 Slovenes and 30,000 Serb collaborators - the latter mostly in Belgrade.

Camps and prisons
The gathering of Hungarians and Germans into camps began in October 1944. About 140,000 Germans and hundreds of Hungarians were working in the 41 Vajdaság labor camps; many Germans perished. The labor camps were active until 1947-1948. Following the deterioration of the Yugoslav-Soviet relationship in 1948-1949 (in the so-called period "Tito - the chained up dog of the imperialists"), again many Hungarians were arrested.

Reorganization of the administration
The Vajdaság (Voivodina) was declared to be an autonomous province in Serbia. Its borders were changed and the Drávaszög was attached to Croatia while the mostly Serb Szerémség was made a part of the Vajdaság.

As part of the administrative reorganization, and starting in the 1950s, regional centers were developed. By the end of the 1980s, these resulted in the formation of 8 independent economic units, existing within the socialist economic system, in almost complete isolation from each other. The new Serb constitution, enacted in 1989, placed Kosovo and the Vajdaság completely under Serbia and did away with their autonomy. In the Vajdaság, this autonomy was always largely a matter of form. The majority of the population was Slavic and thus the autonomy was essentially self-government, ruled by Serbs.

Settlements
Between 1944 and 1948, 40,000 Yugoslav, mostly Serb, families were given land in the Vajdaság and in Slavonia, mostly from former German or ecclesiastic (Roman Catholic) estates.

The large-scale migration from the south continued. Between 1953 and 1971, more than 500,000 settlers arrived in the Vajdaság. A new wave of migrant Serbs arrived after the civil war broke out in 1991 and during the Kosovo troubles of 1999. According to some estimates, these later migrations led to the settlement of 350-400,000 new people in the Vajdaság.

---

[125] Ferenc Kubinyi: 50,000 Hungarian Martyrs. Report about the Hungarian Holocaust in Jugoslavia 1944-1992. P. .3;
Márton Matuska: Days of the Revenge. From Publisher Novisad, 1991.

Exclusion of the Churches

The pressure on the Churches was similar to the one in the Soviet Union. In 1944-1945, many clergymen were murdered on trumped-up charges, regardless of denomination. Later, they were persecuted for standing up for their ethnic group against the Yugoslav ideal. The teaching of religion was forbidden and to practice religion was considered to be incompatible with Party membership. The absence of an independent Hungarian ecclesiastic hierarchy caused problems from 1918 onward and the Croat priests sent into the Hungarian villages could not preserve and protect the national identity. It was only at the end of the 1980s that the Pope appointed a Hungarian priest to the bishopric of the Bácska-Bánát. For historical reasons, there were very few Protestant congregations in this area.

Curtailment of industrial development in this area

The growth of 5.1%-6.2% of the gross provincial products in the Vajdaság, between 1948 and 1972, was well behind that of any other province in the country. The entire North Bácska region, with a Hungarian majority, was left behind in its economic development between 1918 and 1970. In the 1970s and 1980s, the investment per person was at the national average and the situation was even better in agriculture.

The number of unemployed rose more rapidly during the 1980s than in the other provinces. This led to migration, emigration and guest worker jobs in the West.

Education in the mother tongue, the level of schooling and the position of the intellectuals

Hungarian public schools reopened in 1945 and there were Hungarian high schools and teacher training programs. The University of the Vajdaság opened in 1954 and three years later a Chair of Hungarian was established. It was placed in Újvidék where there were very few Hungarians. In 1969, an Institute of Hungarian Studies was opened and similar steps were taken for the Slovak and Ruthenian minorities as well.

Due to the decrease in the population and because of assimilation, the number of schools decreased from year to year after 1950. Today, only the schools in the Vajdaság have a Hungarian section. A significant portion of the previously autonomous Hungarian schools were fused with Serbo-Croat schools and a significant percentage of the students chose to continue their education in the Serbo-Croat sections. Approximately 25% of the pupils did not study in their mother tongue. The school buildings were old and not up to standards.

In the distribution of scholarships and dormitory space, the Vajdaság, and particularly its minorities, were in a very disadvantageous position when compared with the Montenegrins and Bosnians. The Universities of the Vajdaság trained a leadership class that had a completely foreign mentality and did not return to its native South. It stayed in the Vajdaság and assumed leading positions in business and administration, further adding to the discriminatory practices against the Hungarian, Slovak and Romanian minorities.

The number of unskilled workers was very high and the ratio of blue-collar and white-collar workers was very unfavorable when compared to the Yugoslav averages. The number of high school or university graduates was much smaller than in the other provinces. According to 1981 data, the number of Hungarian high school or university graduates was about half of the Yugoslav average.

Separatism

The crisis of the socialist economy became acute during the 1980s, particularly after Tito's death. In 1987, inflation exceeded 100%. In 1989, armed conflict began in Kosovo, where the Albanians were in majority, upon which Belgrade rescinded its autonomy.

During the same year, the Slovene parliament declared that Slovenia had the right to secede and, in 1990, this parliament placed the Slovene law above the Yugoslav one. In 1991, a plebiscite decided to secede from Yugoslavia. The Federal Yugoslav army attacked Slovenia in 1991, after Slovenia declared independence. At the Bosnia-Herzegovina elections, the Communist party was defeated by the nationalist Muslim forces.

A plebiscite in Croatia, in 1991, declared independence for the country. The ensuing bloody civil war and genocide made the European Union to enter the fray and, in January 1992, Slovenia and Croatia became, in fact, independent.

At the 1992 elections, boycotted by the opposition, Montenegro decided to remain a part of Yugoslavia. Starting in the fall of 1992, armed conflicts erupted in Bosnia between the Croats and the Muslims.

Decrease of the population and solution

Since 1961, the Hungarian minority in Yugoslavia has gradually decreased. The reason for this was not only the low birth rate, the mixed marriages and the forced migration in search of employment but also the independently hierarchical ecclesiastic organization, the forced separation from the mother country, the gradual suppression of Hungarian language instruction in the schools, the lack of economic strength for ethnic Hungarian organizations and the politically centralized government which was opposed to the minority for 40 years.

According to the research of Antal Biacsi, the number of Hungarians in the North Vajdaság was steadily decreasing since the middle 1960s. Between 1948 and 1991, the population of the Vajdaság increased by 23%, but the Hungarian population of the area decreased by 21%. In the case of children born of mixed marriages, 45% of the children opted for the nationality of the non-Hungarian parent, 29.2% opted to be Hungarian and 20.4% chose to be considered Yugoslavian. "Yugoslav" is a new nationality category, introduced after World War II. As the number of Yugoslavs grew, the number of other nationalities declined. As a consequence of the minority policies discussed above, the number of Hungarians declined by 14%, between 1910 and 1991. The Germans have practically disappeared (22% decrease), while the Serb population of the area increased by 18%. During the wars of the 1990s, the flood of refugees entering the Vajdaság from the South changed the ratio of the Serbs in the area from 56.8% to 64.3%. Inevitably, the ratio of the minorities, vis-à-vis the Serbs, decreased proportionately.

The lack of economic maturity and growth, as well as the future industrialization and urbanization, will promote assimilation unless the macro-economic process can be stopped by the establishment of autonomy for the ethnic minority. Such autonomy must *include Hungarian ecclesiastic autonomy and territorial self-government for the territorially contiguous communities; Hungarian local government authorities for Hungarian fragments; and personal autonomy in the cultural sphere, education and language-use.*[126]

Even during the past eleven years of warfare in the country, the deliberate change of the ethnic ratio continued, taking advantage of the suspension of the activities of the autonomous organizations. The demographic structure of the Vajdaság underwent a complete change and the Serbs became a majority with 64.3% of the population. Thus, the autonomy of the Vajdaság, guaranteed in 1974, would no longer grant protection to the minorities and must be reviewed according to the declarations and recommendations of the international documents, particularly in the North Vajdaság where most of the Hungarians live. One wonders how much the prohibition of changing ethnic ratios is worth if Yugoslavia, having forced such changes, cannot be made to reestablish the status quo ante. A solution may be a territorial autonomy for the area where the Hungarians live in a bloc and cultural and personal autonomy in the other areas. The non-territorial, cultural and personal autonomy would be based on personal civil rights and it should be organized similarly to the ecclesiastic autonomy as far as supervision of education in the mother tongue and learning in general are concerned. Local self-government in villages where the minority nationality represented the majority would guarantee minority rights to the minority ethnic groups living among national majorities. *The Hungarian Autonomous district would include the seven contiguous areas where the Hungarians represent a majority of the population. It would form a single administrative unit containing the most important settlements. Hungarian, Croatian and Serbian would be the official languages. It would be this threefold, mutually complementing autonomy that alone could guarantee practical realization of individual and collective rights.*

---

[126] Memorandum on the self-government of Hungarians in the Republic of Serbia by Sándor Hódi. Working document at the General Assembly of the DCHV,1992. Agreement on the political and legal frameworks of the self-government of Voivodina. Tóthfalú, 1999.

Civil Rights Battle for Territorial Autonomy in Great Britain

Population (1994): 58,394,000
Ethnic groups: English - 80%, Scottish - 10%, Irish - 4%, Indian and Pakistani - 2%, Welsh - 1.9%
Official language: English.

The 19th century is called the era of the nation states. Yet, parallel with the movement that propagated the development of the majority nationality's language and culture as elements of their national integrity, there arose, in the minority nationalities, the desire to get to know themselves, write their own history, have their own language, customs and cultural values.

The historian, István Diószegi, distinguished four levels at which nationality policies were handled in Europe in the 19th century:

1. Discriminatory - One part of the population was excluded from the practice of their civil rights on the basis of ethnicity or religion. This was seen in the case of the Catholics in Ireland, the Jews in Russia and Romania and the Christians in Turkey.

2. Restrictive - Instruction in the mother tongue was prohibited by statute and use of the official language was made mandatory in administration and legal practice. Use of the mother tongue was limited to the family circle. This was seen in Ireland, in Brittany, in Germany with the Danes, in Poland and with all minorities in Russia.

3. Permissive - Education in the mother tongue was authorized in the constitution, by law and by ordinance. Administration was bilingual and cultural and political organizations were permitted. This was seen in Austria, Belgium and Hungary.

4. Distributive - The dominant nationality shared the sovereignty and the territorial and political separation of the minority nationalities was acknowledged. This was seen in the hereditary provinces of Austria, the Hungarian-Croat agreement, the Swedish-Norwegian relationship, the Austrian-Hungarian relationship and the federalism of the Swiss cantons.[127]

The distributive approach was employed in the 19th century in those countries where there was a historical tradition for it, such as in Switzerland and in the Monarchy, where a certain religious and territorial autonomy existed historically for several centuries. The example presented by these countries served as stimulus for minority nationalities everywhere.

---

[127] István Diószegi: Nemzetiségi politika Európában (Nationality policies in Europe). Üllő és Kalapács (Anvil and Hammer) Magyarságkutató Intézet, Bp. 1991.

171

At the end of the 19th century, the Swiss and Hungarian types of autonomy were viewed with interest throughout Europe. Thus, one of the leaders of the Irish movement, Arthur Griffith, wrote in 1904, in his *"Hungary's resurrection and its implications for Ireland"*, that the solution of the nationality issue in Hungary could serve as a model for Ireland. The development of the modern bourgeois state, at the end of the 19th century and the beginning of the 20th and the introduction of universal franchise, opened the possibility that the parliamentary representatives of the minorities, working for the decentralization of the national authority, initiated the establishment of territorial autonomy and of an independent administration financed by local taxes. This would represent a change in these countries where previously only individual, personal, political rights were recognized

In spite of the fact that the union and economic integration with England produced a rapid improvement in the economy of Scotland and Wales, these peoples were able to preserve their identity. This was largely due to the forceful activities of the Churches, which worked for the autonomous structures, of which they were the centers in the Middle Ages, and for the preservation of the cultural heritage of their people. The growth of the capitalistic society led to an almost total assimilation. Only about 100,000 Scots preserved their Gaelic mother tongue. In spite of the fact that the politically active Irish aristocracy became largely assimilated, the Irish development differed markedly from that in Scotland and Wales. In Ireland, the differences between English and Irish economic maturity were significant and the brutal colonization led to an upsurge in the struggle for independence. The universal practice of the Catholic religion increased the self-awareness of the Irish and gave them the structural basis for distancing themselves from the conquerors.

Ireland

Population (1995): 3,582,200
Minority groups: None.
Official language: Irish (Gaelic) and English.

Scholars are still uncertain as to when the Celts originally occupied Ireland. The majority opinion today holds that this probably occurred during the second half of the first century BC. The Irish language is a variant of the original, local Celtic from which it has borrowed many words.

During the early Middle Ages (7th - 8th c.), there were a number of local kingdoms. During the 9th century, seven distinct political units began to form. It seems that in the 12th century, Dublin, with its stone fortifications, became the center of the Kingdom ruling all of Ireland. Its central importance was largely due to its rich agricultural background and its successful commercial port.

Unification by Religious War and by Suppressing the Native Language

The idea of conquering Ireland arose as early as the rule of William the Conqueror and Henry I. It became timely in 1154-1155, when Henry II (1154-1189) assumed the throne. When the Archbishop of Canterbury lost his authority over the Dublin diocese in 1152 and the Irish Church seceded, an excuse for armed intervention was found.

Henry II sent John Salisbury, the secretary of the Archbishop of Canterbury, to Pope Adrian IV (1154-1159), the only Pope of English extraction. The King asked the Pope's permission to invade Ireland in order to "introduce there the rule of law" and to "make that uncouth and ignorant people familiar with the verity of the Christian religion". It was agreed that the Pope, who wished to bring the Irish Church under his authority, would confirm Henry and his successors as Kings of Ireland.

The King, at that moment, was fully occupied with consolidating his power in England but, as soon as conditions improved, he intervened in the squabbles of the Irish Kings with armed force and defeated them in 1171. At the end of the 12th century, the population of Europe increased rapidly, leading to a quest for land and for a migration toward the still uninhabited areas. The new immigrants came to Ireland from England, Wales, France and Flanders. The new settlers belonged to the lower strata of society and, while free, lived side-by-side with the small Irish farmers who were tied by feudal ties to the land they cultivated. In many cases, it appeared that the new settlers lived in self-controlled small communities that they established themselves and where the single tax was paid by the community as a whole. A number of the poorer settlers could not preserve their freedom and became feudal serfs. The estates of some of the Irish nobility were separated from the free and unconquered areas by forests, swamps or mountains.

The tribal chieftains could not view their hereditary feudal estates as being secure, even though they could own their land as freeholds and pay an annual tax or annuity to their Anglo-Norman overlords. When the English lords went to war, the Irish chieftains were obliged to bring their armed retainers with them and fight. The English language took root in the cities and among the peasantry. The Norman-French language, which served as the literary language, spread among the upper classes. In the eastern parts of Ireland a purely self-sufficient economy was replaced by the production of export goods and by a fiscal economy. **John I** continued the occupation of Ireland, first as Prince of Ireland and later **as King of England (1199-1216)**. Twenty Irish kings had to swear an oath of fealty before John in Dublin. It was John, who introduced the shire system with sheriffs, county courts and circuit riding judges. Before he left Ireland in 1210, John exacted a promise from the Irish Barons that the English laws and customs would be obeyed in Ireland, as well. From the 12th century on, Dublin never had an archbishop who was born in Ireland. The incumbents were royal appointees who frequently combined the position of the archbishop with that of the chancellor, treasurer or even justiciar of Ireland.

In the middle of the 13th century, a rebellion broke out in the Irish principalities. Edward III and Richard II tried to re-establish English rule over Ireland. Finally, the victory over Ireland, at the end of the Middle Ages, was not the triumph of the English Crown, nor of the Irish princes, but of the English magnates in Ireland. By the end of the 15th century, the English king's rule extended only over the four eastern provinces of Ireland, Louth, Meath, Dublin and Kildare. The independent Irish principalities were strong enough in the first half of the century to attempt the establishment of a union among themselves. By the end of the 15th century, the power of the local magnates was the decisive political force in Ireland. As a result of the mixed marriages, the settlers became increasingly Irish by the 14th century. It was probably this development that the notorious 1366

Kilkenny Ordinance tried to reverse. It stated, "The English must not maintain contacts with the Irish, they may not intermarry with them nor wear Irish dress. The Irish language is forbidden even within the family circle. The Irish clergy must be separated from the English Catholic priests."

In the 16th and 17th century, it was the **Anglican Church** that determined the policy in the areas occupied by the English. In 1536, the Irish National Assembly was forced to accept Henry VIII as the head of the Irish Church. The English Reformation had its effects only in the occupied areas and it was there that the monasteries were despoiled. It is recorded of the monks and other priests living in the ancient Celtic territory that they prayed for everybody to take arms against the English king and suggested that those who would die in this endeavor would die the death of a martyr. The Observant Friars (Franciscans) were the first among the Catholic reformers who served as protectors of the Irish communities and of the Irish church against the incursions of rapacious lords. In religious matters, they opposed the rule of the English Crown. The Observant Friars were the first that opposed the religious reforms proposed by the English government and that also organized support for Fitzgerald, the Master of Kildare, among the people. It was Fitzgerald who led the rebellion against the English Crown in 1507. After crushing the insurrection, only Englishmen were appointed as Viceroys of Ireland and until 1922, British troops were stationed in Dublin.

Queen Elizabeth I (1558-1603) and her successors insisted that all persons appointed to an important position recognize the Crown's authority in religious matters, as well as in political ones. The Irish population, however, refused to participate in Anglican religious ceremonies and, as the public offices in Dublin became vacant, they were filled with English Protestants. The Protestant officials who supported the implementation of the severe punitive measures against the Catholics and who recommended that Catholic landowners be deprived of their estates, intentionally provoked an uprising, expecting it to be defeated and hoping to gain considerable benefits from the ensuing conditions.

When the Pope placed the Queen under anathema in 1570, Munster Province rose in rebellion and was assisted by Spanish and Italian troops coming from the continent. In 1583, the rebellion suffered a bloody defeat and Munster became de-populated. The leaders of the rebellion were killed in battle or executed thereafter. Never had Ireland been the victim of such destruction or of such systematic massacres. About 20,000 English settlers were moved to Munster. Huge areas of land fell into English hands and *the English settlers in Munster perpetuated the presence of Protestant interests in Ireland.*

James I (1603-1625) followed this process which can legitimately be called colonization. The most threatened areas were County Ulster, the adjacent parts of County Connacht, the Gaelic speaking higher regions of Leinster and the uninhabited areas of Munster. The settlement policies practiced in Ulster were similar to those in Munster. The English and Scottish recipients of estates were held strictly accountable. They were expected to erect protective structures and to settle 10 British Protestant families for every 1000 acres of land they had received. The new arrivals built handsome houses, established new towns and villages and created new markets and new branches of industry.

A new society took shape that was sharply divided from its social environment by religion, customs and traditions. The relationship between the original inhabitants

174

and the newcomers worsened under the government of Thomas Wentworth (1633-1640), an appointee of Charles I, who was sent for the specific purpose of fostering the interests of the Crown. He made it painfully clear that the Catholic landowners could no longer count on support from the Court. He worked assiduously to prepare for the confiscation of all Catholic lands. After Wentworth was recalled, and believing that the English-Scottish war was a sufficient distraction, a number of Catholic landowners took to arms in 1641 to protect their interests. *The recognition of the Presbyterian Church in Scotland by Charles I strengthened the resolve of the leaders of Ulster.*

The relationship between Ulster natives and Protestant settlers continued to deteriorate and, in the resulting upheaval, about 2,000 Protestant settlers were murdered. The rebellion, based on the situation in Ulster, rapidly extended to the whole country. The fear that eventually all Protestants would be massacred in Ireland triggered the demands by the English and the Scots that the participants in the rebellion be punished immediately. Only Cromwell could accomplish this. He carried the war to Ireland in 1649 and his campaign left an indelible mark in Irish collective memory. His plans included the removal of the Catholic clergy and landowners and forceful, state-sponsored missionary work to convert the Irish to Protestantism. The latter plan misfired because the Protestant preachers could not address the natives in their own language. Not until the restoration of the Stuarts did the Catholic Church again become active in Ireland. Nevertheless, it seemed that, in Ireland, the Catholic Church has been pushed aside. The Protestants not only owned the majority of the land but they also filled the most important positions in the administration and in commerce. It seemed that with the accession of **James II to the throne (1685-1688)**, better times would come again. In fact, a Catholic Viceroy, judges and Privy Councilors were appointed.

In the meantime, a new revolution was beginning in England and, in **1688, William of Orange**, the husband of James' Protestant daughter Mary, was invited to the throne. When James fled to Ireland in 1689, he was forced to call a National Assembly and declare its independence from the English Parliament. The supporters of William were declared to be rebels and their land was about to be confiscated. A number of laws favoring the Irish Catholics were drafted but all this depended on the outcome of the war against William. In reality, the war in Ireland was fought between the Protestants and the Catholics, between the original inhabitants and the new settlers. The Peace of Limerick, signed in 1691, had serious consequences. The Catholics only owned about 15% of the land and the new penal laws extended to all Catholics.

After 1690, all Irish deputies had to take an oath, denying the doctrine of transubstantiation and the supremacy of the Pope. The Popery Bills of 1703-1704 limited the rights of the Catholics in inheriting and leasing land. In 1729, Catholic landowners were deprived of the franchise and in Parliament only Protestant voices were heard. *By 1778, only 5% of the Irish lands remained in Catholic hands. Commercial restrictions, lack of mineral resources and a vestigial industry forced a very large percentage of the population to eke out a miserable existence on the land.*

In the second half of the 18th century, there were many hidden tensions in Irish society. The rapid increase in the population and the high taxes led to increased restlessness. At the same time, the bonds between Ulster and the United States became stronger from generation to generation and strengthened the radical, anti-Westminster sentiments.

In 1782, the Irish Parliament was given the right to enact legislation independently but only the small Irish Protestant minority of English extraction might participate in this activity because the Catholics were excluded. The events of the French Revolution resulted in an intervention of the British government and this caused the English Conservatives to view the Irish Catholics more favorably. In 1793, the Conservatives passed a law that granted civil rights and the franchise to the Irish Catholics. At the same time, the liberalization of the Land Act increased the tensions. Secret societies were formed and became increasingly politicized. In Belfast, the radical Presbyterians, leaning toward equality before the law, became enchanted with the French enlightenment. The United Irish Movement planned an insurrection for the summer of 1798, but it was so poorly organized that the scattered uprisings could be easily put down. Following this insurrection, the Act of Union was proclaimed in 1801. The Irish Parliament was disbanded and declared that it had become one with the English Parliament. The English Prime Minister, William Pitt, was confident that, after the Union was declared, the Westminster Parliament would have a solid Protestant majority and that this majority would make it possible to rescind some of the earlier discriminatory legislation. In 1829, most of the restrictions imposed on the Catholics were removed. In 1830, the Young Orange Ireland party was created. Based on the ideas of William of Orange, it was clearly Protestant in intent and included a number of Irish Protestant intellectuals who were, in many respects, anti-English.

At about the same time, unemployment, poverty, the feudal land conditions and the absence of industry, combined with the "Potato Famine" of 1840s, led to a desperate situation. The famine and the ensuing epidemics caused mass emigration to Australia, Canada and the United States. Between 1845 and 1851, the population of Ireland decreased by about 2 million with almost 250,000 emigrating each year.

In the 1850s, a new type of Irish national political movement emerged, called the Fenian Movement, which led to the formation of a secret society, the Irish Republican Brotherhood. Convinced that Great Britain would grant independence only if forced to do so by arms, the formation of secret military organizations began. *In 1879, Isaac Butt founded the Home Rule Society that later became the Irish National Party.* Under Charles Parnell, it gained increasing support from the British Liberals between 1879 and 1891. Parnell's tactics were successful in getting the electoral laws modified, allowing his party to send 80 representatives to the London Parliament. In 1860, Palmerston, the British Prime Minister, suggested to the Austrian government to return its constitution and privileges to Hungary so far as consistent with the integrity of the Monarchy. *As a curious reaction, Kálnoky, the Austro-Hungarian Joint Minister of Defense, urged London in 1886 to grant the same degree of independence to Ireland that Hungary enjoyed within the Monarchy, if Great Britain wished to avoid a serious diminution of its powers.*[128]

The struggle for autonomy

It was the Fenian uprising that convinced W.E. Gladstone, the greatest Liberal British politician of the period, to begin to implement his "Justice for Ireland" policy. The first step was the 1869 Ecclesiastic Law, which deprived the Irish

---

[128] István Diószegi: Külső tényező - kisebbségi politika (External factors - minority politics) Historia, 1994/2 p. 22.

Anglican Church of its position as "State Religion", even though it had been one of the most important buttresses of the Union. Parnell, the leader of the National Land League, organized in 1879, repeatedly negotiated with Gladstone and afterwards with Prime Minister Balfour. These negotiations resulted in the 1891 and 1903 Acts, under which the Irish peasants could purchase the lands they worked on, either by making small payments or with governmental subsidies.

In 1886, the Liberal government introduced the Home Rule Bill, in order to re-establish the Irish Parliament. The plan guaranteed independence in most areas, except in foreign policy and defense. These endeavors led to a split in the Liberal Party and, ultimately, the proposed bill was rejected. The second Home Rule Bill, in 1893, was approved in the House of Commons but was defeated in the House of Lords. The Protestants opposed the Home Rule Bill and made it a condition of endorsement that certain parts of Ulster be given a special status. The Irish Party insisted that the Law apply to all of Ireland and the only concession it was willing to make was an inclusion in the Bill of a guarantee of the Protestant interests. The Ulster Unionist Council, created in 1905, and the Irish Unionist Alliance created in 1891, demanded that the Union be preserved without any changes. Many of the original inhabitants of Ireland became members of the Sinn Fein, an organization founded by Arthur Griffith that was competing at the polls with the Irish Party in the early 1900s. Griffith wrote a number of articles on Hungary and on the parallelism between Hungary and Ireland. These articles were published in Hungary in 1904 under the title "The Resurrection of Hungary". Griffith summarizes the most important steps leading to the establishment of industry, commerce, education and autonomy and cites the Hungarian Compromise and the Dualist arrangements as acceptable models for Ireland. *At the 1910 General Elections, the Liberal government became dependent on the support of the Irish party, thus leading the way toward the realization of autonomy.* The Catholic-Protestant antagonism became evident after the 1910 electoral victory of Asquith, since it seemed that he wished to follow Gladstone's example with the Home Rule Bill that he submitted to Parliament. Asquith's Liberal government needed the support of the Irish Parliamentary Party and they made their support contingent on autonomy. The attempts to reach an agreement came to naught when World War I broke out in 1914.

In the meantime, the possibility of an agreement radicalized both sides. The opponents of autonomy created the armed Ulster Volunteer Force and this made it evident that granting autonomy would lead to armed conflict in Ulster. On the other side, the Fenian activists set up the Irish National Volunteers as a counterforce to the Ulster Volunteers.

Independence

The 1916 Easter Uprising originated with the anti-war movement and its purpose was the creation of an independent Irish Republic. After the bloody defeat of the rebellion and the execution of 15 of the 90 captured revolutionaries, the survivors were prepared to do anything to re-animate the Gaelic spirit of the country. Their leader was Eamon de Valera, a native of the United States. Arthur Griffith urged the supporters of the republican idea to start an international propaganda campaign seeking support for the legitimacy of the Irish national autonomy.

While the Sinn Fein was strengthening its popular support, the Irish Revolutionary Fraternal Association came under the influence of Michael Collins, a London clergyman, who played a key role in all extreme revolutionary groups. After the return of peace to Europe, the conflict was renewed in Ireland. At the 1918 elections, the Sinn Fein gathered 73 mandates of a total of 105.

Sinn Fein did not wish to be part of the London Parliament and, in 1919, created the independent Irish legislature, the Dail Eireann, hoping to gain international support for the creation of an independent republic. They organized the Irish Republican Army (IRA). After renewed armed conflicts, *Lloyd George introduced a Bill, in 1920, to create autonomy for Ireland. This legislative proposal suggested the establishment of two governments and two parliaments, one in Dublin and one in Belfast.* The Bill was enacted in Northern Ireland in 1921 but 6 counties of Ulster Province declared their desire to remain a part of the United Kingdom. At the same time, guerrillas in the South continued the fight for independence. In 1921, the British government and Sinn Fein reached an agreement and signed an armistice. This, then, led to the creation of the Irish Free State with the status of a Dominion in the Commonwealth. The compromise led to a split in the previously united ranks and it was impossible to predict whether or when Irish independence could become a reality. In 1931, on the instigation of Canada and Ireland, the so-called Westminster Statute was created and, after the end of World War II, Ireland became a fully independent republic.

Northern Ireland (Six Counties of Ulster)

Population (1999): 1,600,000 Irish
Protestants 50%, Catholics 40%.

The problems of Northern Ireland can be subsumed under three headings. First, its relationship to the United Kingdom and to the Irish Republic, second, the deep and ongoing division in its population between the Unionist Protestants on one side and the radical Catholics on the other and third, the development of a viable economic system in such a small area and the provision of services and of a standard of living similar to that of Great Britain's.

The constitutional basis was provided by the Act of 1920 that defined the autonomy of Ireland, but that initially was designed to serve the entire country. This Act eventually caused a deep chasm between the 6 counties of the North and the 26 counties of the South, resulting in two separate parliaments and two separate administrations. The events occurring between 1920 and 1922 made it obvious that the Act could be implemented only in the 6 northern counties, if it could be implemented at all. The basis of the limited autonomy of Northern Ireland was the Parliament, the sovereign governor standing at the head of that part of the country, the Senate and the House of Commons. The structure of the local autonomy had changed little, if any, from the time it was established in 1898 until 1969.

Eligibility for election to the local government was limited to local taxpayers and hence favored the moneyed classes. As a consequence, a quarter of the people who appeared on the roster of the National Legislature were not allowed to vote in local elections. The Irish Home Rule Act went into effect in May 1921 and, within months, serious disturbances broke out in the 6 counties and along their southern borders. For this reason, the newly installed government submitted, in 1922, to the Northern Ireland Parliament a legislative proposal with the following items: "The Home Secretary shall have powers to do what he likes, or else let somebody else do what he likes for him." This statute empowered the Minister "to take all such steps and issue all such orders as may be necessary for preserving the peace" (Special Powers Act). The crisis erupted again in the 1960s. The most important external factors were the effects of the evolving civil rights movement in the United States, the growth of religious ecumenicism in the outside world, as well as the renaissance of the republican sentiment in Ireland, the new national state, on the 50th anniversary of the Easter Uprising. At this celebration, the tragic events of the past were recalled leading to three consequences. First, the 1916 ideals were compared with the reality of the divided country and this produced a feeling of kinship with the IRA, an organization that consistently kept in contact with the survivors of the Easter Uprising. Secondly, increased attention was paid to James Connolly, to the discarded, original social program and to conditions prevailing in the South as compared to the North. The struggle was still for civil rights that were available to all British citizens but not to the Irish Catholics. And thirdly, the 1916 anniversary convinced the Ulster Unionists that every nationalist was a covert "Republican thirsting for spoils" waiting for the opportunity to emerge from his cocoon. The members of uprising were glowing, waiting to engulf the entire province in flames.

A study performed during that year showed that two thirds of the Catholic Irish wanted to have the borders opened as soon as possible. The tensions in society grew. The favorable economic situation in the 1960s did not affect the level of unemployment and thus the competition for jobs between the Catholic Irish and the Protestant English continued. The government and the local administration typically had a Protestant majority. Finally the entire province was engulfed in flames by the struggle for housing.

In the village of Caledon, a Catholic Nationalist legislator was unable to secure a council house for a Catholic family. The one house available was reserved for a 19 year-old Protestant woman, a Unionist politician. Mr. Currie, the legislator, organized a sit-down strike at the house, followed by a civil rights march to the neighboring village. This was a well-organized, peaceful demonstration, but the Civil Rights Association decided to expand its scope. A number of groups were formed in Londonderry and new committees were established to conduct the fight for civil rights.

The protests continued in Belfast with the Civil Rights Association and the People's Democracy on one side and the Protestants under the leadership of the Reverend Ian Paisley on the other. The Northern Ireland government announced a number of reforms but it was too late. The next protest march was on January 1-4, 1969, from Belfast to Londonderry and it was organized by the Civil Rights Association. The demonstrators were severely harassed and roughly treated by the Protestant activists in Burntollet village. The arrival of the march in Londonderry served as a signal for clashes with the police.

In 1969, the IRA renewed its terrorist activities in Northern Ireland in order to separate it from the United Kingdom. The Unionists also had their armed organization, the Ulster Defense Association (UDA) that, in turn, engaged in terrorist activities. The British government interfered with armed forces and jailed the leaders of the revolutionary Irish leaders. Nothing helped. In view of the ever-widening disturbances, the British government decided to accept the legal responsibility and, in 1972, placed the Province under its own control. This meant that the laws passed in Westminster became binding in Northern Ireland as well and that the Provincial administration came under the supervision of the Minister charged with Northern Ireland affairs and of his department. Ulster was divided into 26 administrative units, replacing the former 9, and later 6, counties (See map). All of the 26 units had a mixed population. The administration of these 26 units had only limited authority, but were charged with the management of public education, cultural, health and social organizations, housing, canalization and fire protection. The Province could send 18 deputies to the House of Commons, most of whom were Unionists. Direct control from London did not immediately show results and the violence peaked during the spring and summer of 1972. According to the experts, direct control should have been introduced in 1969, when British troops were ordered to Northern Ireland and not three years later, because in 1969 only 3-4% of the Catholic population supported the IRA. The IRA increased the bombing attacks, which resulted in the formation of private Protestant armies. The situation became intolerable. The Irish could rely in their struggle on support from the strong American Irish lobby. The USA supported the Irish, even though it never took an official position, because Great Britain, as a member of NATO, was much more important to the USA than Ireland. In 1984, British Prime Minister Margaret Thatcher and Irish Prime Minister Garett FitzGerald issued a joint declaration, according to which *"the integrity of both the majority and minority must be preserved and this must be reflected in the structure of the institutions of Northern Ireland"*. The Hillsborough Castle agreement, in 1985, gave Dublin the authority to participate in Northern Ireland affairs by establishing an *Inter-governmental Conference* to work with the *Inter-governmental Council*, established in 1981. Recognizing the fact that the majority of the population of Northern Ireland was opposed to any change, it was agreed that the two parliaments would support the unification of Ireland in the future if a majority of the population demanded it. Signing the Anglo-Irish document indicated that the two countries wished to cooperate in any future arrangements. Even though it was proposed that the Minister for Northern Ireland relinquish some of his powers to the two traditional communities, the agreement did not really reduce the power structure but rather gave both the London and the Dublin governments increased opportunities to directly interfere with the administration of the Province.

At the beginning of the 1990s, the IRA started a new terror campaign of bombings and arson. Prime Minister Major and his colleagues escaped assassination by a bomb exploding in Downing Street. This was followed by bombings at the London Stock Exchange, in Manchester and in the North of England. In 1991-1992, the Conservative government started negotiations with the Parties active in the province, without any success. In this atmosphere, the two Prime Ministers, Major and Reynolds, got together in December 1993 and issued the Downing Street Declaration which again declared that the constitutional structure of Ulster could be changed only with the agreement of the population. The IRA hastened to respond and, in August 1994, declared a unilateral cease-fire, to

Northern Ireland
What kind of administrative decision would be ideal for Ulster ?
(The more industrial part of it is the area of Belfast.)

The proportional number of Catholics in Ulster's 9 counties in 1901

The proportional number of Catholics in the 26 counties of Ulster

Atlantic Ocean

Ireland

Derry
Londonderry
Tyrone
Omagh
Enniskillen
Fermanagh
Antrim
Ballymena
L. Neagh
BELFAST
Armagh
Armagh
Down
Downpatrick
Irish
Sea

Protestant majority
R.Catholic majority

which the Loyalists agreed in October. Shortly thereafter, the London government started exploratory negotiations with the Sinn Fein, the Progressive Unionists and the Ulster Democratic Party. The Protestants were divided in assessing the situation but the Catholics were drawn closer together. The Social Democratic Labor Party (SDLP), under John Hume and the Sinn Fein, under Gerry Adams, agreed to cooperate, the Sinn Fein being viewed as the political arm of the IRA. In June 1997, they accepted the principle of equal employment opportunity, regardless of religious affiliation, made it binding for all parties and published it. The all-party discussions, and the forum, were temporarily suspended during the British General Elections. The new Labor Government considered the decentralization of Northern Ireland as the key to a political settlement. This involved the transfer of much of the central government's authority to the local governments, the establishment of a powerful General Assembly, open borders between Northern Ireland and the Irish Republic and a new agreement between the Irish Republic and the United Kingdom. *The so-called Good Friday Agreement, signed in Belfast on April 10, 1998 contained the basic principles of distributing the centralized powers. A 108 member National Assembly would be elected, with proportional representation, and this assembly would have the powers to act in all areas except the army, foreign and national security policy and taxation.* A complex electoral system was to guarantee that the majority could not impose its will on the minority. Appointments to key positions, such as the presiding officer of the Assembly, the Prime Minister and the Deputy Prime Minister, would require the vote of the majority of both the National-Irish and Unionist-Protestant blocs. The same type of vote would be required for major legislation and for the budget. The Executive, or Government, consisted of the Prime Minister, the Deputy Prime Minister and ten other Ministers who were appointed the same way as Parliamentary committee chairs and members, i.e., according to the relative strength of the different Parties. The participants to the agreement committed themselves to disband the semi-military organizations. The agreement was approved by 71% of the voters in 1998 and, at the elections of the same year, the parties endorsing the agreement won a substantial majority. The EU guaranteed 400 million Euros over five years for the financial support of the agreement.

The most awkward point of the agreement was the surrender of arms. The IRA agreed to do this, once the Northern Ireland government was in place. Unfortunately, there still are radical IRA splinter groups and, even though the Sinn Fein is the political arm of the IRA, it cannot make all these groups surrender their arms. Some of them are not satisfied with the agreement and continue their terrorist activities.

The psychological pressures created by 30 years of terrorism, as well as the British policy interpreted by the Unionists as a surrender of territory, led to a defeatist attitude among the Protestants, to an increase in mixed marriages, increasing emigration and a reduction of their numbers. In the meantime, the higher birthrate among the Catholics began to equalize the numbers between the two groups.

Scotland

Population (1993): 5,120,200
Scots - 100% (9% of the UK).

When the Romans occupied Great Britain, the present area of Scotland was largely inhabited by the Picts. The northern part of the occupied area, to the mouth of the Tay, was called Caledonia by the Romans. About 500 AD, four ethnic groups inhabited the area. The warlike Picts lived in the Scottish Highlands, while the Scots lived along the Western coast, in the area today known as Argyll. They were under the influence of the Irish, but it was they who gave their name to the present Scotland. The Brits, who spoke a variant of the Celt-Welsh tongue lived in the area of the present Strathclyde, while the Southeastern area was occupied by the Angles, living in close proximity to the Germanic Anglo-Saxons. It was the arrival of Christianity that signaled the end of the tribal structures and led to the formation of the Scottish state. Around 844, Kenneth MacAlpine could legitimately call himself the King of the Scots. In actuality, the true union of the Scottish nation took a much longer time. The Scottish clans fought each other for supremacy or, jointly, they fought against the invading Danish or English armies. In 1314, Robert the Bruce defeated Edward II, the English King, at Bannockburn. This victory guaranteed Scottish independence for the next 300 years.

Religious wars as instruments of unification

In the 16th century, the Catholic Mary Stuart divided the country, since, at this time, there were already many followers of the Reformation, with John Knox at their head. Her son, James VI of Scotland was crowned King of England as James I. He was the closest relative of the English Queen Elizabeth I, due to the medieval inter-marriages of the English and Scottish royal houses. The two countries formed a Personal Union, which meant that each country had to be governed according to its own institutions. James did not care very much for Scotland and when, after a long delay, the Scottish Parliament was summoned in Aberdeen, in 1616, the King planned to introduce a new Confession, new Catechism and a new liturgy His model was England where the Anglican Church was the primary buttress of royal absolutism. The Presbyterian Scots refused to accept an ecclesiastic system that was under Episcopal control and was strongly reminiscent of Catholicism.

The *Education Act, introduced by James in 1616, prohibited the use of the ancient Celtic tongue.*
James' son, Charles I (1625-1649), prorogued Parliament in 1629 in order to escape the "Petition of Rights" that Parliament had exacted of him. He wished to rule by mandate and, *in 1637, he decided to extend Archbishop Laud's aggressive Anglican ecclesiastic policies to Scotland and regulate the Presbyterian Scots.* He forbade

the use of the Prayer Book, introduced by John Knox in 1560. This was the last straw. The Chieftains of the Clans formed a union, took to arms, and defeated the royal troops sent to re-establish order. After this shameful defeat, and lacking financial resources, Charles was forced into summoning Parliament. Finally, civil war broke out in 1642. During the second phase of this war, an army of 20,000 Scots fought on the Royalist side, but was soundly defeated by Oliver Cromwell at Preston. Cromwell declared that the captives were common criminals and had them executed. He then devastated the country. In 1688, after the "Glorious Revolution", William III (1689-1702) was summoned to the English throne from the Netherlands. An argument broke out among the Scottish clans whether to support the new king or not. In 1692, the Campbells massacred about 200 members of the MacDonald clan for refusing to swear allegiance to William of Orange.

At the end of the 17th century, the internecine war, which followed the Civil War, as well as religious differences, divided Scotland. Nothing was left for the Scots but to seek union with England. The *Act of Union was enacted in 1707* and the two kingdoms became one country with the name of Great Britain. Taxation, custom duties and indirect taxes were regulated jointly, but Scotland preserved her own ecclesiastic structure, legal system and educational system. The laws passed by the British Parliament applied to Scotland, as well. Scotland's trade with England grew rapidly. It prospered at the time of the industrial revolution and Scottish military officers and administrators participated in the building of the Empire. Yet, the Scottish ideal of independence was maintained for 300 years, by national self-consciousness, patriotic literature and four great universities. In the 1880s, the struggle for independence surfaced again and Scotland demanded Home Rule.

The constitutional developments in Scotland in the 19th century generally followed developments in the United Kingdom. Yet, at the same time, the Victorian Scottish social and political conditions varied widely from those in England. In England, the landowner class strongly supported the Episcopal ecclesiastic organization. The Scottish Presbyterians were united in their social demands and expectations. Their leaders emerged from the business environment and the industries of the Scottish Lowlands created an aggressive and self-satisfied bourgeois class.

The United Presbyterian Church
The need for reforming the state was tightly linked with the need to reform the Kirk (church). Most of the supporters of the evolving Liberal Party came from among the separatist, non-conformist Protestants. In 1847, the two leading groups of this set came together to create the United Presbyterian Church (UP) and, taking advantage of the 1843 split in the Church of Scotland, gathered the smaller sects into the Free Church of Scotland Assembly. In Scotland, the movement fighting for political reforms steadfastly fought for religious tolerance, for the University and for the separation of the Church and the State. They also demanded that the London Parliament, and the local legislature, meet yearly and that the UP hold a synod every year. It seems that the synod was of as much interest to the Scots as were the activities of the Westminster Parliament. As the electoral districts were enlarged, the Scottish representatives could make their political influence count more heavily. The secret ballot was introduced by

Gladstone in 1872. *All these changes made the Scottish (and Irish) deputies realize that they could represent the balance between the Government Party and the Loyal Opposition.*

Education
In 1858, the Conservative government enacted the act dealing with the Scottish universities and the Act of 1872 established the Scottish national system of education. A new administrative unit, the Scottish Ministry of Education, was created. The clergy, the lay patrons, the elders and the urban councilors were replaced by school boards elected by the local population. These Boards gradually assumed supervision over the public schools maintained by the Church of Scotland. *The Anglican Church and the Roman Catholic Church could continue to maintain their schools and also received governmental subsidies for this purpose.*

The fight for autonomy
The most significant step in the modernization of the administration was the creation of the Scottish Office in 1885. Since 1926, its leader was elevated to cabinet rank and, after 1934, he had a governmental office in Edinburgh. His area of authority included Scottish legislation, agriculture, education, healthcare and supervision of the local administration. The 1900 Act on Scottish Urban Councils regulated the rights and authority of the mayors, urban councils and village councils.

The Acts of 1889 and 1894 permitted the organization of local self-governing bodies. These gradually took over the responsibilities of the rather arbitrary Supervisory Bodies and took control of many areas of health-care. Gladstone opposed the separation of State and Church. *Many of his followers did not support his proposals for Irish autonomy. This led to a split in the Liberal Party and to the formation of a Unionist group within the Party.* At the beginning of the 20th century, the Liberal Party maintained its majority among the Scottish electors. The Scots suffered from the split in the Party and also from the debates within the Presbyterian Church. In 1900, a strong drive began among the Scottish Presbyterians for creating a unified Church and this resulted, during the same year, in the fusion of 1,100 congregations of the Free Church with 600 congregations of the United Presbyterian Church, thus creating the United Free Church. After World War I, the Scottish political parties became more radical and, in 1934, the Scottish National Party was born striving for radical changes. In the 1960s, unemployment in Scotland was twice as high as in England and about three times as high as it had been in 1948.

In 1969, oil and natural gas production from Scottish offshore wells began. The Westminster government considered the income from these wells as a gift from heaven. Thus, by the end of the 1970s, the Scottish economy came increasingly under a foreign control. The leadership of the United Kingdom was much more interested in the creation of a Western European super-power, under the auspices of the European Economic Union, than in the de-centralization of the Scottish and Welsh administration. From 1979 on, 100 billion Pound Sterling were taken from Scotland which, according to the Scottish National party, would have made Scotland the world's 21st richest country, if Scotland had retained the right to dispose of its own oil and gas.

The 1973 Kilbrandon report, recommending devolution and an independent Scottish Parliament and government, received less than a third of the vote at the 1979 plebiscite. Even the Labor Party was divided on this issue and only the Scottish

National Party was fully in favor of it. At the 1990 National Conference of the Labor Party in Scotland, the leadership of the Party finally agreed to support a proportional representative system and it was just on the eve of the 1992 national elections that the new system under the Scottish Constitutional Agreement was confirmed. After the elections, the establishment of a Scottish Parliament became the center of the constitutional struggle and the Labor Party included it in its legislative proposal on autonomy. The people were convinced that the creation of a Scottish Parliament was imminent. The leaders of the opposition in Westminster were convinced that such a move was the only way in which British politics could make a new beginning in the 1990s.

At the national elections, on May 1, 1997, the Labor Party won such an unprecedented victory that the Conservative Party lost every single seat in Scotland and Wales. Of the 72 Scottish parliamentary seats, 56 were won by Labor and 10 by the National Party. *In the European Parliament the Scots are represented by 6 Labor and 2 National Party deputies.*

Autonomy - Devolution

Decentralization of Scotland and Wales was an important part of the British Government's program of revising the constitution. The Government proposal to establish a Scottish Parliament was published in the "White Paper" in July 1997. At the September plebiscite, 74% of the Scots voted "Aye". The Act, dealing with the Scottish constitution, was enacted in 1998. The first parliamentary elections in Scotland were held in May 1999 and, on July 1 of that year, the Scottish Parliament was convened, for the first time in 300 years, with great solemnity. The authority of the Scottish Parliament extends over legislation, local self-government, police, fire protection, supervision of public collections, health, education and training, housing, economic development, transportation, environmental protection, agriculture, animal husbandry, fishing, forestry, sports and the arts. The Parliament sits in Edinburgh and it is there that the Scottish Executive functions. It is headed by a Prime Minister, who is also the leader of the parliamentary majority party. The Secretary of State for Scotland Ministry represents the interests of Scotland within the British Government. According to the agreement, the Parliament of the United Kingdom annually provides a budget of about 14 million Pound Sterling, over which the Scottish Parliament has unrestricted control.

The Scottish Parliament had the right to increase or decrease the UK income tax by 3%. The Parliament can dispose of its funds on the basis of local or regional budgets. It may also determine the form of local taxation and may revise the community development taxes and the tax on commercial establishments. Even though External Affairs is among the joint activities, with constitutional revision, defense, internal security, railways, transportation security, etc., there are 8 representatives of Scotland who sit in the European Parliament since the late 1990s. *The delegates of the Scottish Ministries participate in the activities of the Brussels Committee, representing the interests of their country.*

In 1999, there were more that 1,800 students attending the 56 Gaelic schools. In the academic year 2000-2001, the UK Government gave 2.8 million Pounds to the local self-governments to maintain, and further, education in Gaelic in the elementary and middle schools.

Wales

Population (1994): 2,913,000
Welsh – 100% (5% of the UK).

After the collapse of Roman power in Britain, Wales survived as a Celtic settlement, protected by fortresses. Changes came only after the Norman conquest and mainly in the areas abutting on England.

In the 11th century, Wales consisted of three regions, Gwynned, Powys and Dehuebarth. These three areas maintained their independence, did not unite and frequently fought with each other. In 1267, Llywelyn, as the ruler of Gwynned, could call himself the Prince of Wales. Llywelyn took an oath of fealty to the King of England but, when the number of those who objected to the English overlordship grew, Llywelyn rejected the English suzerainty and war broke out between England and Wales in 1277. This first conflict ended with a treaty and peace returned but a second conflict a few years later led to Llywelyn's death in 1282. The fall of the House of Aberffraw meant that the attempt to create an independent Wales failed. Until the middle of the 16th century, the domestic policies of Wales lacked consistency.

After Llywelyn's death, Edward I succeeded in conquering Wales. Daffyd, who also styled himself Prince of Wales, led the resistance but was captured in 1283 and later executed. In 1294, all of Wales rose against England.

Unification by war and oppression

Edward led an army of 35,000 to conquer Wales and only five days after the defeat of the Welsh forces, 500 Welshmen were slaughtered in their sleep. After the uprising of 1294, an ordinance prohibited the Welsh from holding any major position and only few of them even held low-ranking positions for a generation after the conquest.

Edward I was the first English King who named his oldest son Prince of Wales, in 1301. This was the future Edward II, who was born in Caernarvon.

The Hundred Years War, between England and France, affected Wales as well. The suffering and misery led to the *uprising of Owain Glyn Dwr in September 1400*. It was reported to the English Parliament in 1400 that the Welsh tenants were leaving their English masters to return home and participate in the rebellion. The lower clergy, oppressed by their lack of advancement and by the rapacity of their embittered superiors, also supported the rebellion. The rebels declared Owain, Prince of Wales. In a letter written to the King of Scotland, Owain explained that his intent was to raise Wales from the oppression and captivity from which his people suffered ever since Cadwaladr. Owain even had French support against England. The rebellion was defeated in 1415 and for the next generation the Welsh lived in its shadow. *In 1431, 1433 and 1447, the English Parliament renewed the penal code that remained in effect until 1624*. The Code stated that the Welsh people, who were unfaithful to the King, were not allowed to bear arms when in town, in church or on the highway. Welsh could not be appointed to any position accountable to the Crown and could not serve on juries. Marriage between Welsh and English was prohibited and if it nevertheless occurred, the English marriage partner and the children were subject to the same restriction as the Welsh partner.

In the middle of the 15th century, Wales was still a divided country with the Crown lands on one side and the border principalities on the other. At the same time, the Welsh administration showed unmistakable signs of change, due to the long-lasting agony of the War of the Roses. *The Tudors were of Welsh origin and hence many Welshmen fought in the armies of Henry Tudor.* For Wales, the battle of Bosworth, in 1485, was of major significance. Henry's troops went into battle under the red flag of Cadwaladr and, after the victory, the Welsh were entitled to assume positions of power in the local administration. Henry appointed four bishops of Welsh extraction and in Northern Wales the sheriffs, appointed to head the counties, were Welshmen. It seems odd, but the restrictive laws against the Welsh were never annulled. It seemed unnecessary and the Welsh were welcomed at Court. When Henry VIII started a war against the Scots and the Irish in 1533, he wished to protect his back and hence he ordered the unification of Wales and England in 1536.

Religious wars as instruments of administrative unification
The goal is stated in the preamble of the 1536 Act of Union:

"Albeit the Dominion, Principality and Country of Wales, justly and ever hath been, incorporated and annexed, united and subject to and under the Imperial Crown of Realm as very member of the same, wherefore the King's most royal Majesty is very head, king, lord and ruler, yet not withstanding, because in the same country divers rights, usages, laws and customs be far discrepant from the laws and customs of realm and also because the people do daily use a speech nothing like or consonant with the mother tongue used within this realm, some rude and ignorant people have made distinction between the King's subjects of this realm and his subjects of Wales... His Majesty ordains... that Wales shall for ever, from henceforth, be united and annexed to and with his realm of England."

The shire-system, initiated by Edward I, was now extended to the entire country. English descent was an automatic qualification for public office. The second Act of Union was planned by Cromwell and intended to create complete equality with the English system. It was implemented by the legislature after Cromwell's death and regulated life in Wales in minute detail. Wales was given its own system of higher courts with the Courts of the King's Session sitting in Wales and totally independent of the English high courts sitting in Westminster. Wales was divided into four circuits but Monmouthshire was attached to the Oxford circuit. The 1542 Act assured the continued operation of the Council of Wales and Marches and charged it with the responsibility of reviewing the existing laws and ordinances. The Wales Council survived until 1689 and the Wales Supreme Court until the 19th century. The counties of Wales had their own representatives in Parliament and, more importantly, eight Justices of the Peace were appointed in every Welsh county. The Justices of the Peace controlled everyday life and, therefore, their support was extremely important for Cromwell when he initiated revolutionary innovations and the reform of the Welsh Church.

Between 1529 and 1534, the strengthening of the royal power over the Church was the goal of every new law. There was no social group in Wales that would have rebelled or even protested when the royal hand dismantled the existing ecclesiastic structure. There were a few scattered murmurs but no Welshman took to arms in the defense of his church. The abbot of Walle Crucis was jailed for highway robbery in 1535 and a monk in Strata Florida was arrested for coining money in his cell. The monasteries were dissolved.

There were only a few Welsh scholars among the reformers. One of the greatest, William Salesbury, undertook the publication of the first printed books in Welsh. Between 1547 and 1553, a number of books were printed in Welsh, including the first English-Welsh dictionary, Cranmer's Book of Prayers and small volume entitled after its opening lines "Yn Yllyn Hwn", containing a translation of the Nicene Creed, the Lord's Prayer and the Ten Commandments.

In 1553, Mary succeeded to the throne and this led to renewed religious upheavals in England that affected Wales equally.

In 1650, the so-called Rump Parliament passed a law "For the better propagation of the faith in Wales". Colonel Thomas Harrison and 70 commissioners were charged with reorganizing the ecclesiastic and educational structure in Wales. They had no luck in establishing Puritanism but made great strides in education. They added 60 new grammar schools to the existing ones. Education was free and the commissioners took the revolutionary step of opening the schools for girls. Yet, the Welsh language was not taught.

The pertinent paragraphs of the law placed the Welsh language into a subordinate position in both legislative and administrative usage, endeavoring to promote the unification of the country. There was no attempt among the gentry to preserve the ancient language and the land-owning nobility spoke English. Among the middle classes, the language of the printed books slowly replaced the old Welsh.

Prior to the 18th century, there were three revolutionary movements in Wales: religious, cultural and industrial. Finally, the three united to accomplish their joint purpose. Autonomy could not be the slogan for this movement and, therefore, the endeavor appeared in a religious guise, namely a separation from the Church of England. The non-Conformists were persecuted under Charles II and it was only after the *Act of Toleration was enacted in 1689* that this group could start to make progress. They were not numerous, but the Baptists, Unitarians and other small denominations felt that their faith had to be placed on a stronger intellectual basis. They started academies throughout Wales and these were so successful that many Anglicans sent their children to these schools in preparation for entry into the universities.

One language and one Church

The origins of the Methodist religion go back to 1735. Under Queen Anne (1702-1714), the Society for the Propagation of the Christian Faith became very active and was strongly supported by Sir John Phillips of Pembrokeshire. The real prophet of the religious renaissance was the vicar of Llanddowror in Carmarthenshire, Griffith Jones. He organized the remarkable group of Traveling Masters who went from diocese to diocese, spending three months in each, teaching the illiterate children and adults to read. It was *Griffith Jones who made Wales literate* and this literacy was in Welsh. Jones also preached in Welsh - and preached extremely well.

The reformers brought to life not only the ancient culture of Wales but its history as well. The Welsh became aware of the fact that they were indeed the original inhabitants of Britain, the "Ancient Brits". One of the *major contributions of the 18th century was the renaissance of the Welsh literature*.

An independent Calvinist-Methodist Church organization started in Wales in 1811. Only the Anglicans continued to be subservient to the Archbishop of Canterbury. *Sunday schools* were started and so were literary associations. The ancient bardic poetry competitions, *the eisteddfodd*, were renewed, the very first of which was actually held in 1450. It is characteristic of the situation *that Gladstone considered it important* to participate in an eisteddfodd, where he addressed the multitude in Welsh.

Education
The educational system, with both primary and secondary schools, was organized in the 19th century. A Society for the Use of the Welsh Language in Education was formed, which recommended that history and geography be taught in Welsh.

The Liberal Party was much more supportive of autonomy for Wales, Scotland and Ireland, than the Conservatives. For this reason they were delighted when Tom Ellis defeated the Conservatives at the 1886 elections. The political goals, at this time, included the separation of the Anglican Church and the State in Wales, land reform, educational reform and the fight against alcoholism. *The first fruit of the cooperation between the Welsh non-Conformists and Gladstone was the passage of the "Sunday Closure Act" (1881),* which ruled that the pubs had to remain closed on the Sabbath. Even more important was *the introduction of complete local control over education.* The *Welsh University System* was introduced in the 1890s, with the opening of universities in Bangor, Aberystwyth and Cardiff, with Swansea joining the group in 1921. The professors of these new universities, and their students, created a new intellectual atmosphere for the Welsh-speaking population. *In 1907, a Department of Welsh Education* was established and this was followed by the teaching of Welsh in every county. *In 1924, the National Party (Plaid Cymru) was organized, demanding full autonomy for Wales.*

At the beginning of the 20th century, almost one half of the population spoke Welsh.

What was the role of the Church in all this? The poet-preachers came from the churches and this was the group that kept alive the ancient poetic traditions of Wales and thus wakened the slumbering national consciousness.

Autonomy
The Welsh Office and the Office of Secretary of State for Wales, were established in the mid-1960s and signaled an increase in Welsh administrative independence. *An Act on the Use of the Welsh Language, introduced in 1967, allowed the use of Welsh in administration.* Thus, instructions in the kindergartens and primary schools became bilingual, and so were announcements and place names. On radio and television, there were daily programs in Cymri. The *1993 Act on the Welsh Language extended its use to the courts and to all public business but maintained the right to choose between Cymri and English.*

Among all parts of the UK, including Northern Ireland, Wales was the economically most depressed. The principal activities that occupied and fed most of the population, coal mining, smelting and ship building for the past 200 years, were all in trouble, even though Wales furnished one third of the steel produced in the UK. The Anglicized southern area viewed the Labor Party's plans for autonomy with suspicion, fearing that the Welsh-speaking northern and western clique would control the legislature. It was this fear that kept the vote for a limited Home Rule to barely 12%. A repeat plebiscite in 1997 produced a thin majority of 50.3%.

190

The White Paper, containing the government's plans for autonomy, was published in 1997. It included plans for a directly elected legislature. The 60-member assembly was first elected in May 1999. It only had secondary legislative powers. It determined the tasks of the public offices active in Wales, gave direction and basic concepts to the local administrative units and to the National Health Service. It could arbitrate in contested cases. The chairmen of the legislative committees form the membership of the Executive Committee that functions as a regional government with all members being from the majority party. It can also setup regional committees. The Assembly also assumes the following responsibilities from the Secretary of State for Wales: planning, economic development, agriculture and forest management, fishing, supervision of the local administrations, health and welfare, housing, environmental protection, support of the mother tongue, protection of the monuments, sports and recreation. The local administrative bodies are in charge of the schools, welfare, environmental protection, housing, local roads, libraries, museums, galleries and economic development. The police and fire protection are under separate supervision. London preserved only the following functions: foreign policy, defense, taxation, central economic policies, social insurance and broadcasting. Wales maintains its full complement of deputies in the Westminster parliament. The First Secretary continues to represent the interests of Wales and serves as an advisor to the Monarch. He serves as liaison between the Welsh Assembly and Westminster and continues in his duties as Cabinet Minister. The Welsh Assembly elects the president of the local government. The leaders of the other committees are appointed proportionately according to the results of the national elections. The President of the Assembly is elected from the Majority Party, while his deputy is chosen from the Minority Party. In the assembly, both Cymri and English may be used. The Welsh National Assembly was opened in Cardiff in June 1999 by Queen Elizabeth.

Today, in 500 primary and secondary schools, 80,000 students are taught in the Welsh language, with English being taught as a second language. In the English language schools, teaching the Welsh language is mandatory until age 16.

The reason why the autonomy of Wales is not as complete as the one in Scotland is the fact that Scotland was always a separate nation in the British Isles and entered the 1707 "marriage of convenience Union" as an equal partner, while Wales was a conquered component of Great Britain, ever since 1282.

Autonomy and the Politics of National Security Conclusions

At the present time, we know of about 3,600 nationalities and other minorities throughout the world, located within 200 countries. Their number increased markedly after the peace treaties following World War I.

The delayed and stunted national evolution within the multinational empires, the collapse of the colonial empires and the boundaries drawn without regard to ethnic lines after World War I and World War II resulted in the situation where, today, there is not a single linguistically, culturally or religiously "pure" nation state. Some of them, like Romania and Serbia, have minorities of a million people. Governments and governmental philosophies endeavoring, at all costs, to create national states with a single language and a single history introduced exclusion, deprivation of civil rights and ethnic cleansing into everyday practice. These practices were particularly acute where the leading nationality and the minority belonged to different cultural heritages. Thus, while the Hungarians in Transylvania and the Délvidék had belonged for centuries to the Austro-Hungarian, Latin and Western cultural circle, the Romanians and Serbs were firmly wedded to the Southeastern European, Orthodox, Slavic way of life. The Turkic nations of Central Asia and the Eastern Caucasus were tied to Pravoslav Russia by force, while their cultural roots were firmly attached to the Islamic cultural heritage.

Methods of Assimilation and their Sociological Consequences

The examples discussed earlier show clearly that, in the absence of a constitutionally regulated system of self-government, the guarantee of only individual citizenship rights is insufficient to protect the minority nationalities and fragments against the various methods of forced assimilation.

Legal Discrimination
The international, signed agreements are either not transferred to the codes and legislative practices of the country, or if the text of the agreement is accepted, its implementation into daily practice takes a back seat, is negated by local ordinances or instructions and is frequently countermanded by assimilative steps. This is made possible by the fact that these countries are strongly centralized or are decentralized only *pro forma*. In Romania, for instance, the Prefectures always put the directives of the central authorities above the local administrative interests. In minority areas, the police are dispatched by the central government and function strictly on its behalf.

Economic Discrimination

With the excuse of a land reform, the minority was deprived of its land, banks and companies. There was discriminatory taxation, credit, investment, industrial growth and a *numerus clausus* for the higher positions. The number of the minority population finding employment in industry was small compared to the other nationalities, the minorities did not participate equally in the benefits of economic growth and their settlements and employment practices were antiquated. In the employment of workers and in their training, discrimination was shown in favor of the members of the majority population who had been settled in the minority area. The minority was forced to accept an unfavorable division of labor and in the exploitation of the minority's raw materials environmental protection considerations were ignored. The greater than average unemployment in the minority area led to emigration, to a reduction in birth rate, to social tensions and to a decrease in the minority population. For all these reasons, the capitalist group emerging after the change in the economic structure of the country came largely from the majority nationality, even in a minority area. In fact, they blocked the path of the minority toward economic growth and even survival.

Cultural Discrimination

The most common forms of cultural discrimination were: the curtailment of language through language laws or by the imposition of taxes, the elimination of newspapers and periodicals in the minority language, the reduction in the number of cultural institutions, the starving of the educational facilities by withholding subsidies, the introduction of bilingual education to replace education in the mother tongue of the minority to be followed by a switch to the exclusive use of the official language, higher salaries for the imported teachers and officials, the move of minority intellectuals to majority areas, the replacement of the leaders of the educational and cultural institutions, the use of the *numerus clausus* in admission to the universities and discontinuation of teaching in the mother tongue of the minority at all institutes of higher education.

Unless they have strong, community social and cultural organizations that could counterbalance those of the majority, the minority groups would inevitably find themselves at a severe disadvantage.

Political Discrimination

This could take the form of canceling citizenship, reorganizing the administration, replacing public officials, gerrymandering voting districts and limiting the franchise. Additional steps could be the making employment in the executive being limited to the majority ethnic group, manipulating the ballots so that mostly majority ethnic group representatives were elected to the legislature, assigning majority ethnic group members, loyal to the central powers, as law enforcement officers to the minority areas, granting the local administrative units minimal authority and subsidy, making the life of minority political parties impossible and intimidating the minority with indictments, arrests and labor camps.

Changing the Ethnic Ratios

The purpose of this move was to change the composition of the population and thus make a redrawing of the boundaries along ethnic lines impossible. It could be accomplished by a fraudulent census and statistical manipulation of the figures, by granting employment and housing to majority workers following industrialization, settlement of majority populations along the borders, by population transfers, by genocide, by denying that the minority was a separate ethnic group, by resettlements under the guise of land reform, by excluding the minority from the professions and from official positions, by forceful transplantation of populations and by spontaneous emigration resulting from the discriminatory economic policies.

Loss of Identity
Prohibiting or changing personal names and community names and determining ethnicity on the basis of "name analysis".

Destruction of the Church
The various social and Party organizations did not represent so strong and cohesive an ethnic force as the Church, built on the tradition of centuries and acting as the guardian of cultural values and traditions. The Church covered the entire society and its role in preserving ethnic identity was uncontroversial. Realizing this, the central organizations of the state, representing the majority population, would do everything to get control over the Church or destroy it. Such actions might include removing the economic bases of the church, jailing its ministers, destroying the ecclesiastic buildings, forcing conversions, building churches for the majority denomination in minority areas, as for example Greek Orthodox churches in Transylvania. Additional actions might include subjugating the minority dioceses to the majority ecclesiastic organization in order to atrophy language and ritual, by discriminatory financing of the Churches and by discriminatory compensation for confiscated property, as happened in Russia, Slovakia, Ukraine, Romania and Serbia.

The methods to break or assimilate a minority became increasingly refined as the governmental bureaucracies evolved. In fact, the various countries seemed to borrow such methods from each other as shown by the treatment of the Poles, divided among three other countries (in 1772, 1793, 1795.) or the fate of the Hungarians in the successor states after 1920. *The examples could be prolonged indefinitely since the individual, belonging to a minority devoid of self-government and autonomy, stood helplessly before the governmental structures devoted to the interests of the majority.*

The last 70 years of the Saxons in Romania can serve as an example. Three quarters of a century have elapsed since 1918 and this was sufficient for the complete economic destruction of the Saxons, the dissolution of their 800 year-old institutions and the crushing of their ethnic integrity, forcing them eventually to emigrate.[129] In the 1930s, a large number of Bulgarians moved back to Bulgaria from the Bánát. The reason for this move was stated in 1994 thus: "Our old people liked the Hungarians very much and were with them all the way. For this reason, they always wanted to belong to Hungary again. When they saw that this was not possible, many of them returned to Bulgaria."[130]

---

[129] Annemie Schenk: Deutsche in Siebenbürgen. München, Verlag C.H.Beck 1992. In Regio 1994/3, p. 133.
[130] Vivien Zatykó: Magyar bolgárok? Etnikai identitás és akkulturácio a bánáti bolgárok körében. In: Regio 1994/3. p. 133.

The Sociological Consequences of the Loss of Identity

The identity of the people living today is a function of the identity of the group, just as it was prior to the evolution of modern capitalism. The individuals are linked with strong, unbreakable bonds to the community to which they belong. The families are linked to the larger, national community through local churches, organizations and schools that use the mother tongue of the minority and that are the solid moral buttresses and the cultural developmental forces of the local community. The extended families represent the traditions and serve as examples for the young. The so-called secondary affiliations, i.e., professional ones, always take second place behind the primary community group affiliation. It is the primary affiliation that determines the self-identity of the individual and what happened in recent years in Central Europe, namely the disintegration of the Soviet Union, of Yugoslavia and of Czechoslovakia must serve as a cautionary mark for the future.

A number of investigators have confirmed that individuals fallen away from the group representing linguistic-cultural and religious identity and a solid set of moral values and forced to become part of a foreign environment, struggle with a large number of psychic and social problems. Among these individuals, there is a far greater incidence of adaptation difficulties, economic and lifestyle disadvantages, poorer school performances, unemployment, alcoholism, suicide and crime than in the general population. This, in turn, placed a major burden of unresolved social problems, societal tensions and huge financial responsibilities on the governmental structures of the country. It required the establishment of a separate network of organizations, at huge cost, and with no guarantee that it would be able to cope successfully with the social problems that had been generated.

The Conditions Required for the Self-Preservation of an Ethnic Group and for its Internal Development

The Hungarian endeavors at the end of the 19th century, complete with Liberal legislative practices and flashes of positive discrimination in their practical implementation, particularly in the Transylvania of the 1870s, failed completely. The reasons for this failure included the rejection of the overt territorial principle, the centuries-old practice of the Imperial government to set ethnic group against ethnic group, the Russian expansion toward the Balkans, the Pan-Slavic movement and the endeavors of the Balkan national states to attach the neighboring territories where people of their ethnicity lived. The nationalities broke away from Hungary in 1918 but helpful conclusions can be drawn even from failure:

The territorial and autonomous ecclesiastic organizations established with governmental guarantees, such as charters, ordinances, laws and constitutions, can assure the preservation and internal growth of fragmented nationalities, groups of people and nationality minorities.

The regional units, differing from the general administrative system, such as the Székely seats, the Saxon seats, the Cumanian districts and Croatia, assured the self-governance of their autonomous territories by using their own administrative structures and their own officials.

Where territorial autonomy was linked with ecclesiastic autonomy, such as the Transylvanian Saxon territories, survival and the preservation of national identity was assured for centuries.

Ecclesiastic autonomy could assure not only the preservation of the nationality group, but also its cultural and economic growth, provided that an independent diocese could be organized and that ecclesiastical leaders, independent of the dignitaries of the majority Church, could be selected by the independent diocese. Other critical factors included that the minority lived in a compact block within the diocese, that the State guaranteed the financial support required for the maintenance of the ecclesiastic organizations and structures, as it was done in the Kingdom of Hungary for the Serb, Romanian, Slovak and Ruthenian Churches and that the minority was able to involve the lay intellectual leaders in the management of the Church and in active participation in the economic and cultural life of the minority. *As we have seen, the Catholic, Protestant, Unitarian and Greek Orthodox Churches not only worked for the maintenance of the religious community, but often and even in opposition to each other, they worked very hard to protect and preserve their ethnic group and to foster its mother tongue and its cultural traditions.* This role is important even today, as shown by the effect that Papal visits have had in Poland before the change in the regime, more recently in Cuba and in some of the former Socialist countries. Religious freedom rests on more than words. To exist, it must have an ecclesiastic organization using its mother tongue and both higher and lower clergy fluent in the language of the minority. If we examine the current situation of the Csángós or of the Hungarians in Slovakia, we see that the mother tongue has been forced out of the churches and that Hungarian language instruction in the parochial schools is impossible in the absence of Hungarian bishops. The Vatican should see to it that minority nationalities and groups be supplied with priests having the same mother tongue and with bishops responsible only to Rome.

As earlier examples have shown, the local ecclesiastic organizations can assume a leadership role in the struggle for autonomy.

Achievement of the above criteria led to the emergence of an independent capitalist-entrepreneur. With its help, a network of economic and cultural establishments could be instituted that eventually led to self-rule. From a sociologic perspective, we cannot ignore the role of the Churches in this struggle. Their effect is not only on education, on morality and on refraining from sinful activities but also on the establishment and cohesion of small communities.

How Autonomies Were Achieved in the 19th century

According to historic experience, autonomy could be gained in the modern bourgeois society by two routes.

1. In those countries where, earlier, the collective rights of the minority were guaranteed by granting ecclesiastic or territorial autonomy, the bourgeois state itself initiated the process. With wide legislative regulation, the state guaranteed independence for the administration subject to a regional government responsible to the regional parliament and funded by local taxes and revenues. This was the pattern for the Hungarian-Croat agreement of 1868 and for the Swiss Federation. Ecclesiastic autonomy, with its own system of parochial schools, was fixed by law and free use of the native language was assured by a separate, specific Language Act that

applied to all legal, legislative and administrative areas. Legislation of this type could be found in the 1868 Hungarian Nationality Act.

2. In those countries where the legislative practice of the majority nationality did not recognize collective rights, only individual rights, and thus autonomy could not be established on an ethnic basis, territorial autonomy could be achieved only after severe civil rights battles resulting in the decentralization of power. The civil rights battles took several forms:

- Rebellions and insurrections against the increase of feudal obligations.
- War of Liberation where social tensions and ethnic oppression triggered a response from the entire ethnic group.
- The right to use the mother tongue within its own ecclesiastic system. Translations of the Bible after the 16th century stimulated the growth of the national linguistic culture.
- The creation of independent cultural institutions for the care and propagation of the mother tongue and of the national literature in the mother tongue. This literature was clearly influenced by the leading intellectual trends of the 19th century, namely nationalism and liberalism.
- The strengthening of the economic structures and undertakings of the minority did make it possible to finance its politicians and national parties.
- As a result of the universal franchise, the oppressed and economically underdeveloped minorities would form their own organizations that could then manage their fight for civil rights. In this phase the ethnic groups frequently joined forces with each other and with the liberal parties in their political struggle for parliamentary mandates.

We saw this happen in Scotland, Wales and other Western European countries. It is this alliance that eventually forced the liberal parties into a position where they had to join the fight for minority rights. It is not surprising that this chain of events resulted in a domestic crisis in the British Liberal Party at the turn of the century. This crisis finally led to the emergence of a new party willing to endorse radical changes, the British Labor Party. Ever since the turn of the century, the number of radical minority representatives in the Parliament was increasing. These deputies formed independent national parties in order to achieve some level of autonomy.

In the modern bourgeois state, autonomy can be achieved only by decentralizing the administration and by devolution, i.e., by the division of power. In this case, the central government grants proportional participation in legal affairs, ministerial areas and the budget to the local authorities. This is precisely what happened in the past in the Austro-Hungarian and Hungarian Croat agreements. A modern version of this can be seen at the end of the 20th century in Scotland and Wales where industry, agriculture, commerce, environmental protection, health care, education, etc., were transferred to the control of the administration responsible to the local parliament, or to the locally elected self-government. Most of the taxes collected in the given territory remained in that area to support the tasks that the central government had transferred to the local powers. Only that part of the taxes has to be forwarded to the central government that has been earmarked, on a proportional basis, for the so-called joint expenditures. There may be some differences in the systems, as shown by the Scottish and Welsh examples. In Wales, the economic and fiscal matters cannot be handled totally independently from the British government, while in Scotland only foreign affairs are considered to be a joint endeavor. This democratic functioning may become illusory if the central government appoints its own representative to be in a controlling position over the local self-government. This is what happened in Romania with the Prefect system. A similar situation arises when certain portfolios can function only as part of central organization, e.g.-when there is no independent educational network. The British practice could serve as a model for bringing the protection of the minority rights to the level of an international matter. This could be accomplished by having Scottish and Welsh representatives sitting in the parliament of the European Union.

Decentralization of administration can lead to full autonomy, guaranteed by international agreements, if said autonomy is endorsed by an agreement between the majority state and the mother country of the minority. It seems that, today, only those minorities are satisfied with their situation where this path was followed, even though struggles over several decades may have preceded the final agreement. This is what happened in Ireland, with the German population in the South Tyrol, the Danish population in Schleswig-Holstein and, currently, in Northern Ireland. It is evident that the minorities can peacefully coexist with their neighbors even though their mother country is on the other side of the border.

In those countries where the government tries to drown in blood the fight for civil rights, the bitterness eventually will lead to the formation of secret, armed groups fighting for full independence. This happened in Ireland, South Tyrol, Northern Ireland, Kosovo, Chechnya, Tibet, etc. Naturally, for the separatist movements to be successful, a favorable foreign policy must prevail, as it did for Ireland during World War I. In other cases, it may have been a civil war that created conditions favorable for a minority's independence.

The situation becomes even more complex if, in the minority area, there is yet another, smaller minority. In such a situation, the majority nation may play one minority against the other. It is another matter that the hatreds, so engendered, actually assisted the separatist forces in the Austro-Hungarian Monarchy and also in the post-1919 successor states and, given favorable economic conditions, might lead to the dissolution of the given country. This is what happened in Czechoslovakia, Yugoslavia and the Soviet Union.

In summary, we can say that on the basis of our examples separatism has two principal causes:

The lack of autonomy, and

Governmental violence to force the minority to assimilate, prohibition of the mother tongue in schools and actions to forcefully changes the minority population ratios in the economic, cultural and political sphere.

The Europe of Autonomous Minorities – the Pre-requisite for a Peaceful Europe

The preservation of the identity of the minority groups and the prevention of the complete assimilation into the ruling majority nation is possible only if there is economic, cultural and administrative self-governance, i.e., autonomy. In practice, the area inhabited by the minority group or nationality community is fiscally, economically and administratively controlled by the decisions made by the central government and by the parliament representing the majority nationality.

Hence, as we have seen in Corsica, Great Britain and South Tyrol, representation in Parliament was insufficient and a resolution of the problem came only with territorial self-government, i.e., independent government and legislature. In areas with a mixed minority population, a special form of autonomy is required and the solution reached in Finland may serve as an example.

As we have seen, the settlements in Finland are divided on a linguistic basis. A settlement is bilingual, Finnish and Swedish, if one of the linguistic groups reaches 8% of the total population or a number in excess of 8,000. If there is one bilingual settlement in the county, the entire county is considered to be bilingual. The ratio between the linguistic groups is determined by the decennial census on the basis of the entry made on the census questionnaire by the individual citizens. Every citizen may state his or her linguistic preference on the census form. The Finnish solution of the problems of the scattered original inhabitant minorities can also serve as a model for other countries with similar problems.

In the absence of self-government, there will always be serious tensions between the minority, fighting for its survival, and the ruling nationality. The security of the given territory is always under the shadow of war. It is enough to refer to the consequences of the peace treaties that closed World War I and redrew the map of Eastern and Central Europe. The Peace Conference promised the nationalities the possibility of autonomous development, destroyed the only multi-ethnic empire and created five small countries of mixed ethnicity without in any way assuring a realistic evolution of autonomy for the minorities. We have also seen how easy it was to hide the interests of the majority behind the verbal smoke screen of protecting the minority. The peace treaties at the end of World War I reflected the pre-war ideas of France and Russia. They led directly to World War II and, after a 40-year interval, to the collapse of Czechoslovakia and Yugoslavia, the independence of Moldavia, the war in Kosovo, the renewal of the Kurdish problems in Turkey, etc. All this seems to justify those who speak of the inevitability of territorial autonomy as the key condition for general European security.

The current practices, regretfully, have not brought any significant improvements, even though the fear of territorial autonomy as a path leading to separatism is anachronistic under the European economic integration of the late 20th century.

The situation is even worse as far as the recognition of minorities as autonomous groups in international law is concerned. The legal protective devices designed by the League of Nations were totally ineffective but the legal situation introduced after World War II was a giant step backward. *After World War II, all endeavors were focused on the equality of the citizens before the law and on the civil and other rights of the individual. The existence or concept of a nationality or minority was not even recognized.* This attitude was reflected very accurately in the census questionnaires used by the various countries and the methods whereby the gathered data are published. Generally, the forms reflected only citizenship, as in France, or autonomous provinces in Western Europe, occasionally the country of origin of immigrants. No questions referred to nationality or native language. An exception was presented by the Swiss census forms that asked for mono-linguistic or multi-linguistic identification, fully recognizing the collective rights of the linguistic groups. It seems that the aims of the international organizations fighting for equal rights for minorities *should include the democratization of the census forms and insist that the forms ask for nationality and mother tongue*.

The concept of a minority nationality first appeared on the present international scene in the 1992 declaration of the UN dealing with the Rights of Individuals belonging to a national, ethnic, religious or linguistic minority. In 1994, the UN accepted an addendum to the above, which contains Article 27 of the International Agreement on Civil and Political Rights and which is used as a permanent legal reference for minority problems. The addendum states categorically that the guaranteed rights are individual rights but that they must be used in such a fashion that the minority groups may preserve their identity. Yet, international law to this day refuses to recognize the demand of minorities for recognition as independent nationalities or minority groups, when this was already a major issue in the rejection of the Hungarian 1868 Nationality Act by the minority nationalities of the day. In view of this, *it is worthwhile to mention the Hungarian Act 1868/IX that strengthens ecclesiastic autonomy*, in fact recognizes autonomous ecclesiastic organizations and, implicitly, the nationalities they represent.

The UN Agreement on the Protection of Minority Nationalities recommends to UN member nations to create a cultural and educational network for their minorities but does not go so far as to recognize that these minority taxpayers are equal to the majority only if the maintenance of their institutional network, using the mother tongue, is maintained and subsidized by the state the same way as the comparable majority system. In Article 13 of Section II, this is stated as follows: " The execution of these rights does not impose any financial burden on the Parties."[131] By comparison, the Recommendation of the Regional Committee of the European Union is a step forward. It makes it possible that the various regions of the member countries cooperate directly with each other. This makes it possible for the mother country to assist its nationalities living as minorities or fractions in other countries. Needless to say, this path also has fairly tight barriers.

Distinctions must be made between the legal situation of the original inhabitant minorities and the status of the foreign workers or political refugees. In Austria, the latter make up 12% of the population and similar problems are caused in Germany by the numerous Turkish foreign worker-immigrants. Resettlements have to be handled and controlled carefully since once the number of settlers passes a certain minimum, they will not assimilate with the majority population and the cultural, religious and other differences will lead to conflicts. A new minority will be created, just as it was in Hungary in the 16th - 19th century or as it happened in Central Asia. Considering that the resources of the country cannot be divided infinitely, a line must be drawn somewhere. This is in harmony with the current strategy of the European Community vis-à-vis migrations, which allows distinctions to be made between the legal situation of the original inhabitant minority and the new arrivals. The settling of guest laborers must be regulated by quota, if necessary, and every effort must be made in order that the existing minority problems are not aggravated by new ones. Perhaps in the future, a solution may be found whereby the industrialized nations will participate more vigorous-

---

[131] Agreement on the Protection of Minority Nationalities. In: Regio 1994/4, pp. 157-166

ly in reforming the economic conditions of the developing countries and so control the migration from "South to North". In actual practice, we see several approaches to this problem in Western Europe. **The Icelanders gained self-government in 1918** and became totally independent from Denmark in 1944. **The Faeroe Islands became self-governing in 1948 and Greenland in 1979.** Today, Greenland is so independent that it makes no sense to speak of Greenlanders as a minority. In fact, it is the Danes living in Greenland who constitute a minority. Greenland is so independent that they could hold a plebiscite to decide whether they wished to join the European Economic Community or not.

The territorial autonomy of the South Tyrol is guaranteed by a treaty between Italy and Austria. In Italy, the **Valle d'Aosta** is a French-speaking autonomous territory.

In Finland, the Swedes have an autonomous university. In spite of the fact that the Swedes represent only 6% of the population in Finland, the country is bilingual in every respect.

The 200,000 **Rhaeto-Roman minority in Switzerland** maintains its schools and publications from a fund established by the members of the Swiss Federation. Since 1996, all Parliamentary decisions and government edicts must be published in Rhaeto-Roman and this language may be used by the local administration. **In Belgium, the Flemish and the Walloons** have territorial autonomy and even the Germans living there have their own Ministries.

In France, Alsace-Lorraine has not only full linguistic autonomy but its legal system may differ from the French one. **Corsica has partial autonomy.** In this regard, the decisions of the French Constitutional Court agree with the stated foreign policy of the French government, according to which France is entitled to set conditions every time it is asked to sign an international agreement granting special rights to ethnic, religious or linguistic minorities. Even today, France does not distinguish between citizenship (citoyen) and nationality (nacionalité). The two words mean precisely the same thing in France.

Spain has been a Federation since 1976, composed of autonomous territories. The constitution guarantees the right to use the minority language in the areas of the individual regions. The 1987 Constitution made substantial changes by accepting the multiplicity of cultures and languages within the Spanish Federation and divided the country into 17 autonomous parts in which the minorities have an official status. In the areas of minority languages, there are language laws that define the ground rules of language use. Both public affairs and private life are bilingual. Thus, for instance, in Catalonia both Catalan and Spanish are official languages. Since September 1, 1994 Catalan, Basque or Galician may be used in the Spanish Parliament with the state guaranteeing immediate translation. In Catalonia, the Basque Country and Galicia territorial autonomy was established while maintaining the concept of the "United Spanish Political Nation". This explains why the separatist EPA movement has steadily lost its appeal in the Basque Country, as may be seen by the results of its parliamentary elections.

In the Netherlands, Friesland enjoys cultural autonomy.

In Eastern Europe, the example of **Moldavia** serves as breakthrough as far as collective rights are concerned. There the Christian Turks, the Gagauz, can prepare their own minority budget and thus realize their own administration in their own territory. In Slovenia the original Hungarian and Italian minorities have been granted cultural autonomy.

The Hungarian Minority Act, 1993/77 (which is good for minorities living non compact-zones, separately) guarantees collective rights for the scattered minorities and states, "Being aware of the fact that the peaceful coexistence of the national and ethnic minorities with other nations is the key to international security, the law regards the right to national and ethnic identity to be a part of the general human rights. The collective and individual rights of the national and ethnic minorities are fundamental freedom rights that it respects and to which the Hungarian Republic will grant full recognition." The act makes it possible that the minority settlement administration and the local minority self-government be elected by direct or indirect ballot. Generally, only 100 valid votes are required today in Hungary to elect a minority self-government. The Act not only guarantees cultural autonomy, but it provides a legal situation that is practically equivalent to territorial autonomy wherever half of the representatives are elected from among the ethnic minority. In these settlements, an ethnic self-government can be established and a mayor may also be elected. The 1989 Hungarian Constitution, in Section 68, Paragraph 2, assures the minorities the right to teach their mother tongue and the Education Act of 1993, Paragraph 81, makes it possible that not only state or self-government supported educational institutions be established, but that foundations and Churches also have the right to establish and maintain such institutions. In the latter case, if the sponsor of the educational institution is prepared to follow government guidelines and include the recommended basic curriculum in the proposed lesson plan, the institution becomes eligible for a public education contract under which the sponsor is entitled to the same per student subsidy as the public schools. It was this arrangement that made it possible for the penniless teaching orders to reopen their parochial schools. According to Item C. of Paragraph 86, the self-governments must provide for the middle and technical schools of the national and ethnic minorities. Other paragraphs direct that separate ethnic classes may be started for as few as 8 students, that the history of the mother country must be taught and that minority language textbooks be provided. The Act also provides that the additional costs of providing instruction in the mother tongue must be born by the State and by the local self-government. The annual state budget and management acts determine the annual subsidies granted to the nationality and minority kindergartens, elementary and secondary schools. This sum usually represents about 30% of the cost. The remainder is generated from foundations, scholarships and ministerial and governmental subsidies. The total funding amounts to a positive discrimination in favor of these educational institutions. Minority book publishing is almost entirely underwritten by the national budget. The new Romanian constitution excludes such support by stating that support of the minorities must not be different from the support given to other Romanian citizens and any discrimination against them is forbidden. The Bulgarian constitution specifically forbids the creation of autonomous territorial self-governments. As may be seen from the above, Hungary continues the minority practices that were used in the Austro-Hungarian cultural area while Romania and the other Southwest European countries pursue the practices of the Orthodox world to this day.

The *new British Labor government chose to grant autonomy* in trying to resolve ethnic difficulties. Why then is the Northern Ireland problem so difficult to resolve? It is because of the mixed ethnic of the population. Wherever the state chooses assimilation as the instrument for resolving this problem and does everything in order to change the majority-minority ratio in favor of the former, it is extremely difficult to find a form of autonomy that may, in fact, resolve the problem. The post-Trianon successor states evidently had this in mind when they tried to assimilate the minority Hungarian population by ordinance, threats and constant intimidation. In addition they also used resettlement practices to change the ethnic ratios.

In Kosovo, where the native Albanians make up more than 90% of the population, it was much more realistic to strive for autonomy. Because of a long history of oppression, the Albanians demanded full independence. The bloody civil war could be brought to an end only by NATO bombings. In 1999, a compromise was found and territorial autonomy was established under international supervision. It remains to be seen whether this solution will be satisfactory in the long run.

The events in Central Europe, subsequent to the collapse of Soviet Russia, Czechoslovakia and Yugoslavia, should serve as a warning for the future. The Serbian-Bosnian, Serbian-Croatian, Serbian-Albanian and Chechen-Russian conflicts and all the Central Asian trouble spots must not be forgotten. In the Soviet successor states, there are 25 million Russians who now, for the first time, experience the fate of those in a minority. Because of the changes in frontiers, there are 3.5-4 *million Hungarians who live as minorities beyond the borders of their motherland. This makes them the second largest group after the Russians. Even though in the plebiscite held in the Kárpátalja on December 1, 1991 78% voted for a self-governing and self-administrating territory, i.e., autonomy, Kiev refused to listen.* They denied that the Ruthenians differ in any way from the Ukrainians and therefore refused to consider any autonomy for them.

Between 1988 and 1992, approximately 120,000 refugees entered Hungary from the neighboring countries. The Hungarian organizations and parties in the countries beyond our borders demand a legal solution and personal and property security consistent with European standards. They demand free use of the mother tongue in administration and jurisdiction, a network of educational institutions with all instruction being done in the mother tongue, a Hungarian press and publications, a proportional participation in the taxes, decentralization and a personal-cultural and territorial autonomy.

The fate of about 20 million Kurds is unresolved and we must also remember the one million peaceful Tibetans who are oppressed under Chinese rule. They cannot practice their religion freely, they cannot live their life as they wish, because of the strategic importance of their land.

The re-drawing of the maps, largely because of internal developments and changes in regime, resulted in large numbers of people wishing to flee from one country to another. Ruthenians fled to Prague from the Ukrainians, many thousands of Polish descendants wanted to leave the Soviet successor states for Poland. The ethnic cleansing in the former Yugoslavia resulted in about 2 million people leaving their former homeland.

Instead of the Europe of national states, a Europe of largely autonomous regions must be formed within a more unified European Community. The examples shown above prove that it is better and easier to first create a well functioning regional cooperative arrangement and to join a broader community only after it has proven successful. **It would be in the best interests of the European Union if they would demand, as a condition for admission to the Union, that the countries applying for admission show a bilateral, solid treaty with their neighbors, assuring a South Tyrol,**

Welsh, Scottish or Irish type autonomy for their minorities. The present sham agreements, making unwarranted claims along these lines, are obviously not in the best interest of the European Union. The autonomy of the minorities can be assured only by devolution. Were this accomplished, the European Union could integrate member nations from Eastern Europe, who are ready for real cooperation and not some who were internally divided by dissension and by separatist movements. When the European Union emphasizes the pre-eminence of social policies *it should not forget the social problems arising from the manifold ethnic groups.* The ethnic fragments lacking higher and technical education in their mother tongue are at a serious disadvantage in the economic race, in their efforts to rise socially or in developing their own structures for the protection and advancement of their own interests. It does not matter whether a government is based on the Christian principles of peace, brotherly love and freedom, on the Liberal principles of individual liberties, freedom and solidarity, or on the Socialist principles of directed economies, it will pursue discriminatory policies if it does not take cognizance of the endeavors of the minorities living in their country. These minorities may have a different language and a different culture, but what they legitimately want is to be able to raise their children in their own language and in their own cultural environment and to control their destiny themselves, without a feeling of guilt, in the land where their ancestors have lived for centuries or millennia.

In a Europe having a unified economic structure, there is no more room for the traditional national economies. Wars fought for markets no longer make sense, nor do the boundaries enclosing the newly conquered lands. **The majorities and minorities in Europe can have security and peace only if there are regional or territorial autonomies**, extending beyond national boundaries and assuring for the minorities or ethnic fractions linguistic and cultural development and self-government. We have discussed the various methods used for forced assimilation and these should be banned by international law. The endless litany of complaints, going from the American Indian tribes to the Tamils of Sri Lanka, cannot be investigated and cured by international organizations.[132] Just as the League of Nations was unable to be effective in this arena, so is the UN after World War II. They cannot be effective in minority matters because they must respect the sovereignty of the State and not the minority or ethnic fragment. When things go from bad to worse, the NATO troops must step in to assist the UN forces.

The legal infirmities of any minority or ethnic fragment can be corrected only by assuring, preferably with an international treaty, that the minority or ethnic fragment will be allowed to stand by itself and have a true self-government.

---

[132] Gergely Ustoros: A béke oltókése (The grafting knife of peace) Püski, Bp. 1999. p. 11.

LEGISLATIVE ACT XLIV/ 1868

"On Equal Rights For the Nationalities (Minorities)"

Pursuant to the basic principles of the Hungarian Constitution all citizens of Hungary constitute a single nation, the indivisible, united Hungarian nation, every citizen of which enjoys equal rights regardless of his or her nationality.

Furthermore these equal rights may be judged by different rules only as pertains to the official use of the various languages being practiced in the country and, even there, only to the extent as required by national unity, the requirements of governance and administration and the fair delivery of justice.

Maintaining and preserving the total equality of the citizens in all other respects, the following regulations will serve as a standard as to the official use of the various languages:

§ 1. In view of the political unity of the nation, and Hungarian being the official language of the country, Hungarian will remain the sole language for the deliberations and administrative activities of the Hungarian parliament. The laws are enacted in the Hungarian language but shall be officially translated into and published in the language of every nationality; the official language of the national government in all branches of government will remain Hungarian.

§ 2. The records of the municipal authorities shall be kept in Hungarian but may in addition also be kept in all such languages that no less than one fifth of the members of the municipal authorities or administrative bodies request to be used for the records.
If there are discrepancies between the various texts, the Hungarian text will be considered to be the correct one.

§ 3. At any session of the municipal authority all persons endowed with the right to address the meeting may do so in Hungarian or their mother tongue if that is other than Hungarian.

§ 4. The municipal authorities will use the official language of the state in all communications addressed to the national government; but may also, in a separate column, use any of the languages used in their records. In communications with other municipal authorities the official language may be used or any other language may be used that, according to §2, has been approved for the maintenance of the records by the addressee authority.

§ 5. In the area of domestic affairs, the municipal officials will use the official language of the country, but in case this would present any difficulties to the municipality or to its officials, the officials may, as an exceptional situation, use any of the languages approved for the maintenance of the records.

When, however, required by state supervision or administration, the reports and documents must be submitted in the official language as well.

§ 6. The municipal officials, in all their official contacts with communities, assemblies, associations, institutions or private persons shall use their own language whenever possible.

§ 7. Every citizen of the country in all cases where they appear without the benefit of an attorney be it as plaintiff, defendant or applicant may or shall, personally or through an agent, benefit from the protection of the law and the assistance of the judge:

a) Before the community court the mother tongue may be used

b) Before the court of another community the language used in administration and in keeping the records in the said community shall be used

c) Before the local district court the language used in administration and in keeping the records in the home community shall be used

d) Before other courts, regardless whether they are courts of the local municipality or of another municipality, the language used for the records in that municipality shall be used.

§ 8. In case of §7, the judge shall settle the complaint or petition in the language the complaint or petition was made; hearings, the examination of witnesses, inspections and other judicial actions – both in judicial, extra-judicial and criminal cases – will be conducted in the language of the litigants or of the persons being examined. The records of the legal proceedings, however, will be kept in one of the languages authorized for use in keeping the municipal records, subject to mutual agreement between the parties. If the parties are unable to reach an agreement in this matter, the judge may keep the records in any one of the languages in which the municipal records may be kept but must explain the contents of the record to the litigants, with the assistance of an interpreter, if necessary.

The judge is also required to explain, or have translated, the important documents of the case, should these be written in a language that is not understood by one or both of the litigants.

In the interest of the party to be summoned, the summons shall be written in the mother tongue of the party, if immediately known, or in the language in which the records of the municipality are kept where the party resides, or in the official language of the state.

The judicial decision shall be written in the language used in the court records but the judge shall also announce or publish it in the language requested by each party, provided that this language is one of those authorized to be used for the records in the municipality where the judge is sitting.

§ 9. In all civil and criminal cases conducted with the assistance of an attorney, the language used by the lower court in the proceedings and in the sentence shall be according to the current practice until the legislature sees fit to make changes in the administration of the lower courts and in the management of the verbal processes.

§ 10. The ecclesiastic courts shall determine their own administrative language.

§ 11. In the Registry of Deeds, as far as the language of the supervisory Court is concerned, the administrative language of the Court is to be used, but if the parties request it, both the decision and the abstract may be written in the official language of the state or in one of the languages authorized for the keeping of the municipal records in the municipality where the Registry of Deeds is located.

§ 12. In cases under appeal, if these had not been conducted in Hungarian or are accompanied by documents not in Hungarian, the Court of Appeals shall, if necessary, have both the transcripts and the documents translated into Hungarian by certified translators, employed by the Court of Appeals at public expense, and will then consider the cases in their official translation.

The Court of Appeals will always render its conclusions, decisions and judgments in the official language of the state.

The action being remanded to the lower court, said court shall announce the conclusions, decisions and judgments of the Court of Appeals to every party in the language requested by said party provided that said language was one of the approved languages for the administration of the lower court, or for the records of the municipality.

§ 13. The official language of every court appointed by the national government shall be the Hungarian language.

§ 14. Provided that they do not interfere with the legal rights of the ecclesiastic authorities, the congregations may decide the language in which the registers are kept, in which their ecclesiastic business is conducted and also, within the limits permitted by the National Education Act, in which instruction is provided in their schools.

§ 15. The higher ecclesiastic bodies and authorities shall determine the language used in their deliberations, their records, their administration and their contacts with their congregations. If said language was not the official language of the state, in order to provide appropriate state supervision, all documents shall also be submitted in a certified translation, in the official language of the state.

If various Churches or higher ecclesiastic authorities wish to communicate with each other, either the official language of the state or the language of the Church to which the communication is addressed shall be used.

§ 16. The higher and highest ecclesiastic authorities, in their submissions to the national government, may use their administrative or record-keeping language and, in a separate column, the official state language. In their submissions to the municipality or its officials the official state language shall be used. If there are several authorized languages any of these may be used. The congregations in their official communications with the state government or with their own municipalities shall use the official state language or their own administrative language. In communications with other municipalities the official administrative language of said municipality may be used.

§ 17. In the educational institutions already established by the state and by the government, or to be established as need be, the determination of the language of instruction is the duty of the Minister of Education, unless previously ordained by law. The success of the educational endeavor, general education and the public good being the highest goals of the state, it must, as far as possible, see to it that in the public schools any nationality, living in larger numbers in any given area may receive instruction in their own mother tongue in said area, up to but not including post-secondary education.

§ 18. In public secondary and higher educational institutions, existing or to be established in areas where more than one language is in common use, a department of language and literature shall be established for each and every one of said languages.

§ 19. In the National University the language of instruction is Hungarian, however, where this has not been done to date, a department of language and literature shall be established for all the languages in common use in the country.

§ 20. The municipal councils shall choose the language for their records and administration. The records are also to be kept in any language that is requested by at least one fifth of the eligible voters.

§ 21. The municipal officials are required to use the language of the inhabitants of the municipality in all discussions with said inhabitants.

§ 22. In their submission to their own administration, to its officials or to the national government, all municipalities shall use the official state language or their own approved administrative language. In their submission to other municipalities or their officials, the official state language or any one of the approved languages of said municipality may be used.

§ 23. Every citizen of the country may use his mother tongue in any submission addressed to his/her municipality, ecclesiastic authority and legislative bodies.

In submissions to another municipality, administration and its officials, the citizen shall use the official state language, or the language of record of the municipality or administration or any one of the approved languages of record.

In the area of legislation the language to be used is determined by § 7-13 above.

§ 24. In municipal and ecclesiastic meetings, those entitled to address the meeting may do so in their mother tongue.

§ 25. If individuals, religious denominations, private corporations, private educational institutions or unincorporated communities do not use the official state language in their submission to the government, any decision resulting from such submission must have its original Hungarian language text accompanied by an authorized translation into the language of the original submission.

§ 26. As it has been the right of every citizen, regardless of their nationality, just as it has been the right of communities, Churches and congregations to establish private educational institutions at the lower, middle or upper levels, of their own efforts or as a joint venture, this right will be maintained in the future. For this purpose and also for the purpose of establishing other institutions for the promotion of language, art, science, economics, industry and commerce, the individuals may, under the legal supervision of the state, join in associations or corporations, and so having united may establish by-laws, and act on these by-laws under the regulations approved by the state. They may collect funds and these funds may be used according to the legitimate needs of the nationalities and under the supervision of the national government.

Educational and other institutions so established enjoy the same rights as government institutions of the same type and level, with the schools required to follow the mandates of the laws regulating public education. The language of the private institutions and organizations will be determined by the founders.

The associations and the institutions established by them may use their own language when communicating with each other; in their contacts with others § 23 of this Act will govern the use of language.

§ 27. In filling official positions in the future also, only individual ability will be used as a guideline; nationality will not be considered a detriment to the ability of occupying any position or of rising to any dignity. Furthermore the state government will endeavor to fill judicial and administrative positions, particularly lord-lieutenancies, as much as possible, with persons from various nationalities who are fully conversant with the required languages and who are otherwise suitable.

§ 28. Any ordinances of previous Acts contrary to the above decisions are herewith rescinded.

§ 29. These acts do not extend to Croatia, Slavonia and Dalmatia, having extraterritorial rights and being politically independent, but as far as language is concerned in these countries, the agreements made between the Hungarian Parliament, on the one hand, and the Croatian-Slavonian Parliament on the other hand, shall be determinant and, according to which the representatives at the joint Hungarian-Croatian Parliament may speak in their own language.

Bibliography

Arató Endre: A nemzetiségi kérdés Magyarországon.1790-1848. I-II.köt.Bp., 1960.
Arday Lajos: A mai Vajdaság (a történelmi Bács-Bodrog, Torontál, Szerém vármegyék) rövid története. kézirat.
Ács Zoltán: Nemzetiségek a történelmi Magyarországon. Kossuth Kiadó. Bp., 1986.88-89.pp.
Altermatt, Urs: Svájc - az európai modell ? in: Regio,1944.2.sz. 19-30pp.
Anderle Ádám: Megosztott Hispánia. Államfejlődés és nemzeti mozgalmak Spanyolországban. Kossuth, Bp., 1985.
Balassa Zoltán: Hogyan változik tájaink nemzetiségi összetétele. Szabad Újság,1992.julius 25.
Barabás Béla - Joó Rudolf: A kolozsvári magyar egyetem 1945-ben. Magyarságkutató intézet, Bp., 1990.
Bánffy Dezső: Magyar nemzetiségi politika.Bp.1903.
Beksics Gusztáv: A román kérdés és a fajok harca Európában és Magyarországon.Bp.,1895.
Bellér Béla: A magyarországi németek rövid története. Bp., 1981.
Bellon Tibor: Nagykunság.Gondolat.Bp.,1979.
S. Benedek András: Kárpátalja története, és kulturtörténete. Népek hazája sorozat. Bereményi könyvkiadó, h.n.é.n.
Bényei Miklós: Oktatáspolitikai törekvések a reformkori Magyarországon, Debrecen, Csokonai Kiadó,1994.
Bethlen István gróf: Az oláhok birtokvásárlásai Magyarországon az utolsó öt évben.Bp.,é.n.
Biacsi Antal: Kis délvidéki demográfia.Életjel, Magyarságkutató Tudományos Társaság, Szabadka, 1994.
Bíró László: A szerbek és 1848. in: História 1998/3 23-25.pp.
Biró Sándor: Kisebbségben és többségben (Románok és magyarok 1867-1940) Európai Protestáns Magyar Szabadegyetem, Bern,1989.107-108.pp.
Boia, Lucian: Relationships between Romanians, Czechs and Slovaks,1848-1914. Bucuresti 1977.
Bolyai Társaság-RMDSZ: A romániai magyar főiskolai oktatás, Kolozsvár, 1990
Bonkáló Sándor: A rutének (Ruszinok).Franklin Társulat. Bp., 1941.
Bulla Béla: A Ruténföld. Magyar Szemle,1939.4.sz.
Bruckner Győző: A szepesség múltja éa mai lakói. in. dr. Loisch János: A Szepesség.Kókai Lajos kiadása,Bp, 1926.10-11.pp.
Angus Calder: Revolving Culture, London, 1994 (Scotland)
R.H. Cambell: Scotland since 1707.Edinburgh,John Donald Publishers LTD,1985
Constantinescu, Miron (szerk): Erdély története. 2. kötet. Bukarest, 1964.

Connert János: A székelyek intézményei a legrégibb időktől az 1562-iki átalakulásig.Kolozsvár,1901.

Edmund Curtis: A History of Ireland, Routledge, 1992

Csehák Kálmán: A szerb nemzeti egyházi és iskolai autonómia a dualizmus kori Magyarországon a dokumentumok tükrében, Létünk, 1992.4-5.sz.

Csuka János: A délvidéki magyarság története 1918-1941. Püski kiadó, Bp., 1996.

Georg Brunner: Nemzetiségi kérdés és kisebbségi konfliktusok Kelet-Európában. in: Magyarságkutatás Könyvtára Bp., 1995

John Dawes: A History of Wales, Penguin Books, London,1994

T.M. Devine and R. J. Finlay: Scotland in the 20th century.Edinburgh University Press,1966

T.M. Devine and Rosalind Mitchison: People and Society in Scotland I. 1760-1830 The Economic and Social History Society of Scotland, Bristol, 1988

Diószegi István: Nemzetiségi politika Európában. in: Üllő és kalapács, Magyarságkutató Intézet,Bp.,1991.

Diószegi István: "Külső tényező"- kisebbségi politika, in: História,1994/2.sz

Domokos Pál Péter: Rendületlenül. Eötvös-Szent Gellért kiadó. 20-21.pp.

Stefan Geosits: Szentpéterfa, Tusch Druck GmbH, Wien, 1996.

Gordon Donaldson: Scotland. The Shaping of a Nation. David St John Thomas Publisher 1974, 1980,

Ian Donnachie and Christopher Whatley: The Manufacture of Scottish History, Polygon, Edinburgh, 1992

Dudás Gyula: A bácskai és bánsági szerbek története a XVI-XVII.században.Zombor, 1896.

Duray Miklós: Kettős elnyomásban. Madách-Posonium, Pozsony, 1993.

Dus László: Dalmátia a magyar közjogban.Bp.,1906.Grill

Demkó Kálmán: A szepesi jog. Keletkezése, viszonya országos jogunkhoz és a németországi anyajogokhoz.. Bp., 1891. Akadémia

Edelényi Szabó Dénes: Magyarország közjogi alkatrészeinek és törvényhatóságainak területváltozásai. Bp., 1928. Horánszky Viktor RT.

Eszterházy János: Cselekedjünk mindannyian egyetértésben és szeretetben. Panónia könyvkiadó, Pozsony, 1992.

Faragó Béla: Van-e korzikai nép? in: Regio kisebbségi szemle, 1992/2.sz. 36-58.pp.

Fehér István: Az utolsó percben. Magyarország nemzetiségei 1945-90. Kossuth kiadó, 1993.

Alan W. Fischer: The Crimean Tatars. Hoover Institution, Stanford University, California, 1978.

R.F.Foster: The Oxford Illustrated History of Ireland. Oxford University Press, 1989

Fügedi Erik: Szlovák telepítés a török alól felszabadult területeken. in: Agrártörténeti Szemle, 1966.3.sz.

Füves Ödön: A ráckevei görögök nyomában. in: Antik Tanulmányok,VI.köt/1-3.sz. Bp.,1959.

Gáldi László-Makkai László (szerk.): A románok története különös tekintettel az erdélyi románokra., Magyar Történelmi Társulat, h és év nélkül.

Gazdag Ferenc: Az 1994. évi francia nyelvtörvény.in:História, 1996/1.sz

Gerencsér Balázs-Juhász Albin: Működő Autonómiák I-II.Bp., 1998. (kézirat)

Gergely Jenő: Az erdélyi görög katolikus román egyház. in: Regio, 1991. 3.sz. 106-117pp.

Gratz Gusztáv: A dualizmus kora.Magyarország története 1867-1918. 2.kötet.Bp.,1934.

Glatz Ferenc (szerk.): Magyarok a Kárpát-medencében. Pallas Lap- és Könyvkiadó Vállalat,1988.

Goldis, Vasile: A nemzetiségi kérdésről. Bukarest, 1976.

Gondos Albert: Az öreg hárs faggatása.Csikszereda,1994.(a szerző magán kiadása)

Gömöri János: Eperjes és az evangélikus kollégium története.Evangélikus Országos Muzeum, dr.Fabinyi Tibor (szerk) Bp.,1994.

Gyönyör József: Határok születtek. Madách kiadó, Pozsony, 1992.

Hadrovics László: A déli szláv népek kultúrája. szerk. Szekfű Gyula, Bp.,1942.

Hajnóczy R. József: Szepes vármegye történeti változásai. in: dr.Loisch János: A Szepesség...

Hanzó Lajos: Az erdélyi szász önkormányzat kialakulása. Értekezések a Magyar Királyi Horthy Miklós Tudományegyetem Magyar Történeti Intézetéből, Szeged, 1941.

Péter Hidas: The Greeks of Hungary, Gieben, Amsterdam, 1991. in: Mc Gill University Monographs in Classical Archeology and History

Hodinka Antal: A munkácsi görög katolikus püspökség története. MTA, Bp.,1910.

Hóman-Szekfú: Magyar történet IV.köt. Királyi Egyetemi Nyomda Bp.,1935.

Hunfalvy János: Magyarország és Erdély. I-III.Darmstadt,1856,1860,1864. Lange Gusztáv György kiadása

Janics Kálmán: A hontalanság évei. Hunnia kiadó kft, Bp., 1989.

Jancsó Benedek: A román irredentista mozgalmak története. Bp.,1920.

Jakabffy Elemér: Adatok a románság történetéhez a magyar uralom alatt. Lugoj,1931.

Jávorszky Béla: Észak-Európa kisebbségei. Magvető, Bp., 1991.

Joó Rudolf: Etnikumok és regionalizmus Nyugat-Európában. Gondolat, Bp., 1988.

Joó Rudolf: A Nyugat-Európai Kisebbségek sajátosságai és típusai.Bp., 1983, Akadémia in:Nemzetiségi füzetek"

Péter Hidas: The Greeks of Hungary.Gieben,Amsterdam,1991.in: Mc Gill University Monographs in Classical Archeology and History

Hunyady Béla: A hajdúvárosok régi közigazgatási és igazságszolgáltatási szervezete. Bp.,1934.

Kafer István: A miénk és az övék. Magvető, Bp., 1991.

Karsai László: A nemzetiségi kérdés Franciaországban. Kossuth kiadó, Bp.,1983

Katona Tamás: Nemzeti összeütközések 1848-49-ben.MOK 148-155.pp

Katus László: Egy kisebbségi törvény születése. Az 1868. évi nemzetiségi törvény évfodulójára. in: Regio,1993.4.sz.

Keken András: A magyarországi evangélikusság történeti statisztikája. Bp., 1932

Dermot Keogh and Michael H. Haltzel: Northern Ireland and the Politics of Reconciliation. Cambridge University Press,1993

Kemény G. Gábor: Iratok a nemzetiségi kérdés történetéhez Magyarországon a dualizmus korában. Bp., 1952,1956.

Kiss József: A jászkunok meghonosodása. História. 1991. 2-3.sz.

Kniezsa István: A szlávok. Magyar Szemle Társaság,Bp., 1932.

Koch István: Az erdélyi szász iskolák a nemzeti fejedelmek korában. Barcza J. Könyvnyomdája, Bp., 1906 in: Müv.tört.Ért.

Kordé Zoltán: Besenyők az Árpád-kori Magyarországon. História. 1991. 2-3.sz.

Köpeczi Béla (főszerk): Erdély története I-III. Akadémiai Kiadó, Bp., 1986.
Lipcsey Ildikó: Erdélyi autonómiák (Történeti tanulmányok) Bp., 1990.
F.S.L. Lyons: Ireland since the Famine. Fontana Press, London,1963
Lozoviuk, Petr: Tirol - Kettéosztott tartomány az egyesülő Európában? in: Regio, 1993. 3.sz.
Macartney, C. A: The Habsburg Empire 1790-1918. London, 1970.
J.D. Mackie: A History of Scotland. Penguin Books,London, 1991
Magyarok Szlovákiában (adatok, dokumentomok), *szerk. Varga Sándor,* Pozsony, 1993
Magyarországi örmények vázlatos története (*összeállította az V. ker-i Örmény önkormányzat anyaga alapján Hévizi Józsa*) in: Belváros, 1995/1.sz. 5-6.pp.
Andrew Marr: The Battle for Scotland.Penguin Books, London,1992
E. W. McFarland: Ireland and Scotland in the Age of Revolution.Edinburgh University Press Ltd, 1994
Makkai László: Magyar-román közös múlt. Teleki Pál Tudományos Intézet, Bp., 1948
Makkai László: Erdély betelepülése. História, 1986
Mandl Bernát: A magyarhoni zsidók tanügye II.József alatt. Bp., Lampel R. ,1901.
Manga János: Palócföld. Gondolat. Bp.,1979.
Mályusz Elemér: A középkori magyar nemzetiségi politika. in: Századok,1939.
Medvetánc könyvek: Jelentések a határokon túli magyar kisebbségek helyzetéről, Bp., 1988.
Mikó Imre: Nemzetiségi jog és nemzetiségi politika. Minerva Kiadó, Kolozsvár 1944.
Miskolczy Gyula: A horvát kérdés története és irományai a rendi állam korában. I-II.kötet.Bp.,1927.
Moldován Gergely: A románság. Politikai, történelmi, néprajzi és nyelvészeti közlemények.I.köt. Nagybecskerek, 1895 II.köt.u.o.1896.
Nagy Lajos: A kisebbségek alkotmányjogi helyzete Nagyromániában. Minerva-nyomda Rt., Kolozsvár, 1944.
Niederhauser Emil: Illirizmus és nagyszerb tervek, in: História 1992/4. sz. 11-12.pp.
A.J. Otway - Ruthven: A History of Medieval Ireland.Barnes et Noble Books, 1993
Ölvedi János: Napfogyatkozás. Magyarok Szlovákiában, püski, New York, 1985
Pach Zsigmond Pál: Magyarország története tíz kötetben, Akadémia kiadó, Bp., 1978
Raymond Pearson: National minorities in Eastern Europe 1848-1945. The MacMillian Press LTD, 1983.London
dr.Pechány Adolf: A tótokról. Bp.,1913.
dr. Pecze Ferenc: Szerbek és Magyarok a Duna mentén I-II (1848-1867) Századok, Bp, 1988/3
Omeljan Pritsak: Prolegomena to the National Awakening of the Ukrainians during the 19th century. 96-110.pp. in: Culture and Nationalism
dr.Pirigyi István: A magyarországi görögkatolikusok története. Görög katolikus Hittudományi Főiskola, Nyiregyháza,1990.
dr.Pirigyi István: Kárpátalja. Keresztény Magyar Vetés újság, 1994. május-szeptember
Polányi Imre: A szlovák társadalom és polgári nemzeti mozgalom a századfordulón. Akadémia, Bp.,1987.
Popély Gyula: A csehszlovákiai magyarság a népszámlálások tükrében 1918-1945. Regio Könyvek, Bp., 1991

Puskánszky Béla: Erdélyi szászok és magyarok. H.n.1943.

Raffay Ernő: A vajdaságoktól a birodalomig. Az újkori Románia története. JATE. Szeged,1989.

Roland Sussex and J.C.Eade: Culture and Nationalism in 19th century Eastern-Europe. Slavica Publishers, Inc, Columbus, Ohio, USA,

Romsich Ignác: Helyünk és sorsunk a Duna-medencében, Osiris, Bp., 1996.

Dr. vitéz Ruttkay László: A felvidéki szlovák középiskolák megszüntetése 1874-ben. in: Felvidéki Tudományos Társaság kiadványai. Pécsi Egyetemi könyvkiadó, Pécs, 1939.

Sárközi Zoltán: Az erdélyi szászok a nemzeti ébredés korában (1790-1848). Bp.,1963.

R.W.Seton-Watson: A History of the Roumanians. Cambridge, 1934.

Ljuba Siselina: A volt Szovjetunió nemzeti politikája és a kárpátaljai magyarság.in:Regio, Írók Szakszervezete Széphalom Könyvműhely, Bp., 1992/2.sz.

Dusan Skvarna: A szlovák nemzeti mozgalom 1848-ban. in: História, 1998/3.sz

Sipos Péter - Horányi István: Szemelvénygyüjtemény az 1917-1945 közötti történelem tanításához (kéziratként) Bp., 1990.

Sokcsevits Dénes-Szilágyi Imre- Szilágyi Károly: Déli szomszédaink története. Népek hazája sorozat. Bereményi kiadó,Bp.

dr.Szabó Oreszt: A magyar oroszokról. Bp., é.n.

Szarka László: Adatok a csehszlovákiai magyar kisebbségről. in: História, 1991/ 2-3.sz

Szarka László: Felső-Magyarország, Csehszlovákia, Szlovákia-II. in: História 1992/8.sz

Szász Zoltán: A románok története. Népek hazája sorozat. Berményi könyvkiadó, h.n.é.n.

Szász Zoltán: A nemzetiségek és a magyar forradalom. in: História 1999/3 15-17.pp

Szücs Jenő: Nemzet és történelem. Bp.,1974.

Szentkláray Jenő: A karlócai patriarchális és fruskagórai monostori szerb levéltárak. Századok. 1883.IV.füzet.

Székely András Bertalan: A Rábától a Muráig. Nemzetiségek egy határ két oldalán. Püski, Bp.,1992.

Székely Marianne: A protestáns erdélyi fejedelmek hatása a román kultúra fejlődésére. Tiszántúli Könyvkiadó Rt ,Debrecen, 1935.

Szentesi Zöldi László: A skót függetlenségi mozgalom,in: Magyar Fórum, 1997.szept.4.

Szokolay Katalin: Lengyelország története, Balassi kiadó, Bp., 1997.

Szongott Kristóf: Arménia folyóirat VII.évfolyama, Szamosújvár, 1893.Todorán Endre nyomdája

Vujicsics Sztoján: Szerbek Pest-Budán. Főpolgármesteri Hivatal és Szerb Főv-i Önkormányzat Bp., 1997.

Taylor, A.J.P: The Habsburg Monarchy 1809-1918. New York, 1965.

Edward C. Thaden: Conservative Nationalism in 19th century. Russia University of Washington, Seattle,1964.USA

Thim József: A horvátok és a hazai szerbség a magyar történetben. In: A magyarság és a szlávok. szerk. Szekfü Gyula, Bp.,1942.

I.Tóth Zoltán: Magyarok és románok.Bp., 1966.

I.Tóth Zoltán: Az erdélyi román nacionalizmus első százada. 1697-1792. Bp.,1946.

Töttösy Ernő: Dalmácia. Mécses kiadó. Bp .,1992.

Trifunovits Andrea: Az olaszországi kisebbségek helyzete. in: Regio,1994.2.sz. 127-144.pp Tustner Ignác: Déli tartományaink földje, népe és jövője. Értekezések a bosnyák jog és balkanológia köréből. Debrecen.,1918.

Udvari István: A ruszinok XVIII.századi historiográfiája. (Tudománytörténeti vázlat)Szabolcs-szatmári Szemle 1991.2.sz. 143-157.pp.

Vadkerty Katalin: A reszlovakizáció. Kalligram könyvkiadó, Pozsony, 1993.

Vadkerty Katalin: Magyar sors Csehszlovákiában. in:História, 1997/2.sz.

Varga E. Árpád: Népszámlálások a jelenkori Erdély területén. Regio Könyvek, MTA Történettudományi Intézet, Bp., 1992

Várady Eszter: A finnországi kisebbségek és a svédországi finnek. VITA, Bp., 1991. in: Kulturális modell kutatások

Vígh Károly: A szlovákiai magyarság sorsa. Népek Hazája sorozat

Zatykó Vivien: Magyar bolgárok? Etnikai identitás és akkulturáció a bánáti bolgárok körében. in: Regio, 1994/3

Hungarian Kingdom in the second half of the 13th century

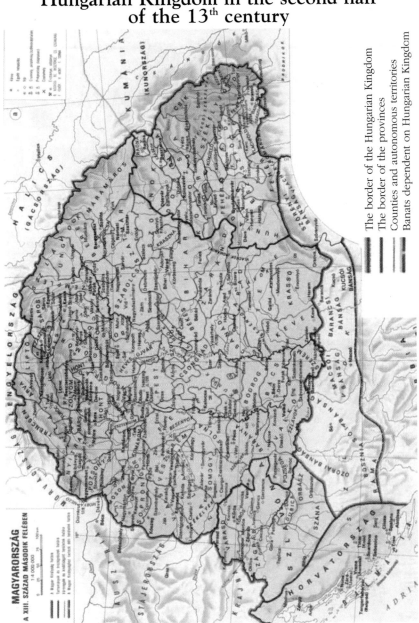

The border of the Hungarian Kingdom
The border of the provinces
Counties and autonomous territories
Banats dependent on Hungarian Kingdom

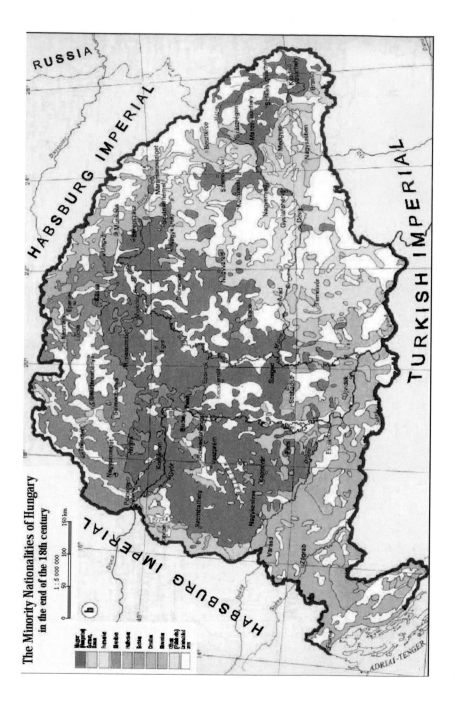

The Minority Nationalities of Hungary
in the end of the 18th century

1 : 5 000 000

0   50   100   150 km

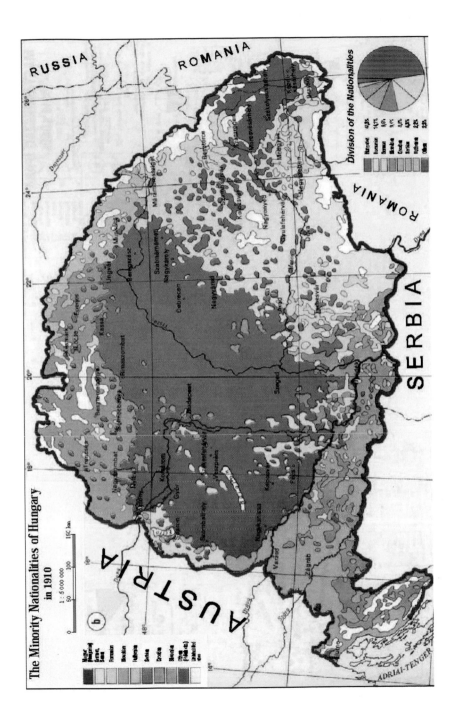

The Minority Nationalities of Hungary in 1910

1 : 5 000 000

Division of the Nationalities

RUSSIA

ROMANIA

ROMANIA

SERBIA

AUSTRIA

ADRIAI-TENGER